S0-AOO-112

TWAYNE'S WORLD AUTHORS SERIES

A Survey of the World's Literature

CANADA

Robert Lecker, University of Maine, Orono

EDITOR

Gwen Pharis Ringwood

TWAS 602

Photograph by Irene Stangoe

Gwen Pharis Ringwood

GWEN PHARIS RINGWOOD

By GERALDINE ANTHONY, S.C.
Mount Saint Vincent University
Halifax, Nova Scotia

TWAYNE PUBLISHERS
A DIVISION OF G. K. HALL & CO., BOSTON

Published in 1981 by Twayne Publishers,
A Division of G. K. Hall & Co.

Printed on permanent/durable acid-free paper and bound
in the United States of America

First Printing

Library of Congress Cataloging in Publication Data

Anthony, Geraldine, 1919-
Gwen Pharis Ringwood.

(Twayne's world authors series ; TWAS 602)
Bibliography: p. 176.
Includes index.
1. Ringwood, Gwen Pharis—Criticism and interpretation.
PR199.3.R52Z52 1981 812'.54 80-29011
ISBN 0-8057-6444-5

For Bill Jr., Melanie, and Tom Anthony

Contents

About the Author
Preface
Acknowledgments
Chronology
1. Grass Roots 19
2. "Proff" Koch and the Folk Plays 39
3. Robert Gard and Alberta Folklore 70
4. The Ringwood Musicals 95
5. The Plays of Social Protest 113
6. The Children's Plays 133
7. Novels and Short Stories 140
8. Fragments 159
9. Conclusion 164
Notes and References 171
Selected Bibliography 176
Index 185

About the Author

Geraldine Anthony, S.C., is the author of the book *John Coulter* (Twayne Publishers), the editor of *Stage Voices: Twelve Canadian Dramatists Talk About Their Lives and Work*, and the general editor of the series, *Profiles in Canadian Drama*. As professor of English at Mount Saint Vincent University in Halifax, Nova Scotia, she gives courses in Canadian and American Literature. Although her specialty is the seventeenth century (she has an M.A. in philosophy with a thesis on Descartes, and a Ph.D. in English with a dissertation on Dryden—both from St. John's University, New York) her chief interest lies in drama, and for the past several years she has consistently researched Canadian drama—visiting most of the theater centers across Canada and interviewing Canadian playwrights and others involved in theater. She has published articles in the *Canadian Theatre Review*, *Canadian Drama/L'Art Dramatique Canadien*, *Atlantis*, *Canadian Library Journal*, *Cithara*, *Canadian Theatre Review Yearbook*, *World Literature Written in English*, and *Canadian Children's Literature*. She has been the recipient of Canada Council grants, a fellowship in journalism from the *Wall Street Journal* at the University of Minnesota, and has done postdoctoral studies in seventeenth-century literature at Oxford University, and in modern drama at Columbia University. A native New Yorker and a member of the Congregation of the Sisters of Charity, Dr. Anthony has been a resident of Nova Scotia since 1963.

Preface

Gwen Pharis Ringwood's reputation as a playwright of note has only recently been acknowledged by eastern Canadians although the West had long since discovered her worth in the authenticity, creative qualities, and rich evocation of Alberta and British Columbia's life and people. Yet consider her early play, *Still Stands the House* (1939) which has been performed more often than possibly any other one-act Canadian play in English. Its premiere production took place at the Playmakers Theatre, University of North Carolina, Chapel Hill, in the spring of 1939. That same year, in Ottawa, it won the Dominion Drama Festival Award for the Best Play by a Canadian, and it was published by Samuel French & Company. Reprinted many times, it has also appeared in several American and Canadian anthologies. Since its first production *Still Stands the House* has continued to be produced each year in high schools and universities, drama festivals and community theaters throughout North America. The fact that this superb drama and Ringwood's other fine plays have been largely ignored by professional theaters in Canada is a challenge, not to the quality of her work, but to the judgment of those responsible for selecting Canadian plays in professional theaters.

Ringwood's considerable contributions to Canadian literature—her twenty-four stage plays, four musicals, numerous radio plays, children's drama, short stories, and two novels dealing chiefly with Canadian prairie life are understandably appreciated best by western Canadians who share her rapport with the west and its unique qualities. But the universal nature of her work makes it singularly appealing to nonwesterners as well. To specialists in the field, Gwen Ringwood is a highly respected playwright.

It was only in the mid-1960s that Canadian stage drama began to establish a foothold in theater in Canada. Ringwood is a pioneer in the field. Since 1936 she has been writing, teaching, adjudicating, directing, and producing plays, improvising theater space, and educating whole communities in drama. Forty years of dedicated work in the face of such major obstacles as a scarcity of committed directors, constructive critics, professional companies, and adequate theaters, deserves special recognition; Ringwood has helped to preserve the traditions of theater in remote western Canadian areas since the 1930s.

Early in her writing career Gwen Pharis saw the vast possibilities, the epic qualities of her native Alberta prairie land as both subject and character for drama. Her subsequent work ranged over the wide area of Canada's West—the pioneering prairie folk, the gold miners of northern Saskatchewan, the Ukrainian immigrants of Alberta, the Indian tribes of the Cariboo, the gold miners of Billy Barker's days in British Columbia, the ranchers and cowboys of the Calgary Stampede. Her special qualities of gentleness, warmth, comic instinct for play, and wry sense of humor, made her singularly adept at creating folk comedies. She has used a variety of forms: fantasy, farce, comedy, parody, realism, impressionism, classical tragedy, myth, multimedia presentations, musicals, and poetic drama. Ringwood's talent for experimentation invests her work with freshness and appeal.

The colorful characters who people her plays fall into three categories: larger-than-life folk heroes of western Canada; Canadian personalities magnified by time and history; and fictional inhabitants of farm and prairie. Characters such as Widger the miserly Albertan farmer, Planter the gold miner, Sokolander the politician, Professor Bond the geologist, and Dowser Ringgo the water diviner and pedlar of strange potions—these personalities reflect the land Ringwood knows so well, and their conversations express the folk imagination and idiom with which she is so familiar.

Conflict and paradox are at the root of the Ringwood experience of life on stage, perhaps because they are at the heart of her own response to life. A modest playwright, diffident about her work, she yet has the toughness and resilience of the frontier woman of the prairies. "Writing in a kind of limbo"[1] as she describes it, all her life, removed from the mainstream of significant major theater movements, she has had to fight for the recognition of Canadian stage plays in a country that chose to ignore its own dramatists, preferring instead to produce the plays of British, American, Irish, and European playwrights. An independent, free-thinking liberal, she nevertheless often depicts in her plays unliberated women from traditional backgrounds. Although she is highly sensitive to the tragedies of humanity, Ringwood is often at her best in folk comedy where she can distance herself and use delicate wit to underline the foibles of contemporary society. An ardent Canadian, she nonetheless has espoused a broader, more international spirit. Despite her dedication to playwriting as a vocation, she has always put husband and children first. Yet as a sophisticated woman with her fingers on the pulse of a changing society, she has often espoused new causes and new philosophies, but she is also solidly grounded in tradition. Out of conflict and paradox in her own life, Ringwood has fashioned a rich body of folk and regional literature, produced on stage and radio, and published singly and in anthologies. Her works are preserved at the University of Calgary Library, Calgary, Alberta. Ringwood continues to write at Chimney Lake, B.C. A study of the total Ringwood opus is richly rewarding in its comprehensive picture of the life and people of the Canadian west in this century.

GERALDINE ANTHONY, S.C.

Mount Saint Vincent University, Halifax

Acknowledgments

I wish to thank Gwen Pharis Ringwood for giving so generously of her time in interviews at Chimney Lake, B.C., for free access to all her manuscripts, and permission to quote from her unpublished works. My gratitude also to her husband, Dr. John Brian Ringwood, and to her family for granting me interviews. To her friends, especially Clive Stango, Vivien Cowan, and Sonia Cornwall, my thanks for patiently answering my questions. I am indebted to Dr. Robert Gard for interviews on his assessment of the Ringwood contributions to folk drama and for his descriptions of Alberta folklore and local history. To Elsie Park Gowan, Jack T. McCreath, Walter Kaasa, Senator Donald Cameron, Tom Kerr, and Doris Gauntlett, my thanks for interviews and letters on their close association with Gwen and her plays. To the Carolina Playmakers at the University of North Carolina, Chapel Hill: her professors, colleagues, and friends—Paul Green, the late Samuel Selden and John Parker, Emily Crow Selden, Norma Cartwright Scofield, Walter Spearman, Darice Parker, Elizabeth Lay Green, Thomas Patterson, and Adeline McCall—my gratitude for their valuable insights. For reading the manuscript and offering perceptive comments I thank Dr. Ronald Hatch, Dr. Jeanne Welcher Kleinfield, Professor James Noonan, and Caroleen Marie Browne, S.C. My appreciation also to Michael G. Martin, archivist, University of North Carolina Library, for locating the missing play, "One Man's House."

Permission to quote from Ringwood's works has been granted by the following: Samuel French for excerpts from the plays *Still Stands the House* and *The Courting of Marie Jenvrin;* the *Montreal Star* for passages from the short stories "Some People's Grandfathers" and "Little Joe and the Mounties"; the University of North Carolina Press for excerpts from *Pioneering a People's Theatre,* edited by Archibald Henderson.

Chronology

1910 Gwen Pharis born in Anatone, Washington state, 13 August, daughter of Leslie and Mary (Bowersock) Pharis.

1913 Family moves to a farm near Barons, southern Alberta, Canada.

1914-
1925 Attends elementary schools at Barons and Magrath, and high schools at Crescent Height, Calgary, and Magrath. Family moves to Magrath in 1917.

1926-
1928 Family moves to Valier, Montana. Graduates from Valier H.S. Attends freshman classes at the University of Montana. Obtains position as bookkeeper for Browning Mercantile on the Blackfoot Indian Reservation.

1929-
1933 Family returns to Alberta. Attends the University of Alberta, Edmonton, for two years in the Honours English Program; is forced to switch to a straight arts program for financial reasons. Works part-time as librarian's assistant in the medical library, and as secretary to the director of drama, Elizabeth Sterling Haynes, Extension Department, while continuing with university courses.

1934 Graduates with a B.A. degree from the University of Alberta.

1935-
1936 Registrar of the newly established Banff School of Fine Arts. First stage play produced, *The Dragons of Kent.* Writes ten radio plays for the program, *New Lamps for Old,* CKUA radio, University of Alberta.

1937 Awarded a Rockefeller Foundation Fellowship to the University of North Carolina, Chapel Hill, Department of Dramatic Art, unofficially called the Carolina Playmakers.

1938 "Chris Axelson, Blacksmith" produced at Chapel Hill. Writes the play "The Days May Be Long." Teaches at Olds Adult Folk School and at the University of Alberta's Department of Education Summer School in Edmonton.

1939 Writes the plays *Still Stands the House, Pasque Flower,* and "One Man's House." Graduates with an M.A. in English and drama from the University of North Carolina, winning the Roland Holt Cup for outstanding work in drama. Writes the three-act play *Dark Harvest* for her M.A. thesis. Teaches summer courses in drama and junior acting at Banff School of Fine Arts. 16 September, marries Dr. John Brian Ringwood, M.D., in Magrath, Accepts position of director of dramatics (1939-1940) for the Extension Department, University of Alberta. Writes the plays *Saturday Night* and *Red Flag at Evening.* Gives correspondence course, *So You Want to be an Actor,* on CKUA, University of Alberta radio station.

1940 Writes and stages in Edmonton an historical pageant on the Methodist missionary John MacDougall and Indian Chief Maskapetoon for a huge outdoor audience on the seventieth anniversary of the Methodist Church. Moves with her husband to Goldfields on the north shore of Lake Athabasca, northern Saskatchewan.

1941 22 April, first child, Stephan, born. Awarded the Governor-General's Medal for outstanding service in the development of Canadian Drama. Writes the play, *The Courting of Marie Jenvrin.*

1942 19 November, second child, Susan, born. Returns to Lamont, Alberta. Dr. Ringwood enlists in the Canadian Army Medical Corps as captain and goes overseas.

1943 Moves to Edmonton. Writes a pageant, "Christmas 1943," for the University Women's Club. Receives word that her two younger brothers have been killed in action.

1944-1945 Awarded a grant to write plays dealing with native Albertan material: *The Jack and the Joker, The Rainmaker,* and *Stampede.* Writes the short story, "The Little Ghost," the radio play, "The Fight Against the Invisible," and the stage play, "Niobe House." Appointed to the Administrative Board for the Allied Arts Society under the sponsorship of the Allied Arts (War Service) Council of Edmonton for which she gives a course in playwriting.

1946 Husband returns from the war. Moves back to Lamont in a Ukrainian area. 15 December, third child, Carol, born.

1947 Writes the short stories, "Get Along Little Dogie" and "The Last Fifteen Minutes."

1948 Returns to Edmonton where Dr. Ringwood sets up a private practice. Writes the play, *The Drowning of Wasyl Nemitchuk or A Fine Colored Easter Egg.*

1949 13 January, fourth and last child, Patrick, born. With Elsie Park Gowan, writes the short story, "The Truth About the Ten Gallon Hat." Teaches playwriting and short-story writing at the Banff School of Fine Arts.

1950 Plays the title role in *Anna Christie* at the University of Alberta.

1952 Writes the play, *Widger's Way* or *The Face in the Mirror,* and the radio plays "Right on Our Doorstep," "Health Scripts for Children," and "Frontier to Farmland."

1953 With composer Bruce Haack, writes the political musical, "The Wall." Writes the radio play, "The Bells of England." Moves with husband and children to Williams Lake, B.C., where Dr. Ringwood practices surgery. Helps to revive The Players Club and initiates the popular "Coffee Houses."

1954-1955 Writes the short stories "So Gracious the Time," "Home Base," and "Supermarket."

1958 Composes the poem, "The Road," for the B.C. centennial.

1959 Her first novel, *Younger Brother*, written. Dramatizes *Heidi* for serial radio production. Writes the play, *Lament for Harmonica or Maya.*

1960 Gives workshops in dramatics and adjudicates numerous plays in the British Columbia Dominion, Provincial, and School Drama Festivals, 1960-1970.

1961-1962 Commissioned by the 50th Anniversary Committee of Edson, Alberta, to write a play based on the early days of Edson. With Chet Lambertson, composer, writes the musical, "Look Behind You, Neighbor."

1963 Writes the short story, "Some People's Grandfathers" or "Sammy Joe and the Moose."

1964-1966 Volunteers services to the Cariboo Indian School, Saint Joseph Mission, Williams Lake, for a program in speech arts. Writes an adaptation of "The Lion and the Mouse," and an Indian version of *The Sleeping Beauty*. Travels with her husband to England, Ireland, and Italy. Publishes impressions in letters to *Williams Lake Tribune*. Edits a two-volume work *My Heart Is Glad*. Writes the children's play, "The Three Wishes." Gives workshops in dramatics for teachers at Williams Lake Schools, 1966-1968.

1967 Travels with husband to California and Mexico. Gives summer course in speech for student actors at Notre Dame College, B.C. Awarded Certificate of Merit for outstanding contributions to the British Columbia Centennial Celebrations of 1966 and the Canadian Confederation Centennial Celebrations of 1967. Writes the play, *The Deep Has Many Voices*. With composer, Art Rosoman, writes the musical, "The Road Runs North."

1968 Dr. Ringwood retires from the medical profession and they move to Chimney Lake, B.C. Gives courses in modern drama, playwriting, acting, and freshman English to the students at Cariboo College, Williams Lake, 1968-1975.

1970 Writes a series of short, satiric plays, "Encounters." Writes the novel, "Pascal." Her brother Bob Pharis dies. Delivers the banquet address at the 50th Anniversary of the Carolina Playmakers, Chapel Hill, North Carolina. Present when her mother, Mary Pharis, in her eightieth year, receives B. Ed. degree at University of Lethbridge. Gives writing workshops and judges the high school playwriting competitions for the Spring Festivals at Victoria, New Denver, Dawson Creek, and Prince George, 1970-1974.

1971 Honored by the people of Williams Lake with the opening of the Gwen Pharis Ringwood Outdoor Theatre in Boitanio Park, for which she produces the plays *The Stranger* and *The Deep Has Many Voices*.

1973 Awarded the Eric Hamber Trophy by the British Columbia Drama Association for commitment to theater as teacher, director, adjucator, playwright emeritus, and Renaissance lover of life and people. Adapted for stage the children's fable, *The Golden Goose*. Adjudicated the Prince Rupert Drama Festival.

1974 Invited to be a member of a panel at the "Theatre Before the Sixties Conference," Hart House, University of Toronto Graduate Centre for Drama.

1975 Elected to the Central Interior Arts Panel for British Columbia and the British Columbia Arts Board. Made honorary president of the B.C. Drama Association for Amateur Theatre. Visits Russia with her husband. Gives lectures on drama at the University of Toronto and York University. Receives second place award at the New Play Centre's Women's Playwriting Competition, Vancouver, for her play "The Lodge."

1976 Wins first prize for the children's play, *The Magic Carpets of Antonio Angelini*, from the Ontario Multicultural Theatre Association 1976 National Playwriting Competition; travels to Winnipeg to assist in its production at the National Multicultural Summer Festival. Writes the play, "A Remembrance of Miracles." Goes on a playwrights' speaking tour, arranged by Playwrights Co-op, to the universities at Calgary, Edmonton, Saskatoon, Sudbury, North Porcupine, and Victoria.

1977 Gives a lecture on drama to theater students at Dalhousie University, Halifax, Nova Scotia. Writes the short story, "Restez, Michelle, Don't Go," which is subsequently read on CBC radio, Vancouver.

1978 Invited to take part on a Panel of Women Writers at the Intercontinental Conference of Women Writers of North and South America, University of Ottawa. Begins writing myth and memory book, "Scenes from a Country Life."

1979 Writes the play *Mirage* for production at the Association of Canadian Theatre History, meeting at the University of Saskatchewan, Saskatoon, where she addresses the members with a lecture on mid-twentieth-century Canadian Drama in western Canada. Gives a lecture on Radio Drama to the members of the Association of Canadian Radio and Film Researchers at the same conference in Saskatoon.

1980 Finishes the first draft of a one-act tragedy, "The Furies," the last of the trilogy of Indian plays.

1981 Writes a one-act play, *The Garage Sale*, which is to be produced at the Du Maurier Festival in Vancouver in April. It has been bought by CBC radio for their "Sunday Matinee" program. *Mirage* will be published by Borealis Press, in *The Collected Plays of Gwen Pharis Ringwood* (adult plays) edited by Enid Delgatty Rutland.

CHAPTER 1

Grass Roots

TO CONJURE up a picture of Gwen Pharis Ringwood at the present time is to see a slender, vibrant woman in her early seventies standing in boots and slacks and an old woolen jacket on the shore of Chimney Lake in the ranch country of northern British Columbia, triumphantly displaying a rainbow trout she has just caught or a flaming blossom she has nurtured. For Gwen Pharis Ringwood will always be associated with the land, whether it be the prairie country of Alberta where she grew up, or the gold fields of northern Saskatchewan where she went as a young married woman, or the rough ranch country near Williams Lake, B.C., where she and Barney brought up their four children. It is this closeness to the grass roots of Canada that made her so accessible to the ideas of regional and folk drama.

A happy chain of circumstances led to Ringwood's involvement with a new style of theater. First her upbringing on a farm in the heart of the Canadian prairie; then her friendship with Elizabeth Sterling Haynes and their quickening interest in community and prairie theater; subsequently her introduction to "Proff" Koch and his influence in the writing of folk plays; and finally her meeting with Dr. Robert Gard and his encouragement of her work in the direction of Alberta folklore and local history. The miracle of it was that a talented prairie girl moved unwittingly through ideal channels to become a gifted playwright, offering Canadians a new style of regional drama especially adapted to the portrayal of western Canadian life.

From Ringwood's family background, her involvement in community theater, her education in folk drama, and her interest in the land and its people, a body of work has evolved which, after forty years, is still developing and making its gradual contribution to Canadian literature. Ringwood is a kind of magical person, inspiring others with belief in themselves, while she herself, with no apparent effort, produces an abundance and variety of literary works. A slight woman, quick, still attractive, with bright, searching eyes and throaty voice, she wins over the visitor immediately. One caller noticed that she used to smoke continually, striking matches quickly and unthinkingly on the underside of any available piece of furniture, while she discussed intently some idea or responded to some question. Dressed casually in slacks and sports shirt, she treats cooking and gardening with careless ease—a casual throwing together of ingredients produces a tasty, gourmet dinner while a seemingly unplanned scattering of seeds yields an abundance of wildly beautiful plants and flowers harmoniously blended. Perhaps this is symbolic of a woman really in touch with the land. Her friend, the artist, Vivien Cowan, describes Gwen Ringwood's occasional experiments with paint as imaginative, fanciful things in brilliant colors conjured up from a fertile mind. Many of her plays have that same quality about them. Her sensitive affinity with nature expressed in passages of lyric beauty possess the same kind of magic which we see in, for example, W. O. Mitchell's *Who Has Seen the Wind;* the spirit and color of her writings bear a close resemblance to the paintings of the Group of Seven; her deep understanding of prairie people is closely related to the work of Frederick Philip Grove. Ringwood's work forms a significant part in a tradition of Canadian prairie writing and painting. It is important to know something of the early biography of Gwen Pharis Ringwood in order to understand her prairie roots and the regional character of the land out of which she came. This mystique of the prairie had a deep influence on the developing writer.

I *Biographical Background*

Gwen Pharis was born in 1910 in Anatone, in the state of Washington. Her father, Leslie Pharis, a farmer and teacher from Missouri, was of Irish-American and French Huguenot stock, while her mother, Mary Bowersock, was originally of Pennsylvania Dutch and English-Irish extraction. Their marriage was happy, perhaps because both were intelligent, stimulating people who complemented each other—she with her thirst for learning, he with imaginative, romantic, philosophic, and liberated sensibilities. They instilled in their three sons and daughter a love of nature, a freedom of outlook, and right values.

In 1913, when Gwen Pharis was three years old, the family moved to Canada where they had purchased a farm outside of Barons about fifty miles north of Lethbridge, Alberta. Across the treeless prairie they journeyed from Lethbridge in two horse-drawn wagons with one cow. Mrs. Pharis described that procession which consisted of a wagon with hay rack driven by her husband and a wagon containing a large green box loaded with miscellany—household goods—which she drove. Tied to that was a respectable buggy with a gentle cow tethered behind. Their dog Trixie added to the procession. They rode "fifty miles due north to a P.O. called Barrhill," as Mrs. Pharis relates it, where their half-section was located. Arriving late at night, they were reluctantly permitted to stay by the erstwhile owners who had lost the land by default. At Barons they established their wheat farm and Gwen's father also opened a school in a one-room schoolhouse. Later the family moved to Magrath where Mr. Pharis was again successful at both teaching and farming. A crowning achievement of his later life came when, as one of the initiators of the United Farmers Organization in Alberta, he was elected as an Alberta advisor to the federal government's Agricultural Advisory Committee Program, meeting four times a year in Ottawa with the minister and deputy minister of agriculture. Gwen's attachment to her father and her rapport with his affinity for the land is easily discernible in her plays.

Gwen was greatly attached to her three younger brothers, Blaine, George, and Robert. She was crushed by their premature deaths—Blaine and George overseas in the Canadian Air Force in World War II, and Robert in a sudden death many years later. As children they had explored the area around the St. Mary's River across from the Blood Indian Reserve, where their parents' ranch and farm were located. They knew every inch of the coulee, the sweep of prairie, the Indian tepees in the distance. Often walking through the gulley and into the deep ravines, they would delight in examining the creeping cedars, fir, and spruce, the fern, and lady slippers in the stream opening out into the St. Mary's River. These were magical places and the source of Gwen Pharis's personal body of myth. Each day in summer Gwen Pharis and her brothers explored the ravines and coulees through this prairie land, picked black-eyed susans, walked past the mysterious well, conscious of the stimuli of winds, grass, and river, struggling to find meaning in these things and in their relationship to each other. In her novel *Younger Brother* she comes to grips with this land and its influence on their young lives. And in her plays she recreates the prairie again and again, stressing the qualities of beauty and solitude, of violence and terror which informed the lives of the prairie people, showing how nature in all its varied aspects was responsible for their strengths and weaknesses.

Early in life Gwen Pharis's future career was influenced by theater and also by the community in which she lived. Every year from age seven she was treated to the mystery and excitement of theater. At the annual five-day period of the Chautauqua festival of the arts in Magrath, the artistic level was always high in the presentation of world-famous lecturers, outstanding musicians, and classical dramas. Gwen Pharis's parents also took her to theater in Lethbridge to see professional British and American companies of actors.

Religion had little influence on her life. Her parents were Protestants but were not strongly affiliated to any particular church. Her father had been brought up a Baptist but he worked hard to rid himself of the rigid Baptist training which he considered narrow and cruel. He was a true romantic with little patience for the trivial. He leaned always toward a philosophical point of view. Gwen Pharis became a Unitarian for a short time but returned to her original agnosticism. The community in which she lived as a child was predominantly Mormon and she therefore always had the feeling of being an outsider, a Gentile. In the village of 1800 people, only one hundred were not Mormons. She tells us that this experience of seeming to look on life from the outside gave her the objectivity she would later need in her work. As a writer she has always remained aloof from her material, never subjectively involved. Even in those plays where she has used family as characters and family incidents as plot she remains a detached observer with the true objectivity of the artist.

Further influences on her work were those teachers who encouraged and inspired her. Her schooling was diverse and stimulating for it brought her to Calgary; Valier, Montana; and Edmonton. When she finished elementary school in Magrath in 1923 Gwen was placed in ninth grade in Crescent Heights High School, Calgary, while her mother was pursuing her education in normal school. Gwen Pharis found the large school very challenging with principal and mathematics teacher William Aberhart, later the first Social Credit premier in Canada (Alberta), and Miss Allard, English teacher, who encouraged her to write the short stories later dramatized on radio.

She returned in 1924 to Magrath High School for tenth grade

where her father was vice-principal and teacher. Gwen Pharis delighted in his mathematics and English lessons because he expanded her vision and revealed to her the excitement of exploring knowledge, instilling in her a love of math. She likened plane geometry to music, soaring with triangles, and she began to understand the feelings of mathematicians who use math formulas to send rockets soaring through the sky. Gwen Pharis achieved top marks in her high school math courses, and she captured her sense of excitement in the mysteries of math in the short story "The Death of Einstein." Her play *The Deep Has Many Voices*, written fifty years later, contains again her feelings of wonder at the vastness of the universe and the ability of mathematicians to harness some of its power.

Gwen Pharis was sent in 1925 to Crescent Heights High School in Calgary for eleventh grade. Here she made a lasting friend, Dorothy Thomas of High River, for whom, many years later she wrote the Edson story in the play, "Look Behind You, Neighbor."

In 1926 Leslie Pharis took his family to Valier, Montana, where he invested his money in an irrigated farm. Gwen Pharis attended twelfth grade in Valier High School and then spent one year at the University of Montana where she wrote essays on Yeats, scraped through in physics, refrained from joining a sorority, dated the boys from ethnic neighborhoods, and generally attempted to be very avant-garde. Her saving grace was her creative writing in the English courses. She delighted in European writers, especially Chekhov. This early affinity for Chekhov revealed itself years later in the characters and structure of some of her plays, notably "The Lodge." Chekhov's detachment from dependency on any one main character can also be seen in several Ringwood plays, especially *The Rainmaker,* and in her three musicals, "Look Behind You, Neighbor," "The Road Runs North," and "Mirage."

Gwen Pharis was forced to leave the university in 1928 when she was not yet eighteen years of age, due to the failure of her father's farm. She applied and obtained a job as bookkeeper with Browning Mercantile on the Blackfoot Indian Reservation. Despite the aloof attitude of the white community toward the Indians whom they served, Gwen Pharis made friends with both Indians and Metis. Cora Welch, a half-Irish, half-Indian girl, later to be made princess of the Blackfoot Tribe, became her friend. Cora's Indian boyfriend was the personality Gwen Ringwood used, many years later, to create the title role of her novel "Pascal." It was here on the

Blackfoot Indian Reservation that Ringwood's genuine interest in Indians developed. Ten years later at Chapel Hill, she tried to utilize the myths of the Blackfoot mythology in a drama of ancient Indian rituals and long poetic speeches but she failed to capture the mystique. She was to succeed some forty years later when she wrote her two successful Indian plays, *Lament for Harmonica* and *The Stranger*.

After three devastating years in Montana, Leslie Pharis was forced in 1929 to sell the farm and their household furnishings at auction and to bring his impoverished family back to Alberta. The three years of fruitless labor; the early loss of an expensive uninsured bull, struck by lightning (depicted in Ringwood's play *Widger's Way*); the resultant inability to carry out his intention to raise blooded cattle; the successive crop failures—reduced the family spirit and income. It was the depression years, and both Mr. and Mrs. Pharis immediately applied for teaching positions in Spring Coulee near Magrath, where they lived with their sons in the teacheridge, meanwhile sending Gwen for her sophomore and junior years to the University of Alberta as a second year student in the Honours English program. Professors at the university who influenced her thinking were Dr. W. G. Hardy, novelist; Professor William Hardy Alexander, classicist, Unitarian minister, and active member of the Socialist CCF; and Dr. Broadus of English language textbook renown. Dr. Alexander became her good friend. This great classical scholar was to remain a long time family friend of the Ringwoods. A key figure in the humanities, Dr. Alexander, who eventually departed for the University of California at Berkeley, was Alberta's loss. Dr. Hardy influenced Gwen to become a Unitarian for a time; Dr. Broadus, a brilliant, sardonic man, encouraged her to write and often addressed her in class with the words' "And now are we to have a purple passage, Miss Pharis?" After finishing her junior year Gwen Pharis was forced to give up university and to look for a job. Her family had moved back to the farm outside Magrath. The depression had caused more financial losses. Gwen obtained a full time job as assistant to the medical librarian at the university and was able to continue her education sporadically, taking a course occasionally.

But the turning point in her life came two years later, in 1933, when she began work as secretary to Elizabeth Sterling Haynes who, by means of a Carnegie grant to the Department of Extension of the University of Alberta, was initiating a development of theater in the province of Alberta. Five years of total immersion in drama with Elizabeth Haynes decided Gwen Pharis's future. Her first play, directed and produced by Elizabeth Haynes at the newly opened Banff School of Fine Arts, launched her stage and playwriting career. During those five years she wrote thirteen half-hour radio plays for the CKUA program, *New Lamps For Old*, directed by Sheila Marriot. Unfortunately, Gwen Pharis failed to keep the scripts so we have only the titles listed in the bibliography of this book. In 1933 Mrs. Haynes and E. A. Corbett established the Banff School of Theatre which later in 1935 became the Banff School of Fine Arts. In the summer of 1937, Frederick Koch, chairman of the Department of Drama at the University of North Carolina, taught playwriting at the school. Becoming aware of Gwen Pharis's talents, Professor Koch was instrumental in her obtaining a Rockefeller Foundation grant to the University of North Carolina at Chapel Hill for her M.A. degree in drama. She left Alberta in 1937, leaving behind Brian Ringwood, the young medical student to whom she had become engaged. She returned to Edmonton in the summer of 1938 to teach at the University Summer School before leaving for her second year at U.N.C. The two years at Chapel Hill were prolific in the writing of six plays and the successful production of five of these. All of these plays are extant and in published and manuscript form. Gwen Pharis assisted also in the preparation, editing, and proofreading of Fred Koch's quarterly magazine *The Carolina Play-Book* to which she also contributed articles, poetry, and plays. In June 1939 she graduated with an M.A. degree in English and drama, winning the Ronald Holt Cup for outstanding work in drama, and having her play *Still Stands the House* produced for the commencement performance.

The years following her graduation were personally fulfilling for Gwen Pharis in her professional life, her marriage, and the birth of her children. Returning to Alberta in the late fall of 1939, she married Dr. John Brian Ringwood. She was appointed director of drama for the Department of Extension at the University of Alberta while her husband interned in the Misericordia Hospital.

The next move on the part of the Ringwoods was highly significant as it resulted in her coming to a recognition of the Canadian spirit, of discovering Canada, its unique terrain and impressive beauty, and of making it her own. Her writings henceforth are rich in this recognition. In October 1940 the Ringwoods chose to move to northern Saskatchewan at Lake Athabasca. In winter there was light only from 10:00 A.M. to 3:00 P.M. but in June there was light all day and night. Life at Goldfields was a Spartan existence as evidenced by the modified bunkhouse in which they lived on the north shore of the lake. It was so cold that Barney Ringwood had to cut a hole in the ice for water and then, clad in a great buffalo coat, he would carry buckets of water to the bunkhouse and attract Gwen's attention by bumping the door with his head, his coat meanwhile covered with icicles. While Lake Athabasca was frozen there would be no plane or boat and no mail but only radio messages from the outside world. Barney, the only doctor for the goldmining community, went by dog team, plane, boat, or freight canoe to see his patients. The people were tough, hard-rock miners used to the pioneering life. On 22 April 1941 Gwen and Barney Ringwood's first child, Stephan, was born; the following year Susan was born. For both these deliveries, Barney sent Gwen back to the hospital in Edmonton, Alberta. The two years spent in Goldfields formed an exciting and adventurous period in their lives. It was here that Gwen Ringwood was inspired by the colorful character of a neighbor to write the successful play, *The Courting of Marie Jenvrin.* Here also her imagination was fired by the vivid beauty of the Canadian northwest. Her later affinity for the paintings of the Group of Seven may well have had their origin in her experiences in Goldfields.

Leaving Goldfields in 1942, the Ringwoods carried with them wonderful memories. Gwen Ringwood described it in a letter to Robert Card written many years later in 1952:

> In a long freight canoe with an outboard engine, my husband who was the mine doctor and I travelled along the lake between the hundreds of small rocky islands that rose clean and sheer out of the water. On the islands were tangled vines, wind-racked jack pine and the graceful mountain ash with its white blossoms in the spring and the crimson berries in the fall. When we left the Lake to "come outside" we knew that we would probably never again live in as beautiful a place.[1]

Here is a description that might easily have been a summary of one of the paintings of the Group of Seven. Ringwood's conception of the primitive beauties of Canada, and that expressed by the Group, are identical. We are also reminded here of A. J. M. Smith, of F. R. Scott, and of many other Canadian writers' versions of Canada as the "lonely land"—this land which served as a source of inspiration for a people's values and which is so evident in Ringwood's plays.

The challenge of the environment, hard and lonely and tragic as it appears in her prairie plays, is still the cause of a spiritual communion with that mysterious force, the source of life on the prairie. In this she shares the vision of Canada's older poets: Charles G. D. Roberts, Bliss Carman, Archibald Lampman, D. C. Scott, and others whose communion with nature nourished, rather than deadened, sensibility and inspiration. Her work also reminds us of the narrative poet E. J. Pratt, who wrote of the heroic struggles of man with his environment, as did Ringwood in her prairie plays. Like Pratt, she also believed that in the final analysis man's salvation lies, not in nature, but in himself. Pratt's relationship with the Group of Seven in the decade of the twenties, when the relation between art and poetry in Canada was being strongly emphasized, resulted in a close affinity between their work and his poetry. The same is true of Ringwood's drama. Also, Pratt's and Ringwood's confrontations with the cruelties of nature and their attempts to relate these with a Christian view resulted for both in a reconciliation with the mystery of the universe. Garth in Ringwood's *Dark Harvest* comes to an acceptance of this mystery and immolates himself to it. It is the view of the agnostic who yet hopes in the possibility of meaning behind the force. Both Pratt and Ringwood are concerned with man's struggle against nature and his gradual coming to terms with it.

The next three years' artistic endeavors were fraught with loneliness, for her husband had enlisted and departed overseas for World War II. But her meeting with Dr. Robert Gard who offered her a grant to write Albertan folk plays was the inspiration she needed to bring her vision of Canada to other Canadians. During this period Gwen and her two small children lived in Edmonton, Alberta. In the same letter to Robert Gard, already quoted above, Gwen speaks of having "discovered Alberta, made it our own." She refers to the fact that Canadians at last are becoming conscious of their national heritage, and continues: "I know the Canadian West and each year I have come to a deeper appreciation of its many-sided character, its infinite variety." In the same letter to Robert Gard she writes of the people of Canada:

Our population is a heterogeneous one and our manners and customs vary greatly from community to community, from region to region. We have villages where speech and action and thought is in the light, quick rhythm of the French. Again a Ukrainian town seems to have a slower, outwardly stolid rhythm but underneath run the deep, passionate undercurrents of feeling and a lusty, broad humour. We have towns with the flavour of a quiet English village or a slightly aggressive American town; we have industrious German settlements, mining towns with a preponderance of Latin names, the cow towns where the flavour and play-acting of the ranching industry have their way, the northern town with its feeling of the fur trade and the dog team. There are towns where the talk is of jumping horses and polo, and towns where the talk is of an historic past. And a few ghost towns—in the desert or at the site of a defunct mine.

Of Barney and herself she tells Robert Gard:

So we have travelled through mountains and muskeg and the great silent forests of lofty spruce. We have hunted or picnicked along the shores of the many lakes that are in the parkland area. We have seen the wheatfields green in the spring and golden in the fall, have watched cowhands drive cattle over the rolling foothills and have heard the coyotes howling from hill to hill across the gaunt, duncolored sweep of the unbroken prairie. We have marveled at the twisted conformations of the Badlands and hired a car to pull us out of the sand when we ventured too far into the Sand Hills. And as we travel over the country we begin to sense all that lies under the earth—coal and gold and uranium and oil and fresh spring water and bitter alkaline water and hot sulphur water and the bones of the dinosaur and the buffalo and the flint arrow head and the bones of men who died looking for gold or a passage to India or for souls to save. And over the earth is the blue and grey and crimson of the Western sky, the flashing jet plane and the big bellied Air Liner.[2]

She concludes this letter with the words: "And for the most part these are the things I have written about. Most of my plays, I suppose, could be called 'regional.' " It is as a regional writer that Gwen Ringwood is able to direct the attention of Canadians to their land and people; it is as a regional writer that she is able to dispel the myth that regional writing can be neither universal nor of first-rate quality; it is as a regional writer that she is now at last being recognized. Her finest plays to date are regional, giving us the character of the land and its people, whether it be in the western Canadian prairies, the ranch land of British Columbia, or the valleys of the Fraser Canyon.

The years from 1946 to 1968 were productive for Gwen Ringwood in writing and in community theatrical activities. Dr. Ringwood's medical and surgical practices dictated their moves first to the Ukrainian district of Lamont, Alberta, then to Edmonton, and finally to Williams Lake, northern British Columbia. Two more children were born, Carol in 1946, and Patrick in 1949. Gwen, her husband, and children finally settled in 1953 in the fast-growing community of Williams Lake, where Dr. Ringwood's surgical skills were sorely needed by the loggers, the ranchers, and the Indians. A large portrait of Dr. Ringwood, astride his horse, now graces the wall of the lobby in the new hospital at Williams Lake—a tribute to his long and devoted service.

Gwen Ringwood's growing role in the life of the community was clearly evidenced in her service to the people of Williams Lake as wife, mother, teacher, actress, director, and playwright. She initiated here the popular "coffeehouses" or evenings of dramatic entertainments, and with others, revived the community theater. She did not ignore the Indians in her growing awareness of service to the community but donated a portion of her time to the Cariboo Indian School located at Saint Joseph's Oblate Mission. On Fridays she collaborated with Sister Germaine on a Language Arts Program. Gwen adapted plays for the Indian children and helped seventh- and eighth-grade students compile two books of their stories and legends. Despite her community involvement, her devotion to her own children took precedence until they were finally grown up and settled in their own careers.

Then came another major move. Retirement for Gwen and Barney Ringwood in 1968 meant more time to devote to their special interests at their cottage on Chimney Lake where they had previously acquired 140 acres of property. Here Gwen Ringwood now has her own little cabin a few paces from the house, where she can write undisturbed. Barney pursues his sportsman's interest in fishing and riding, chopping the winter's wood, mending the fences, and managing most of the practical business matters. Gwen frequently interrupts her quiet life at Chimney Lake to give college courses in drama at Cariboo College, to conduct workshops on theater in various areas of British Columbia, to adjudicate amateur productions, to participate on various provincial panels for the arts, to attend drama association meetings, and to lecture at various Canadian universities in the east. Her plays continue to win prizes in drama competitions. For her outstanding contribution to Canadian Theatre she was the recipient of the Eric Hamber trophy from the British Columbia Drama Association in 1973. *The Magic Carpets of Antonio Angelini* won first prize from the National Multicultural Theatre Association in 1976 and was produced for six weeks at the Winnipeg Multicultural Festival the same year. *Widger's Way* was revived for the 1976 Kawartha Festival in Ontario. "The Lodge" was presented in Vancouver in 1977, having received second prize at the New Play Centre Competition for Women Writers in 1975. Two stories and a play were produced on CBC radio in 1978; two more plays were broadcast on CBC radio in 1979; and her musical play *Mirage* was produced at the University of Saskatchewan in Saskatoon in the spring of 1979. With this brief introduction in mind, let us turn to a study of the crucial drama experiences and influences in Ringwood's life.

II *The Prairie and Community Theater and Elizabeth Haynes*

Within the community of Alberta, Gwen Pharis's writing was directly affected by Elizabeth Haynes and her ideal of community theater; the views of a colleague, Elsie Park Gowan, also contributed to her development; an indirect source of inspiration were the paintings of the Group of Seven.

Ringwood maintains that the strongest force in her becoming a playwright was her friend, director of drama, and teacher, Elizabeth Sterling Haynes, who was the first director of Edmonton's Little Theatre in 1928. With her husband she had moved to Edmonton in 1923 after a distinguished career in acting and teaching theater arts in Toronto. In 1933 she was appointed to develop drama throughout the province of Alberta through a grant from the Carnegie Foundation. Gwen Pharis traveled throughout Alberta with her as her assistant from 1933 until 1937. From this association she learned to write plays, to act, and to adjudicate. Elizabeth Sterling Haynes inspired a very different sense of theater than one would get in New York, London, or even Toronto—not theater for a bored middle-class but theater that creates community. This is crucial to an understanding of Ringwood's work. Haynes made the Dominion Drama Festival a reality in Alberta. She aroused small community groups in every area of the province to a total group effort to bring theater to the people. She helped amateur theater groups on depression budgets, and she aided in laying the foundations in 1935 for the Banff School of Fine Arts to which she appointed Gwen Pharis as first registrar. A distinguished pioneer of the arts in Alberta, she was honored by students, faculty, and civic authorities. In 1974, long after her death, a special celebration *Remember Elizabeth* was inaugurated by the University of Alberta, and a booklet recalling her rich contributions to theater in Alberta was published. In it Ringwood wrote: "A western Canada theatre was born during those depression years. It was rooted in Elizabeth's idealism and faith in art; nurtured by her great knowledge and talent; it flowered and dropped seeds in many unexpected places . . . . seeds which still bear fruit."[3] Ringwood also wrote an article, "Elizabeth Haynes and the Prairie Theatre," in which she says of Mrs. Haynes:

> The Prairie Theatre that Mrs. Haynes began, nurtured and sometimes saw come to rich flowering, has the vitality, honesty and the magic of good theatre anywhere . . . . Most of the towns in Alberta, many in Saskatchewan and Manitoba, are a part of that Prairie Theatre. The plays that I, and many other Western Canadians have written were derived from and written for it. To us the Prairie theatre is a reality . . . . Mrs. Haynes willed it into being . . . travelling from one end of the province of Alberta to the other. As the actors and students and writers and directors whom she taught and trained moved on, they took with them her ideal of a theatre big enough to illuminate the pathways of the soul. And so today the Prairie Theatre exists not in one place, but in many.[4]

Community theater in outlying or back country areas of North America was often a rural movement inspired by farmers and ranchers' associations in order to draw people to the local meetings. This happened also in Alberta. Gradually these play groups became more sophisticated and more highly organized. Many writers obtained their first playwriting experiences through these rural groups. Ringwood's work with Elizabeth Haynes brought her into close contact with these community theatrical groups scattered throughout Alberta and the other western provinces. Besides the adjudications Ringwood gave to these aspiring groups to improve their acting and writing talents, she was also led to see the communal value of involving whole communities in the production of a play or musical. It was this concept of communal theater that years later inspired her to write and direct two musicals for communities in Alberta and British Columbia. So successful was she that in 1977, Clive Stango, the editor of the local newspaper in Williams Lake, B.C., described her dedication to the people of Williams Lake and to their theater as having a cumulative effect. It involved first the large casts of amateur actors who would otherwise never have been drawn to theater; then it drew in audiences composed of the actors' families, neighbors, and friends. "Ringwood's expertise and dedication changed the character of Williams Lake" said Clive Stangoe.[5]

The outdoor theater built and dedicated to her in 1971, the Gwen Pharis Ringwood Theatre, in Boitanio Park, Williams Lake, B.C., is a symbol of community gratitude.

Elsie Park Gowan, an Albertan colleague of Gwen Pharis, also influenced her. They collaborated on the radio series, *New Lamps for Old*, each contributing twelve plays on great humanitarian leaders. During the dialogue that ensued, Elsie, who was, even then, a feminist supporter of women's liberation, tried to change Gwen Pharis's very traditional ideas on women. Elsie's ideas were considered but failed to change Gwen's orthodox views at the time. But years later one can observe the change in the roles played by women in her plays. The women in *Still Stands the House*, *Pasque Flower*, *Dark Harvest*, *The Rainmaker*, *Stampede*, and several other early dramas play the traditional roles of housewife and mother. Only in the plays written in the 1960s and 1970s do they break away from these roles to maintain their independence as professional career women. "The Lodge" is a powerful example of this.

A further factor in the development of Ringwood's talents as a folk dramatist was the Group of Seven, those Canadian artists whose work emphasized Canadian landscape. Donald Cameron was able to bring one of these artists, A. Y. Jackson, to the Banff School of Fine Arts to lecture to the aspiring artists and writers there who were interested in native landscape. Jackson broadened their vision of Canada so that their artistic and literary work reflected the same kind of awareness of the Canadian scene. Gwen Ringwood, charged with this vision, wrote plays about prairie life realistically, often poetically, and with vivid imagery.

"The Group of Seven" came into being in 1920 when seven Canadian artists with similar interests and ideas, who had exhibited their paintings together and were fast becoming known for their artistic rapport with the rugged beauty of Canada, decided to establish themselves as a distinct group of artists. Their membership included: Franklin Carmichael, Lawren Harris, A. Y. Jackson, Arthur Lismer, J. E. H. MacDonald, Tom Thomson, and Frederick Varley. Frank Johnston resigned from the Group in 1924. Emily Carr, though not formally a member of the Group, was greatly influenced by them in her art. Lawren Harris was her closest associate. Carr records her impressions of the Group in words that bespeak the sentiments of many later Canadian artists and writers whose works, consciously or not, show the influence of these major Canadian painters:

. . . this Group of Seven, what have they created?—a world stripped of earthiness, shorn of fretting details, purged, purified; a naked soul, pure and unashamed; lovely spaces filled with wonderful serenity. What language do they speak, those silent, awe-filled spaces? I do not know. Wait and listen; you shall hear by and by. I long to hear and yet I'm half afraid. I think perhaps I shall find God here, the God I've longed and hunted for and failed to find.[6]

This is the spirit Ringwood creates in her prairie plays. She sets a giant figure of a prairie farmer against the canvas of a world shorn of detail, a limitless expanse of earth and sky in which the farmer dwindles into a finite creature struggling against the elements, crying out to that God he has looked for and failed to find (cf. *Dark Harvest*) as he realizes the power behind nature and, like Emily Carr, "waits and listens." The Group of Seven tried to convince Canadians that they must have an art of their own if Canada was to be a great country, even as Ringwood and other pioneer dramatists attempted to do with theater.

One of the last areas of Canada to be painted by any member of the Group of Seven was the prairies. A. Y. Jackson went to Alberta in 1937, before Ringwood left for Chapel Hill, and while she was still at the Banff School of Fine Arts where he lectured. Jackson sketched the foothills around Lethbridge and the study for his *Blood Indian Reserve*, that area which could be a perfect setting for her Indian plays, *The Stranger* and *Maya*, the area from which Ringwood came. In later years he returned many times to that place. Lemoine FitzGerald, the last artist to join the Group of Seven in 1932, became known as the "Painter of the Prairies." He truly captured the atmosphere of the prairies in varying light that expressed the changing seasons. His works reveal the same restraint and austerity as does, for example, Ringwood's play, *Still Stands the House*. In his painting *Doc Snider's House*, exhibited in the Group of Seven's 1931 show, he achieves a rapport with the prairie in winter that parallels Ringwood's in *Still Stands the House*. Peter Mellen in his book *The Group of Seven* says this of Fitzgerald's work: "In this painting he uses dry and delicate colours and crystal-clear light to express the frozen quality of the winter landscape. Here he succeeded in capturing the atmosphere of the prairies without having to represent the traditional wide-open spaces."[7]

Harris, Jackson, and MacDonald were fascinated by the Rockies and painted vast mountain landscapes in Alberta and British Columbia. Lismer made one trip in 1928 and painted his famous

Cathedral Mountain. The Group were convinced that it was the rugged northern landscape that truly expressed the Canadian character and identity. Their energy and vitality were reflected in their works of art. Ringwood's musical "The Road Runs North" expresses the same dramatic quality and energy. The paintings of The Group of Seven and the plays of Ringwood and her colleagues reflect many elements unique to Canada.

III *The Carolina Playmakers and Frederick Koch*

A third and highly important factor in the development of Ringwood's talents was her exposure to Frederick Koch's ideas on the folk play. As has been noted, in 1937 Ringwood received a Rockefeller Foundation grant and scholarship to a graduate school education in folk-playwriting at the University of North Carolina in Chapel Hill. The two years with the Playmakers was one of the strongest forces shaping Ringwood's career as a western Canadian playwright. Fred Koch and his fellow professors in the Department of Drama opened to Gwen Pharis the unlimited potentialities of the folk play, and her compassion for western Canada's prairie people and minority groups was intensified as it sought expression in dramatic form.

It is therefore important to examine the folk play as understood by "Proff" Koch and Ringwood's other teachers at Chapel Hill. Frederick Koch derived his ideas of folk drama from the Irish Literary Revival, the plays of Yeats, Synge, and Lady Gregory. What these writers did for theater in Ireland, Fred Koch attempted to do for theater in North America through his students. His enthusiasm for the folk play was so contagious that it prompted the launching of the Carolina Playmakers' School which has continued to operate from Koch's founding of it in 1919 to the present. Koch inspired his students with a vision of the vast possibilities for playmaking embodied in the very character of the land in which they were nurtured. Gwen Ringwood thus became aware of the epic quality of the open prairies and the effect of this vastness upon the human being, its larger-than-life qualities. In *Still Stands the House*, for example, the prairie itself becomes a character in the play, shaping the personae, establishing the plot, and conditioning the outcome. Ringwood's early dramatic inspiration involved an interpretation of this prairie, an examination of the human struggle with the land, and an understanding of the hard work and ingenuity needed to conquer it. Ringwood's very language stems from the land and interprets it. The dialogue which she puts into the mouths of her characters is land-oriented and serves to associate her people with the earth. She is a regional dramatist only if one does not narrowly define "regional" as emphasis on a single locale without relevance to the larger world around it; her plays deal with human conflicts identifiable to theatergoers everywhere because the dramatic value of the folk play lies not in folk ornamentation but in the human problem. As Fred Koch defined it:

> The drama of the conflict of man with the forces of nature may be termed "folk drama." The conflict may not be apparent on the surface in the immediate action on the stage but the ultimate cause of all dramatic action that we classify as "folk," whether the struggle be physical or spiritual, may be found in man's desperate fight for existence.
>
> The term "folk drama" is here used in a new sense, not limited to the communal folk plays of Medieval times (often attributed by scholars to group authorship) which took the form of Christmas pantomimes by village mummers, jigs, sword dances, festivals and various other community celebrations. The term folk drama as here used designates the work of a single artist dealing consciously with his material—the folkways of our less sophisticated and more elemental people, living simple lives apart from the responsibilities of a highly organized social order.[8]

Koch emphasized that it was the new Irish drama which pointed the way toward his initiating folk-playwriting in his course "Native Prairie Plays" which was given for the Dakota Playmakers at the University of North Dakota in 1914, and then at the University of North Carolina in 1918:

> From the first our particular interest was in the locality—in the native materials—and in the making of fresh dramatic forms in playwriting and in acting. For we felt that if the young writer observed the locality and interpreted it faithfully, it would show him the way to the universal. For if we can see the "interesting-ness" of the lives of those about us with imagination, with wonder, why may we not interpret that life in significant images for others—perhaps for all?[9]

Samuel Selden, one of Gwen Ringwood's professors, who worked with "Proff" Koch and later took over the chairmanship of the department when Koch died, defined folk drama in this way:

> The term "folk," as we use it, has nothing to do with the folk play of medieval times. But rather it is concerned with folk subject matter: with the

legends, superstitions, customs, environmental differences, and the vernacular of the common people. For the most part they are realistic and human; sometimes they are imaginative and poetic. The chief concern of the folk dramatist is man's conflict with the forces of nature and his simple pleasure in being alive.[10]

Another drama professor and major American playwright who greatly influenced Gwen Pharis Ringwood was Paul Green, the Pulitzer prize-winning author of the play *In Abraham's Bosom* and the initiator of symphonic drama in the southern United States. Green defined folk drama thus: "The folk are the people whose manners, ethics, religious and philosophical ideals are more nearly derived from and controlled by the ways of the outside physical world (cf. Synge's *Riders to the Sea*) than by the ways and institutions of men in a specialized society (cf. Schnitzler's *Anatol* cycle)."[11] Paul Green taught Gwen Pharis and her fellow students to recognize in the folk heroes of the past the life-giving forces of a nation. Just as he turned for aid and sustenance to the American pioneers and forefathers who defined the ideals of the United States, so Green expected Ringwood to find the roots of her theater by turning to the early settlers and leaders of Canada. Green said, "I find myself turning for aid and sustenance to the pioneers and forefathers who helped define and state and bring forth into living terminology these ideals that are the root of our faith. I find myself going back to the early days of our nation's history, trying to put my ear in tune, as it were, to the speaking of these thinkers and leaders."[12]

Hence from such inspired teachers as Frederick Koch, Samuel Selden, and Paul Green, Gwen Pharis was stimulated to write plays about Canadian folk heroes, pioneers, and immigrant peoples. As Archibald Henderson succinctly put it in his foreword to *Pioneering a People's Theatre:*

Koch presents the ideology of folk playmaking; Selden, the able new leader, offers a thoughtful appraisal and lucid estimate, both of Koch the personality, player, and sower of dreams, and of the place of dramatic arts in the University Curriculum. In vivid strokes are portrayed the original and authentically American contributions of Koch to the American drama and theatre: the meaning and inspiration of the "folkplay" and the democratic technic of critically moulding the creative product. In his inimitable individual way, Paul Green, the most notable playwright to emerge from this aura, describes the birthpangs of dramatic creation.[13]

What a difference there is between this and urban-derived theater! In the regional and folk play, the dramatist is urged to examine the land, the environment from which his characters emerge, and to let that land mold those characters and shape that plot, as indeed it does in real life situations. In urban-derived theater the emphasis is on character and its conflict with other characters, shaped and defined by family and friends, neighbors and strangers. The land is simply not there, or merely peripheral like the backdrop to a theater, motionless, exerting little force. Ringwood, like so many other playmakers, was being formed to a new kind of playmaking that happily was geared to the kind of drama that would recreate the Canadian west.

IV *Alberta, the Land, its History and Folklore, and Robert Gard*

Ringwood's work in folk drama was further stimulated by Dr. Robert Gard (educated in folklore at the University of Kansas and Cornell University) who had been encouraged to come to Alberta in 1942 by Donald Cameron, then director of the Department of Extension at the University of Alberta. A Rockefeller Foundation grant was arranged through Dr. David Stevens, director of the Division for the Humanities of the Rockefeller Foundation, to enable Gard to do Alberta folklore research and to stimulate some movement in local drama and the use of local native materials. Thus the Alberta Folklore and Local History Project was established.

Robert Gard proved to be one more link in the chain of circumstances that led Gwen to develop the folk play in western Canada. He traveled through Alberta interviewing the old-timers who had opened the province, collecting their reminiscences, diaries, and journals, which later became the basis for the books he published: *Johnny Chinook*, a collection of tall tales of the Canadian West; *Midnight*, a story of the Calgary Stampede; and *Grassroots Theatre*, an account of folk drama in the United States and Canada. These books in turn inspired Gwen with the themes for some of her plays; for example, the horse Midnight figures largely in her play *Stampede*. Other examples will be enlarged upon in chapter 3. In offering her a grant to write four plays on Alberta's folk heroes, Gard was the instrument which sharpened Gwen's talent for further development of the folk play. He helped to enrich the regional sources she had already been taught to use at Chapel Hill. His travels, especially through southern Alberta around Magrath and Old Man River, where Gwen Pharis was raised, acquainted him with her background and aided him in exploring with her further themes for prairie plays which she had previously begun at the University of North Carolina.

Ringwood's subsequent success with these folk plays sprang directly from her intimate feeling for her native southern Alberta landscape. This feeling was the germinal source of a new kind of western Canadian literature distilled out of the land and the quality of the land, the sights, sounds, smell, and rhythm of life on the prairies. The very landscape becomes personified in this kind of literature as the writer interprets and transfers the living thing into an art form. The quality of life imposed by the land accounts for all the resulting complexities—the struggle for existence, the interrelationships of various groups of people, the kind of lives they are forced to live. The land becomes an obsession and the base of human conflict.

Thus the land set the tone, and the epic appeal of the open Alberta prairie with its vast spaces and subsequent solitude became the basis of Ringwood's early work. What challenged her was the struggle to get on top of the vastness of the country and the importance of the land, to grapple with the largeness of these considerations and to produce a drama worthy of them.

With this brief introduction to the influences directly bearing on Ringwood's future work—her family background, her work with Elizabeth Haynes, Frederick Koch, and Robert Gard—we will now examine in more detail her plays written under the influence of her two strongest mentors, Frederick Koch at North Carolina and Robert Gard at Alberta. The chapters following these will be devoted to Ringwood, the mature playwright, creating independently her original musicals, plays, novels, and short stories.

CHAPTER 2

"Proff" Koch and the Folk Plays

WHEN Gwen Pharis arrived in Chapel Hill, North Carolina, in the fall of 1937, she responded immediately to the natural beauty of this southern state. She had never seen such heavy foliage nor glimpsed the Atlantic ocean. The first sight of the ocean exerted a mysterious hold upon her. Emily Crow Selden was with her in Wilmington on this day and she describes it: "There's only one word that fits Gwen's expression when, after all those years on the Alberta prairie—she first saw—and experienced the ocean. That word is ecstasy. Her whole being pulsed with it. . . . It pulled her, and she was part of it."[1] This intense response to nature invested her regional and folk dialogue with vivid imagery and a sense of the rhythm of the land itself. Thus she established atmosphere and mood, giving her audience a sensibility for the region out of which her characters emerged. In Chapel Hill the rich foliage of the trees, the scarlet birds, the profusion of colorful flowers deeply moved this young woman who was already sensitive to her own undulating golden prairies at harvest time in western Canada.

Gwen Pharis's fellow students liked her immediately because they found her always friendly and generous. Among her many lasting friends were Emily Crow (playwright and wife of the late Samuel Selden); Rietta Bailey Howard (author of the Negro spiritual, *Washed in the Blood*); the late Betty Smith (author of *A Tree Grows in Brooklyn*); Darice Parker (secretary of the Drama Department and John Parker's wife); Lynn Gault (playwright and brilliant set designer); Sam Hirsch (writer and critic); Robert Dale Martin (casting director of CBS-TV). But in those days these friends were merely novices enthusiastically writing their first plays. Emily, Rietta, and Gwen were inseparable. Together they shared their deepest thoughts and convictions and their criticisms of each other's work. Koch's classes engendered a contagion of enthusiasms and self-confidence. He firmly believed that every person was capable of writing a good play. Those sessions with "Proff" when each student was required to read his or her play before the entire class and then wait for the deluge of youthful criticisms certain to come, were a powerful means of preparation for the years ahead. Far away from Chapel Hill, many of the young playwrights would have to face themselves and their work virtually alone, without the aid of experienced theater critics.

Gwen Pharis was Proff Koch's assistant and "girl Friday." Part of her duties as a Rockefeller Fellow consisted of marking undergraduate assignments and helping to edit the *Carolina Play-Book*, a magazine published four times a year by the Carolina Playmakers. Many of her articles, poems, and plays were Koch's selections for inclusion in those issues.

During her two years at Chapel Hill Gwen Pharis wrote six plays: a farcical comedy entitled "Chris Axelson, Blacksmith"; a folk drama of social protest, "One Man's House"; and three plays exploring serious and tragic themes: *Still Stands the House, Pasque Flower*, and *Dark Harvest*, (her first three-act play). She also wrote a short play on the theme of the possessive mother, entitled "The Days May Be Long."

It is interesting to note the general comments made about Ringwood's work by her friends and professors: Emily Crow Selden, Elizabeth Lay Green, Professor Samuel Selden, and Professor John Parker. These remarks on her 1937-1939 work were made in retrospect, in 1976-1977, in interviews and letters. Their nonspecificity and lack of substantiation may weaken the points made, but it should be understood that their usefulness lies mainly in the comparison which the reader can make between these comments by witnesses of her early work, and the analysis made, forty years later, in this book on her contemporary plays. Emily Crow Selden offers the following recollections of Gwen:

> Proff liked Maxwell Anderson's style (he had taught Anderson at the University of North Dakota) and he urged Gwen to write in blank verse. She had a natural poetic style and her characters came alive. Gwen wrote in a hurry, a weakness, but she accomplished so much of real worth in those two short years—four excellent plays written and produced—besides all the aid she gave Proff and her fellow students. Proff called her "little Gwen." There was a portrait of Gwen painted by a fellow student which caught her real strength. She seemed to us so delicate and frail but he captured the pioneer spirit in her. As for her talents—the dialogue in her plays was not necessarily realistic but the effect came across. Her style and symbolism was good. She could write excellent poetic drama.[2]

Emily Selden is a perceptive critic. The reader will note later on that one of Ringwood's strongest gifts is her poetic response to language. Another friend and critic, Elizabeth Lay Green, Paul Green's wife, herself a playwright, said of Gwen Pharis's work that there was a feminine quality in the plays she wrote at Chapel Hill.[3] This may be true, if, by femininity, Mrs. Green means an ability to create convincing female characters whose sensitivity and response to life is deeply feminine.

Professor Samuel Selden, who was her teacher, said that "Gwen was an exceptionally bright member of our graduate group of students and she was a very talented writer. . . . Professor Frederick Koch was a warm admirer of hers and was very fond of her."[4] Gwen Pharis found Samuel Selden's criticism of her work honest and constructive.[5]

Another professor, John Parker, was a young instructor and theater administrator when Gwen Pharis arrived in Chapel Hill. He was youthful enough to be included in the group of her personal friends in social as well as classroom activites. Of her work at this period of her development he wrote: "Gwen's primary interest was, from the beginning, playwriting; and she excelled in that field. . . . All of her plays are stageworthy—some more than others—but all characterized by their honesty in conception, their fidelity to native locale, and most of all by the poetic quality of the dialogue which revealed the characters and advanced the story."[6] John Parker's appraisal is solidly substantiated when one reads those plays. Professor Parker recalled Gwen Pharis's determination to broaden her talents by increasing her acting experience. She appeared in Lynn Gault's delightful southern plantation farce *His Boon Companions*. This gave her more insight into timing comic dialogue which she handles well in one of her Chapel Hill plays, "Chris Axelson, Blacksmith," and in later comedies and farces such as *The Drowning of Wasyl Nemitchuk or A Fine Colored Easter Egg*, and *Widger's Way*. Parker also remarked on her "keen talent for writing colorful, imaginative, provocative dialogue."[7] He was, of course, referring to *Still Stands the House*, *Pasque Flower*, and *Dark Harvest*. Parker was administrator of the Drama Extension work, traveling throughout the state of North Carolina organizing play festivals and managing hundreds of adjudicators. He considered Gwen Pharis next to Betty Smith, one of his best critics and adjudicators—"a play doctor"—as he termed it. In recalling those days at Chapel Hill Parker remarked that Gwen was fortunate to have come there during a period when they had the greatest number of capable young playwrights who competed with each other and set new and high standards in playwriting.

I *Folk Comedy*

The first play that Gwen Pharis wrote at Chapel Hill in the winter of 1937 was a short one-act farcical comedy entitled "Chris Axelson, Blacksmith." In this little situation comedy, she promptly put into effect some techniques she had learned from Koch. The regional and folk elements are all there—the setting of the blacksmith's shop in a small western Canadian village near Lethbridge, Alberta; the dialect of the Swedish immigrant; the dramatic situation of the new Canadian endeavoring to provide his nephew with an education; the folk characters of blacksmith, slow-witted young man, and townspeople. In "Chris Axelson" she produced an average exercise in playwriting, nothing more. However, in this farcical comedy she does show an instinct for comic dialogue and a natural gift for characterization. Although it is set in Alberta, "Chris Axelson" could be located anywhere and still make a valid statement. What she does with this first play, she carries through in all her future work in drama; Gwen produces, in effect, a universal experience from a particular, regional background. Although all good authors do this, not all are working with a regional and folk play form. The point stressed here is that regional drama is not second-rate drama when it successfully creates a universal experience. In "Chris Axelson, Blacksmith," Gwen Pharis combines comedy and farce which she continues to do in her later work. Within the form of a farcical comedy she creates folk characters involved in situations typical of ordinary people anywhere. The audience is thus able to go beyond the character, beyond the region, in order to empathize with the human condition and the human experience which is only too familiar to them.

Ringwood had known a widower blacksmith in Magrath who was bringing up his sons, and she was fascinated by their loving relationship and their concern for others. On the untimely death of one of the boys, Gwen Pharis wrote the poem, "Sandy," which was published in *The Carolina Play-Book*[8] in December 1937. Her play grew out of this. At a time when many plays were written about leaving home, she pondered over the possibility of writing one about a boy who wanted to stay home. Her plot, which is slight, centers on the attempt by Chris the blacksmith to persuade Sandy, his nephew, to go to art school in Minneapolis; Chris pretends that the money for school was willed to Sandy by his father. Sandy prefers to stay with Chris and add an auto parts shop to the business. He discovers the truth through slow-witted Carl with whom Chris was supposed to travel to Sweden. Chris had given Carl a series of letters to be mailed singly to Sandy over a period of time. Carl, failing to understand the ploy, gives Sandy the first letter rather than keeping it for mailing from Sweden. Thus Sandy discovers that Chris, instead of going on the long-planned vacation, was, in reality using his savings to send Sandy to art school. Sandy therefore returns to Chris, bringing with him a used truck to begin the "new-fangled" auto parts shop.

Proff Koch had taught his students to develop characters who were true to the region out of which they grew. Gwen Pharis is dealing with an immigrant to Canada, a new Canadian, in whom she must combine the typical characteristics of a lower-class Swede and the acquired qualities distinctive to western Canadian prairie folk. She does this admirably in "Chris Axelson" as she depicts the bluff, blunt, hard-working Swede with the instinct, common to western Canadians, of sending their children away from the prairie for an education that will prepare them for a career. Leslie Pharis had done this very thing with his daughter, Gwen, at a time when his income was considerably reduced during the Depression. Added to these characteristics in Chris Axelson is a generosity, a kindliness, and a trust in others that make him a memorable individual. His slow manner of thinking and considering ideas and plans, his lack of trust in change, are also idiosyncratic of his temperament and region. Other characters in the folk play are equally engaging but less individualized: Sandy, a first generation Canadian who has taken on Canadian characteristics totally and who exhibits affectionate patience with his uncle's idiosyncrasies; Carl, the slightly retarded Swedish immigrant; Bennet, the Canadian prairie farmer; and Billy, the little boy. It is obvious that Gwen Pharis cares about the characters she creates. This compassion, devoid of sentimentality, is communicated to her audience. Nor does her audience question the validity of her characters. In a dialogue engaging Chris, the blacksmith, Bennett, the farmer, and Carl, the slow-minded young man, the character of the blacksmith is clearly revealed in his simplicity, generosity, kindliness, and good humor.

The dialogue, which is natural and smooth for the Canadians, is stiff and awkward for the Swedish immigrants. The simplicity and innocence of Carl is revealed when he informs the others that he cannot return the ill-fitting shoes because he has already written his name in them. Gwen Pharis does not give any audible response to this statement but leaves it to the director to suggest mild surprise on the part of the Canadian present, and simple acceptance on the part of the Swedish immigrant Chris.

BENNETT: Hello, Chris.
CHRIS: Hello, Bill. I got your chain-saw all ready—so sharp it cuts right through the sidewalk. (*He sees Carl*). Why, hello, Carl.
CARL: Hello. (He sits down).
BENNETT: I brought Carl in to talk over plans for your trip, Chris. We may not get to town again before Wednesday.
CHRIS: That's fine. How you feel now, Carl?
CARL: Good. (*Carl has a strong Swedish accent too. He is a bit dumb in his head but the most willing and good-natured fellow in the world. He is very conscious of his new suit, new shoes, and a straw hat that is very bright and shiny.*) But those shoes was wrong size that feller sell me. They don't feel so good.
CHRIS: Too bad. You should take them back. (*Wrapping chain saw in sack*).
CARL: (*Sadly*). It is too late. I write my name in them already.
CHRIS: Here you are, Bill. (*Gives him chain-saw*).
BENNETT: Fine. How much do I owe you?
CHRIS: Altogether it's three-eighty.[9]

There follows dialogue on repayment of a debt. Chris shows perfect trust in his fellow Canadian's promise to pay his bill after threshing. This is characteristic of the Canadian prairie dweller's trust, and fundamental to his ability to survive on the land. The added witty dialogue is that Ringwood characteristic humor which makes her folk plays so lively and spirited.

BENNETT: I'll pay you after threshing, Chris, if that's all right with you.
CHRIS: Sure, sure. No hurry.
BENNETT: You're looking hearty these days.
CHRIS: Yah. I feel fine. Ever I quit drinking I'm strong as a horse.
BENNETT: You sure laid off sudden.
CHRIS: I make some big fool of myself, I think. Probably I'd be dead four—five years ago, if I kept on like crazy wild Indian.
BENNETT: Takes will power to stop all of a sudden.
CHRIS: Well, when I take nine year-old kid to raise, I figure it's time to stop. What kind of life for a kid with an old boozer around? So when Sandy's Dad died I just quit. I sure look at that kid

sometimes the first year and think maybe I send him to my sister.

BENNETT: You never touch the stuff now, eh?

CHRIS: I get pretty drunk two times a year now. On the first day of July and the seventeenth of November.

BENNETT: What's the seventeenth of November, your birthday?

CHRIS: Nah. That's the day I quit drinking. I get drunk to celebrate. (He laughs at his own joke). (*A*, 4-5)

In this play we see Ringwood using dialogue to reveal characterization and to provide comedy, e.g., in Chris and Sandy's relationship, in the comic confrontation between the blacksmith and Carl, and in the following conversation between Billy, the little boy, and the middle-aged blacksmith.

CHRIS: You hear that bus blowin' like a ship in the fog?

BILLY: That means the bus is leaving. He blows like that at our corner.

CHRIS: Sandy's on that bus. He's going nearly three thousand miles riding over the country. Then in two days he gets to Minneapolis.

BILLY: Three thousand miles. I guess he'll see the ocean, Mr. Chris. I never saw the ocean.

CHRIS: No. He don't see the ocean but sees a big lake and a river that runs swift as this truck going down hill. And when he gets there he sees high buildings with eighteen stories in him—maybe twenty.

BILLY: Gee that's awful high. (*There is a silence*).

CHRIS: I saw them buildings when I was coming out here from Sweden. I was a young man then, just come from being a sailor on a ship. I was bigger than Sandy but not so smart. He's like his Dad. His Dad was the smartest one in all my family.

BILLY: Aren't you Sandy's Dad, Mr. Chris?

CHRIS: No, Son. I'm his uncle.

BILLY: I've got an uncle, Uncle Jack.

CHRIS: You be good to him then. Sometimes uncles like little boys just like their Dad.

BILLY: Uncle Jack lost his shirt at the races. He told Daddy.

CHRIS: That's too bad. (*Turning with the truck*). Well, Son, there you are. I fix this truck up so it's good like new. You try now and see if old Chris don't fix it. (*A*, 18-19)

Although she was criticized by George Broderson in the *Manitoba Arts Review*[10] for using this latter scene as a "filler" to cover the time gap, it actively serves to highlight the sober simplicity shared by blacksmith and child, both of whom are unaware of the subtleties of language and in particular of the North American idioms. Thus the scene adds to the comedy and to the blacksmith's characterization.

Ringwood's talent as a technical director is evidenced in the stage directions, in the handling of stage business, and in her ability to cope with the sophisticated demands of the stage, e.g., moving characters naturally on and off stage. For this reason, staging her plays never creates major difficulties. Some examples of the above stage directions and character descriptions are the following: "*Chris Axelson is working at a forge, singing his own variation of a lusty sea chanty as he works. Chris is a powerful man of about 65 years. His laugh is a trumpet, his rage is heroic, his gentleness unexpected and full of humility. After a few minutes of pounding and singing, Chris suddenly breaks off and turning from the forge, goes to the door. He speaks with a Swedish accent*" (A, 1). When Sandy has apparently left for Minneapolis, Gwen Pharis offers the following description and directions for Chris: "*The old man sits down dejectedly. After a moment he goes over to the shelf and takes down the bottle he confiscated from Carl. He starts to take a drink from it, puts it down, and once more takes up the pictures of the old Ford. His power is gone from him and he is a lost and lonesome old man*" (A, 20). "Chris Axelson, Blacksmith" won the Gwillym Edwards prize for the best play by an Alberta playwright in the Alberta Provincial Drama Festival in 1939. Produced at the Playmakers Theatre, Chapel Hill, on 26 May, 1938, it was directed by Floyd Childs with David Rosenberg as blacksmith and Carleton Read as the nephew. In August 1938 it was produced at the Rustic Theatre, Banff, directed by Mary Ellen Burgess, starring Donald Cameron as the blacksmith and Jack Tyo as the nephew. Of the reaction of her fellow students to it when she first read the finished manuscript to the class at Chapel Hill, Gwen Pharis says: "I read it in our playwriting class and I discovered that wonderful feeling of the joy of making people laugh . . . a singing feeling of how fine it is to be able to generate that kind of merriment."[11]

II *A Folk Play of Social Protest*

During the Depression Gwen Pharis became absorbed in the ideologies of socialism and communism. Her future mother-in-law was a socialist; her friend and fellow student Sam Hirsch was in touch with the people fighting against dictatorship in Spain. He also was deeply concerned for the liberation of the black people in the south and took Gwen Pharis to several of their meetings. The Depression generated a desperate search for remedies to fear, want, and near starvation at a time when people were losing hope and faith in both themselves and their country. Ringwood's socialism grew also out of her earlier experiences with small communities in Alberta. Her own family life in Magrath, and her later involvement in prairie theater when she and Elizabeth Haynes visited numerous small communities throughout the entire province of Alberta, gave Ringwood the insight she needed and thus strengthened her views on the necessity for a moderate form of socialism. In the small communities in which she worked, she saw individual members of large families who did not leave home to better themselves but remained to help others in the family. Out of her awareness of these difficulties and of the socialist and labor movements in Alberta came the desire to express the dilemma of the dedicated liberal and labor worker. It should be emphasized here that Ringwood writes about the human condition of people caught between differing ideals—probably an unusual attitude in the 1930s.

"One Man's House" (1938) was her second play written at Chapel Hill, and it set the tone for her later plays of social protest. The title comes from the lines in the play spoken by Jan Lodeska, the strike leader, to his wife who protests his involvement in labor disputes which have brought only unemployment and poverty to the family. In reply to his wife's protests Jan says, "What is one family, Martha? One man's house? Beside the thing he knows is right."[12] The play, as Ringwood defines it, "is derived from the life of a Polish reformer whom I knew in Alberta, a man who couldn't keep from making speeches against the economic order upon which he was dependent for a living."[13] As a result this man spent several months in jail; companies refused to employ him, and his family was therefore reduced to poverty. His wife never understood how he could sacrifice his own family for an ideal. Like this Polish reformer, Jan Lodeska was endeavoring to build a new world. Gwen Pharis uses the regional background of new Canadians in Alberta, the dialect of Polish immigrants, and the characterization of a Polish family in Canada.

This drama could have been set wherever there is social injustice. The play is quite simple and straightforward. However, the dramatic material is complex enough to warrant a three-act play because it requires more scope to develop fully the situations and characters. Yet within the strictures of a one-act play, Ringwood develops the plot reasonably well. Jan Lodeska understands his vocation as a labor leader. In the past he had suffered the loss of his job when employers discovered his labor reform plans. Now he decides, for the sake of his family, to go "underground" in assisting labor reforms, rather than risk losing another job. But when his son plans to be a strikebreaker, rather than continue the fight against management, Jan Lodeska comes to the fore openly as leader, and, in so doing, the audience is assured that he will lose everything. Yet the impression given is that the Jan Lodeskas of this world will keep on fighting. Although a lengthier treatment would have given the dramatist scope for more development, nevertheless within the framework of a one-act play, "One Man's House" still makes a valid statement.

This first play of social protest reveals Ringwood's tone in this type of drama. She has no axe to grind but is quietly and compassionately revealing the human situation when men strike. Her voice is not strident. Consider the following conversation between Jan Lodeska and his daughter, Josie:

JOSIE: All that speakin' you done all your life ain't got you nowhere, Pa, except out of work. In jail once even. (*Coming down and facing him*) One man can't change nothin'. He loses every time.

JAN: Not one man alone, Josie,—but many can, they can change things.

JOSIE: (*Arguing*) Seems to me it's dog eat dog in this world.

JAN: (*Leaning forward*) To stand together Josie . . . that is the one way the worker can fight. I hear today the owners of the Packing Plant can't get new men. If the strikers stay out two weeks more, they'll get a good settlement, by God.

JOSIE: (*Sitting down right of table and facing him.*) Well, I'd hate to be picketing in this weather.

JAN: Yah, it is hard on the men now, but soon it will be over and they will forget. They will get their half day off that they should have . . . a little time to rest . . . and better pay. It will be good. (*Leaning back with a satisfied smile*) Yah, good. It was always my dream, Josie, to see the workers one day free from slavery and suffering. I think I see it coming true. Someday the world will be for all men. I will not live to see it, but you will, Josie . . . you and your children. (*O*, 11-12)

This dialogue is quietly making Ringwood's point. Jan Lodeska's tone is not desperate but it is persistent in the face of all obstacles. Ringwood is particularly gifted in the use of dialogue. Several of her lines have become memorable, for example, the following lines spoken by Jan Lodeska to his wife, which Emily Crow Selden remarked had caught the imagination of the audience and were quoted by many playmakers over the years when they gathered together:

> The years they crowd us, Martha!
> Like sheep at a narrow gate. (*O*, 9)

"One Man's House" was produced by the Playmakers Theatre at Chapel Hill on 20-23 April 1938, with Vivien Veach (later state senator in Illinois) as director, Sam Hirsch as Jan Lodeska, and Betty Smith as his wife. Many years later, during the McCarthy era, Sam Hirsch was interrogated and suffered the loss of his job and reputation, as had the character he portrayed in "One Man's House."

"One Man's House" is Ringwood's first play on a social theme; it is unsatisfactory because it does not explore the problem in depth nor does it allow for character development. There is the ultimate clash between two loyalties—the family and the ideal—but the two protagonists, Jan and his son Stas, are not given enough time to reveal their basic attitudes, their emotional reactions, their involvement with the human condition. "One Man's House" is, like "Chris Axelson, Blacksmith," more of an exercise in playwrighting, revealing the skills Gwen Pharis is gradually learning, rather than a solid drama of any depth. Yet both of these plays are links in the development of Ringwood's dramatic skills. Both lead up to her later and better work. In "Chris Axelson, Blacksmith" she explores the uses of comic dialogue later to be perfected in *A Fine Colored Easter Egg* or *The Drowning of Wasyl Nemitchuk* and in *Widger's Way*. She is also testing her ability to depict the relationship between simple, warmhearted people which she develops successfully in *The Courting of Marie Jenvrin* and in *Stampede*. In "One Man's House" poetic dialogue is tried and tested; then developed more fully in the rich poetry of *Still Stands the House* and *Pasque Flower*. Again her emphasis in "One Man's House" on the human condition of people caught between different ideals is repeated more powerfully in the later plays: *Lament for Harmonica*, *The Stranger*, "A Remembrance of Miracles," and "The Lodge."

Shortly after writing "One Man's House" Gwen Pharis was in New York. She tells us that she listened seriously to Communists there but was repelled by the seemingly unreasoned hatred of all middle-class values.[14] As a result, on her return to Chapel Hill, she decided to eschew the theme of social protest in favor of drama about her beloved prairie. Gwen Pharis had done her apprenticeship and was ready to create plays of more lasting value. She wrote *Still Stands the House*, considered by some critics to be her best one-act play, followed by another powerful prairie drama *Pasque Flower* which was later extended into the successful three-act play, *Dark Harvest*.

III *Folk Tragedy*

The sufferings endured by those who live on the prairie, resulting from the loneliness of the life, the blizzards and droughts that left families isolated from one another, was a fact of life for Gwen Pharis. *Still Stands the House* is her response. The influences exerted on her for the writing of this and her other prairie plays was Yeats's poetry, O'Neill's plays, Synge's drama *Riders to the Sea*, and the use of language and peasant themes from the Irish literary revival. "Irish theatre at the University of Montana had become part of my literary consciousness from reading and savouring a way language was used."[15] She goes on to say that she saw in the Irish playwrights how a writer could transmute environment and experience into fictional drama. As Synge had transformed the very hard peasant life in Ireland into drama, so Ringwood hoped to use the great sweeps of the prairie and the difficult life of the Canadian wheat farmers. She says:

> I wrote the first draft of *Still Stands the House* in a kind of poetic blank verse with a great thrust towards the end because my first vision of the play had been of the black-haired woman of forty, mad, rocking a doll in an empty house. I eventually did not use the doll. . . . I wanted to express through images, similes, metaphors that came up out of the land . . . and to use those in the way that the Irish writers had used them. . . . Also there was the feeling for the one-act plays done successfully at the Abbey Theatre. O'Neill had also started the one-act play at the Provincetown Playhouse but it wasn't a popular professional form. . . . Again it seems a movement you could surround and perhaps echo in Canada. . . . There was more of the Irish influence and a little bit of O'Neill in dealing with frustration and eventual madness.[16]

Set in the Depression years of the 1930s, it succeeds in being a powerful, artistic metaphor of western Canadian life. Nature seems deranged when it inflicts the bitter droughts of summer turning the prairie into a dust bowl, or the fierce blizzards of winter that bring death by freezing to those lost in a storm. The land is the protagonist here and the people are reflections of the prairie spirit. Hester is the pioneer figure—harsh, silent, enduring, obsessed by the land. Her sister-in-law, Ruth, represents the gentler, feminine woman nurtured within the more hospitable areas of town life. Conflict is the central note of this play—conflict with the forces of nature reflected in the conflict between Ruth and the Warrens. The elements of tragedy are here. There is rich poetic language; the characters are heroic prairie people; the dialogue is entirely fitting to their particular temperaments; the tragic flaw, an error in Ruth's judgment, brings Ruth and Bruce to their deaths. The effect on the audience is to arouse them to pity for the Warrens' helpless isolation, and fear for their lives; the catharsis or purging of these emotions occurs at the end when Hester buries herself in the house and the audience becomes aware that the house, a symbol of humanity, will survive.

Ringwood is very economical in building up the action to its climax. A real estate salesman brings Ruth a vision of an irrigated farm close to the city, if only she and her husband will sell their land (reminiscent of Gwen Pharis's parents in their move to Montana). Hester stands like a wall before their hopes, claiming the house as her own. The sterility of her life and all she represents is powerfully emphasized by the symbolic pattern Gwen creates of birth versus death, spring versus winter, love versus sexual repression.

The richness of Ringwood's poetic language with its fine rhythms is accountable for the mysterious pull this play has on the reader and theatergoer. So small a play, like a tiny gem gathering within it a reflection of the human spirit, it yet produces a powerful response. Once again Gwen Pharis uses a regional setting, theme, and characters; then she moves away and beyond the Alberta prairies to a universal experience by creating a conflict between Hester and Ruth with which any audience can empathize. The spinster Hester, forced to live with her sister-in-law, sees in Ruth a rival, a usurper of the family possessions, a destroyer of family traditions. The conflict between Hester and Ruth is one with which we are only too familiar whether it be set in prairie or city life. But the force dictating Hester's action is obsession with the land, and the character of Hester has been molded by the harshness of the prairie. Why is she a deranged woman? What strange power had the land exerted upon her so that she has lost her perspective? In Hester, Ringwood has created a most unusual character. Nurtured by the prairie, she becomes symbolic of the prairie in its violence and unpredictableness. Hester is the prairie and she is to be feared. She is the dark haunting spirit of the Depression that deprived men and their families of their sustenance and their lives. Hester is the force bringing death whereas Ruth is the gentle life-giving spirit of love. Bruce is caught between love and death. In the end death wins as does the prairie in the 1930s. Emily Crow Selden says of *Still Stands the House:* "Of all the Playmaker one-acts I've seen over the years, I can remember none that produced such an impact."[17]

The plot revolves around the opposition of the spinster Hester to the selling of the family home and land by her brother Bruce Warren and his fragile wife Ruth. In the midst of their heated discussion, a blizzard attacks the prairie and Bruce therefore takes his lantern and goes out to the coulee to save the mare who is about to foal. After he leaves, Ruth realizes that in her distraction she has forgotten to fill the lamp. In her haste to follow him, she lets Hester fill her lamp while she gets ready to leave. But Hester is losing her sanity. With the grim cunning of the deranged, she only pretends to fill Ruth's lamp. As Ruth, who is pregnant, faces the blizzard, the audience is aware that neither she nor Bruce will ever return. Hester closes the door, blows out the lamp in the window, pulls down the shades, places the symbolic bowl of hyacinths outside in the storm, and locks the door. Like O'Neill's tragic heroine in *Mourning Becomes Electra,* Hester bars herself from the living world outside her house and the play ends.

The audience may question whether indeed a farmer of Bruce's experience would leave the house in a blizzard without personally checking the lantern, or whether Ruth who is just beginning to realize Hester's insane state of mind, would depend on Hester to fill her lantern. Because the play is dependent on this dramatic device it is important to examine this situation. Both Bruce and his father have always left the filling of the lanterns to the women. Therefore it is unlikely that Bruce would check this normal procedure which in the past has never failed. Bruce has not erred. It is Ruth who has forgotten to fill the lamp because of her emotional conflict with Hester. Ruth is also filled with nervous agitation when she realizes Bruce's plight so she allows the deranged Hester to take care of her lamp before she rushes out into the blizzard. The audience should find this conduct normal under stress.

Strong characterizations and rich, poetic language are responsible for the success of this play. The names Ruth and Hester, given to the two main characters, are suggestive of those two women of heroic stature in the Old Testament—Ruth who loved deeply and Esther of the undaunted spirit. Gwen Pharis has created unique characters in the harsh and sterile Hester, the warm and loving Ruth, the weary and frustrated Bruce. Perhaps the strongest character is the dead father Martin Warren whose portrait on the wall dominates Hester's and Bruce's life. One reading or one theater experience of *Still Stands the House* imprints these people indelibly on the mind. There is a strong affinity in Ringwood's style and spirit with the work of Frederico Garcia Lorca. Both are poetic dramatists approaching theater from poetic and philosophic points of view while interweaving their individual views of time and space in a quest to understand the meaning of life. Both develop theater language crafted from poetry; both have a command of poetic dialogue and a respect for the use of the symbol to aid them in their exploration of theme. In Lorca's *Dona Rosita* the symbol of the rose bears a strong resemblance to Ringwood's use of hyacinths in *Still Stands the House* and of the pasque flower in the play of the same name. Both playwrights have a fine grasp of the use of symbol.

The language in *Still Stands the House* is highly symbolic. Ringwood wrote her first plays in poetry and then translated them into poetic prose. Obviously she kept the subtle rhythms, imagery, and symbols of the original version of *Still Stands the House*. Although the play opens with practical dialogue between the real estate agent and Ruth, it begins to build emotionally and dramatically, and the dialogue becomes consistently richer. As death becomes more imminent the symbols increase in vitality. The hyacinths, the wind, the snow, the soil, are all symbolically personified. Hester remarks about Ruth's hyacinths: "You've gone to as much trouble for that plant as if it were a child."[18] The plant symbolizes Ruth's unborn child, and when Hester in a deranged fury breaks off a bud that has not yet blossomed we are sensitively aware of the forthcoming tragedy. The hyacinths are a symbol of spring and new life. Ruth's attempt to put them in the Warrens' Wedgwood bowl is frustrated. Since they prefigure the child Ruth is bearing, this is a second rejection by Hester. This life-giving symbol is reinforced by the mare's foal soon to be born in the blizzard. But all this burgeoning life will never be brought to fruition. Hester destroys the hyacinth bud; the unborn colt and the unborn baby will meet death in the storm, again through Hester's action. The unravelling of Hester's knitting signifies the gradual disintegration of her mind. Ruth is frightened by this and by the winds on the prairie—a portent of the madness and of the blizzard to come. She says: "The wind swirls and shrieks and raises such queer echoes in this old house! It seems to laugh at us in here, thinking we're safe, hugging the stove! As if it knew it could blow out the light and the fire and (*Getting hold of herself*) I've never seen a blizzard when it was as cold as this. Have you Hester? (*SS*, 11). Hester talks of her father who had exerted such a powerful and possessive hold over her. She repeats his description of snow on the prairie: "(*Unconscious of Ruth*) 'He always liked the snow.' (*Her eyes are on the portrait of her father.*) 'He called it a moving shroud, a winding-sheet that the wind lifts and raises and lets fall again' " (*SS*, 12). In a bitter confrontation with Ruth over the land that means so much to him and yet has produced so little, Bruce says: "Yes, it's strange that in a soil that won't grow trees a man can put roots down, but he can" (*SS*, 21). Bruce says of the soil: "When I saw the wind last spring blowing the dirt away, the dirt I'd ploughed and harrowed and sowed to grain, I felt as though a part of myself was blowing away in the dust. Even, now, with the land three feet under snow, I can look out and feel it waiting for the seed I've saved for it" (*SS*, 21). Like the hyacinths, the house and lanterns function figuratively as well as literally. When Hester insists that the Warren family could always stand alone, that they never needed other people for support as Ruth obviously does, Ruth replies: "You'd sit in this husk of a house, living like shadows, until these four walls closed in on you, buried you" (*SS*, 21). Ruth then explains her fears for her unborn child who would find life in such a house deadly. She says to her husband and sister-in-law, "You two and your father lived so long in this dark house that you forgot there's a world beating outside, forgot that people laugh and play sometimes. And you've shut me out!" (*SS*, 21, 22).

The house is both a character and a symbol. It is the house Ruth fights, Hester defends, and Bruce tries to cope with. The house is like a dark shadow cast over their lives: forbidding and authoritarian, it symbolizes the past and a life dedicated to the past. Its silence is loud with meaning. It creates the dramatic tension, and when all the characters are lost, the house remains triumphantly alone.

Hester's reference to herself as a vestal virgin lighting the lamps bestows a strange power on the house. Subconsciously one sees it as a temple—a sanctuary created by the pioneer's dauntless spirit against the ravages of nature. As the lighted sanctuary lamp is a sign of the Divine Presence in Christian churches, so the lighted lamp in this play symbolizes the presence and love of Ruth and Bruce, but, more important, the life-giving spirit of hope which is so integral a part of the pioneer character. The lamp in the window, the lantern in the blizzard—both must be filled with oil if they are to give light and hope to the pioneer. As an unlighted sanctuary lamp is a sign of an empty Tabernacle so the unlighted lamp in this play is a sign of death—the end of love, of life, of hope. Without hope the pioneer would be lost. His courage in the face of all obstacles was fed by hope—hope in the blessings of the land, in the indomitable spirit of his family. When there is nothing left for that hope to feed on, the pioneering spirit dies. One of Hester's last gestures is the blowing out of the lamp. The audience recognizes this as the end of life. The house becomes an empty Tabernacle.

Yet there is a certain exaltation inherent in the play's ending. The Warren family, it is true, will be destroyed but the house remains—perhaps the pioneering spirit will not die. Ruth and Bruce are made nobler by their struggle. Hester, the mad woman, becomes a colossal shadow overpowering and preserving the house. Man's struggle continues on. The house is therefore also a symbol of mankind. Each member of the Warren family found within its walls shelter and support but also the seeds of death. Although death took them one by one, the house (mankind) continues on.

In writing this play Ringwood sought the advice of professionals. For example, in the development of Hester's madness, Gwen Pharis discussed her characterization with the psychiatrist Dr. Frank Tallman who reassured her that Hester's depiction was realistic. Fellow students Betty Smith, Robert Finch, and other playmakers were also helpful and constructive critics. They read the play and discussed with Gwen Pharis the characterization, plot and poetic language. But it was Ringwood herself who created the color and form to accentuate her vivid imagery and to shape the play *Still Stands the House* into the quite perfect one-act play which emerged. To date, *Still Stands the House* remains Ringwood's best constructed one-act play, and Hester one of her finest characterizations.

Gwen Pharis described how *Still Stands the House* should be produced. The setting in winter is somber and austere. She says she can still remember those gaunt wood houses without trees, standing in isolation in the Depression years when the good rich soil was blowing away on the dry land farms. She recalls also blizzards in which she had lost her way. With the falling snow making visibility zero she had walked in circles in deep snow totally unable to discern the right direction. The terror of those blizzards will always remain in her memory. As a result of this austere prairie landscape, Ringwood suggests the best way to produce this play:

> I think the more austere the production the better. If its cadences are softened and the rhythm sounded and savored, the play loses impact. It should be done in a very austere manner, no attempt to try to make this a "poetic" play. . . . If it is done in a restrained manner, especially if the speech is restrained, flattened, then the images come alive and the essential flow of the play is there.[19]

Note that this same quality of austerity, emphasized so strongly by Ringwood, is incisively pointed out by Margaret Atwood and appears in Canadian prairie literature all the way from Frederick Philip Grove through Sinclair Ross and Sheila Watson to present western Canadian writers.

Margaret Atwood in *Survival* notes that Canadians are preoccupied with survival. She says: "In earlier writers these obstacles [to survival] are external—the land, the climate, and so forth. In later writers the obstacles tend to become both harder to identify and more internal; they are no longer obstacles to physical survival but obstacles to what we may call spiritual survival."[20] The dramatization of failure which Atwood sees in so much Canadian literature in which heroes fail or die, is the very quality that vitalizes *Still Stands the House*. It is neither ironic nor pessimistic but rather a cause for hope. Although it is true that the protagonists die in their struggle to wrest life from the prairie, the house, the human race, lives on, continuing the fight for existence despite the odds.

In Frederick Philip Grove's work, the character of austerity in, for example, *Settlers of the Marsh*,[21] can be found in both the people and the land. The two protagonists, Niels Lindstedt and the girl whom he loves, Ellen Amundsen, are each austere in their different ways—Niels in the long years of self-discipline to make ready a home for his future bride, and Ellen in her stern and uncompromising attitude toward life. Her inability to accept her own sexuality leads to her refusal of Niels's offer of marriage. Although tragedy follows, the novel does not end on a tragic note but one of hope with Niels and Ellen sharing an understanding that may develop into a deeper, more lasting relationship. The hardships of life on the prairie are very real but so is the spirit of hope, and it is this added dimension that gives Canadian prairie literature its substance and tone.

Sinclair Ross in the novel *As For Me and My House*[22] presents a husband and wife whose bleakness of existence is appalling. Philip is a minister by circumstances rather than vocation. Poverty forced him into a calling to which he can give only a feeble response. Obsessed by his yearning to be an artist, he drifts along, paying slight heed to his wife for whom he has long since lost any feeling of love. The tragic circumstances of his affair with a young parishioner, and her death in childbirth, end not in despair, as one would expect, but in a return to his wife who freely chooses to care for the baby whom she names Philip. Actually it is a rebirth for the minister, and the reader is aware of a small ray of hope in this painful cry for survival.

Sheila Watson is still another Canadian writer from the west whose work also bears this same mark of austerity of life, of a struggle for existence, and of a final resolve touched by hope. In her novel *The Double Hook* the people of a small village in the Cariboo fight for survival as a community. Madness, murder, and death touch the lives of these people. They live in fear and isolation, blind to the real values of life. Watson, like Ringwood, makes extensive use of symbols, imagery, and poetic prose that sharply delineates her characters and their situation. The end of this story is full of hope as James, the protagonist, returns home. "Out of his corruption life had leafed and he'd stepped on it carelessly as a man steps on spring shoots."[23] James sees the corruption in his own life and he seeks a new beginning. That new beginning is heralded in the last lines of this folk tale: "And from a cleft of the rock she heard the voice of Coyote crying down through the boulders: 'I have set his feet on soft ground;/ I have set his feet on the sloping shoulders/ of the world.' "[24] Ara's cry as James approaches the girl and her baby is an acknowledgment of the quasi-Messianic nature of James's leadership of the community, foretelling, in a sense, that the people will be led out of bondage into the promised land, the community for which they had suffered.

Atwood's emphasis of survival as a Canadian preoccupation, and of a Canadian literature that is "undeniably sombre and negative"[25] is lightened by her final words:

> But in that literature there are elements which, although they are rooted in this negativity, transcend it—the collective hero, the halting but authentic breakthroughs made by characters who are almost hopelessly trapped, the moments of affirmation that neither deny the negative ground nor succumb to it. These elements are not numerous, but they gain their significance from their very scarcity.[26]

The works of Grove, Ross, Watson, and Ringwood suggest that the climactic moments of hope in the future are more numerous (if these writers be typical of the Canadian west) than one would be led to believe. The tragedies of life in the Canadian prairies and in the Cariboo, as seen through the eyes of these western writers, are almost always brightened in the end by that small ray of hope which is also the hallmark of Canadian life.

At the University of North Carolina where *Still Stands the House* was first produced on 3 March 1938, the play was such a popular and critical success that it was chosen for presentation at the fifteenth commencement on 6 June 1938. The original production was directed by Lynn Gault, with Floyd Childs as Hester, Howard Bailey as Bruce, and Ruth Mengel as Ruth. The same cast performed in the commencement production with Harry Davis as director. The following year, on 25 February 1939, it was presented by the Medicine Hat Little Theatre at the Alberta Drama Festival in Edmonton, winning first prize as the best native Canadian play entered in the annual Dominion Drama Festival in 1939. Directed by Mary Laidlaw it included in the cast Kitty White, Ethel Finley, Louis Flath, and Vivian Rodgers. Elsie Park Gowan also played Hester in one of the early productions in Canada. Repeatedly produced in the United States and Canada each year since then, it has also been translated into Gaelic and presented on radio in Dublin. Published by Samuel French, it has gone into several printings and is included in many play anthologies. That the audience response was less enthusiastic in its 1968 revival for the Playmakers' fiftieth anniversary was due to its lackluster performance rather than to the fault of the play.[27]

In 1977 Elsie Park Gowan said this of the play, then in its thirty-eighth year of production:

> *Still Stands the House* is to me the best Canadian one-act play by far and it sums up the whole human experience of farming in that dried-out country. . . . There isn't a single line in that play that is superfluous. Every single speech contributes to the total characterization, the plot, the setting,

which of course is practically a character in it. . . . Gwen's forte in playwriting is her depth of emotion.[28]

Walter Kaasa, a fellow actor with Gwen and director of many of her plays, has described it as a masterpiece. What impressed him was the extent, quality, and control of the symbolism. He particularly noted the starkness: in the colors used, the prairie background, and the character of Hester. Kaasa maintains that the antagonist is the prairie itself, and he feels that it is Ringwood's capturing of the feeling of winter on the prairie within the confines of a one-act play that accounts for its singularly high quality. He also refers to the importance of the lamp in rural life:

If you have ever had the chance to walk out in the bleakness of the prairie at night, the darkness is phenomenal . . . and the importance of that light in the window is breath, is life, is existence; and she captures that. . . . She transports you outside with her images. I think it is by far her greatest play. . . . She is good not because she wrote about the prairie but because of her immense ability to make those characters live in an environment, because of her ability to create a symbolism that is akin to the play.[29]

Kaasa's emphasis on Ringwood's use of symbolism is noteworthy, for as her talent develops it will be observed that it is her insight into the use of symbols and her ability to control them that constitutes one of the essential strengths in her plays. Of Hester and Ruth, Kaasa added that he had rarely seen actresses competent enough to play those two roles because they require an immense amount of study and talent to achieve success. In his experience of play-directing, these are two of the most difficult characters to play. Kaasa says this of the play:

Still Stands the House is a very simple, earthy, grassroots play but highly sophisticated, one of the most complicated plays I know of. Which means while it can be done by people who know little about theatre, for enjoyment and participation purposes, it cannot be well done without knowing a great deal about all the aspects of theatre production.[30]

Tom Kerr, who adjudicated *Still Stands the House* in countless drama festivals over the past forty years, and who directed and produced many of Ringwood's plays in prairie theaters and on CBC radio, observes that one important proof that *Still Stands the House* remains a classic is that now, forty years later, Samuel French still orders publications of it and still sells it. At Kerr's latest production of the play (1977, in Saskatoon, Saskatchewan) he was interested in knowing whether or not the play had dated. At the university theater, students who acted in it were from the prairie and they had absolutely no quarrel with the play; they accepted it totally as a true depiction of life on the prairie. Kerr concludes:

> In *Still Stands the House* Ringwood has the ability to write characters, to write conflicts, to write a situation with a good blending of language. The plot is solid; the structure is solid; the people are believable. . . . Her poetry flows through it. The rhythm is there. She is really at her height encompassing all things of a playwright in that play.[31]

Another one-act play of the Canadian prairies, written by Gwen Pharis at this time, was *Pasque Flower*. She tells us in *American Folk Plays:* "I remember the prairie spring of waving wheat fields. Wild roses everywhere on the unbroken sod and the pale blue pasque flower at Easter time."[32] The recollection of the pasque flower prompted the title.

In *Pasque Flower* Gwen Pharis again examines the pioneer aspects of Canadian prairie life. Explaining why the pasque flower is the motif, she remarked: "When the pasque flowers come out, we know that it's really spring at home. Until then we're never sure. And after the long snow-locked winter, spring means more to us than to any people in the world."[33] The play (which is really Lise's play) involves a marital rift between Jake Hansen, a wheat farmer, and his wife Lise, and the dark rivalry between Jake and his brother David. The gift of a bouquet of pasque flowers from her husband awakens in Lise the realization that their marriage will survive. The flowers are a harbinger of a new spring in their life.

The plot is a simple one. Jake's brother David, a doctor, returns to the family home after years of estrangement to see his sister-in-law Lise, whom he has always loved, before going to a new assignment in the Yukon. David tries to persuade Lise to leave her husband and go with him. He almost succeeds until Lise suddenly sees the pasque flowers and discovers that, not David, but her husband Jake has brought them to her. His surprising sensitivity to her inner needs—for it is the anniversary of the death of their only child—helps her to see his real nature under the hardened exterior. She decides to remain with him because he needs her. This maternal instinct in Lise is to be seen in Gwen's female characters in almost all her plays. Two emotional situations add to the mounting conflict: Jake's heartless appropriation of the land of an old neighbor who could not pay his debts, and the memory of the death of their first and only child. Neither of these situations is totally resolved although, at the end, Jake has decided to give the land back to his old neighbor. Although this plot is entirely adequate for a one-act play, Gwen Pharis later expanded it successfully into the three-act play, *Dark Harvest*.

Pasque Flower was first produced at Chapel Hill on 2-4 March 1939 with Gwen Pharis as director, Earl Wynn as Jake Hansen, Roberta Roberson as Lise, and Allen Andrews as David. It was selected to be presented on 5 June 1939 at the twenty-first season of the Carolina Playmakers with John Parker as director. Of this performance Professor Parker said: "Now *Pasque Flower* is perhaps her second best play of those she wrote at Chapel Hill. It is highly poetic. All her plays had an element of poetry in them. When she writes prose it sounds like poetry."[34]

This is a verse play but it lacks the imagery of *Still Stands the House*. By comparison, the prose in *Still Stands the House* is stronger and more poetic than the free verse form used in *Pasque Flower*. Yet Emily Selden says that some of the lines were particularly memorable such as the following spoken by Jake to his wife:

> Your eyes are blue as a field of flax
> With the dew on it, but in an hour
> The flowers fall as if they'd never been.[35]

The characterization of Jake and Lise is sufficiently well-rounded but David's character is not well explored. All three are demanding love; all three are imprisoned by their own obsessive needs—Jake by the land, Lise by the child she lost, and David by his love for Lise. Their realization of each other's obsessions is ironical for each accuses the other of persistent unreasonable preoccupations; yet no one character is aware of his own obsession. Ironical, too, is David's challenging of the loss of love between Lise and Jake, because it is this very challenge that reawakens Lise's love and maternal instinct for her husband.

The prevailing tone of *Pasque Flower* is austere, somber, sparse, the tone we have come to recognize in Gwen Ringwood's prairie plays. She has captured again the feeling of prairie isolation and hardship, but this time the constant struggle between man and the land results not in destruction but in a spirit of reconciliation with the land even when man fails. The rivalry between Jake and his brother, David, is reminiscent of the biblical Cain and Abel relationship, another instance of the extensive use of biblical names and figures in *Still Stands the House*, *Pasque Flower*, and *Dark Harvest* which enriches and strengthens the mythical relationship of man to the land.

The dialogue in its stark simplicity is expressive of the sterility of Lise's life. It is simple, clear, and almost barren poetry, reminiscent of some of the dialogue used by Maxwell Anderson in his play, *Winterset*. Witness the words of Lise to David who is urging her to leave with him:

> Sometimes, in summer,
> When the wind raises the dust like smoke,
> I've traced your name there on the ledge.
> Tried to hold on to some remembered beauty,
> Something you gave me in your voice and smile,
> When you were here before.
> Then I'd see the dust blot out the name I'd written.
> I took it as a sign it was a dream I'd had,
> Having no meaning. (*P*, 18)

It is significant to note here the creation of an image and then the immediate personification of it. Ringwood continues to do this in her later work. Her gift for metaphor, simile, and symbol; her ability to evoke vivid images in her poetry, is apparent in "the dust like smoke." The dust is personified as it blots out the name of her lover. In another section of the play Jake, in a confrontation with his wife Lise says:

> A man can get more warmth from an unploughed field
> That welcomes his hand
> Than from a woman who shuts herself away,
> Peers at him out of the corners of her eyes,
> Expecting the worst from him. (*P*, 12)

The fertility image which is used here so simply lends a tragic tone to Jake's words. The subtle implications of a frightened animal in the words, "Peers at him out of the corners of her eyes," says more than many lines of poetry could convey. *Pasque Flower* was published in the *Carolina Play-Book* in March 1939.

As a requirement for the M.A. in drama, The University of North Carolina offered the student a choice of writing a thesis or a three-act play. Gwen Pharis chose the latter and decided to lengthen *Pasque Flower* into the full-length drama, *Dark Harvest.* This became one of her finest three-act plays. It won the first prize in the Ottawa Little Theatre Playwriting Competition, was produced at the University of Manitoba in 1945, and was published by Thos. Nelson in the same year. Thirty-six years later the *Canadian Theatre Review* in the winter of 1975, gave *Dark Harvest* its second publication. Anton Wagner reviewed it and commented: "*Dark Harvest* is without question Ringwood's most successful full-length drama to date. Its protagonist, Garth Hansen, the land-hungry Alberta farmer attempting to dominate nature and a hostile God, is perhaps Ringwood's only heroic and tragic male figure."[36]

G. L. Broderson writing in the *Manitoba Arts Review* in 1944 said of *Dark Harvest:* "It is probably the best play that any native-born Canadian author has written. Yet such are the conditions of the theatre in Canada that *Dark Harvest* remains not merely unpublished but also unperformed."[37] The following year it was produced at the University of Manitoba. Of this production, Gwen Pharis said: "It was exciting to see a university production of a full-length play because in the West at that time we hadn't had many. I was quite pleased with the production. . . . With the prairie feeling given it. The reviews were good. Prairie people were excited about the newness of seeing themselves on stage."[38] Influenced by Chekhov's *Cherry Orchard,* Gwen set out to create the epic character of a wheat field, which is as symbolically evocative as was Chekhov's cherry orchard. She revised the play later on, to bring it up to the war years. It is this second version that appears in the *Canadian Theatre Review.*

Gwen Pharis speaks of the difficulties of converting a one-act into a three-act play:

> I have always been trying to learn how to write a three-act play . . . to initiate enough conflict and action between the people to hold and not become repetitive, not just repeat the same conflict, which some long plays do. Well this has always been very difficult for me to find a line of action that is tight and strong and will hold for a whole evening, as Ibsen does. In the end I felt that the conflicts were reasonably strong.[39]

In lengthening *Pasque Flower* to three acts, many significant changes were made. Whereas in the shorter play the theme stressed Jake, Lise, and David's relationship, in *Dark Harvest* the emphasis is on the relationship between Garth (Jake) and his God. Implicit throughout the play is this extraordinary rivalry, like that of the biblical Cain, between the wheat farmer and his Creator. In Act 2 Garth says: "I never found any God except what I found out there, the one that lies in the earth and lets things die. And he's blind! He laughs at you; he makes a man slave for him and laughs."[40] Lise answers that God is not like that. Garth replies that he had hoped Lise would replace God for him. Instead, Lise's lack of love sent him back to confront God again. He says,

> But I didn't go back as a slave. I went back to beat him at his own game. I went back to make the land grow wheat in spite of him, in spite of hail and dust and drought. In spite of anything he could do, I swore I'd find a way to beat him. And I did. I've won.[41]

The plot of *Dark Harvest* follows the development of Garth's strained relationship with his wife Lise and brother David, as it parallels and is subordinated to his relationship with God and the land. As the play opens the audience is introduced to Garth, the land-obsessed farmer, and to his brooding wife Lise who for two years is haunted by the death of their only child, a son, blaming Garth because he had failed to get a doctor in time to save the child. Then David arrives on the scene, home from the war and eager to see Lise whom he has always loved. Garth dislikes him because in his youth he sold half their land to pay his medical school expenses. Garth spent the following years struggling to get that land back. Now David has returned and he remains to practice medicine. The love between himself and Lise, nurtured in their youth, continues to grow. Garth is savagely aware of this but unable to cope with the situation because his struggle with the land is even more overpowering. The town authorities want to purchase some of his land on which they plan to build a hospital and to appoint David the director. Garth is loath to sell it but capitulates finally in an angry scene with David. He tells David and Lise to leave and marry, maintaining that he needs neither of them. Although Lise loves David, her maternal instinct to care for her husband forces her to remain. Parallel with this plot is the feud between Garth and the inept landholder Al Morrow. When Garth legally takes Morrow's land, the latter revengefully sets fire to his own truck at the newly constructed half-finished hospital where Garth's wheat is stored. David is in the building. Garth leaps into the truck, steers it away from the hospital, and plunges with it over the hill to his death. The onlookers are aware that he could easily have jumped to save himself; the audience is left to conjecture the reason. His death would certainly open the way for David and Lise to marry, but Charlie, the farmhand, has the last word when he says that Garth had something in his mind about God. This gradual coming to terms with a force in nature, alluded to several times in the play, makes Garth's death a mystery. One is tempted to think of it as a kind of self-immolation. Garth at the end seems to have discovered within the land a mysterious presence that transcends force. In his last conversation with Charlie, Garth speaks of this mystery. He says:

> It's got to be something better. Do you hear, it's got to be. Or there's no reason for it. If there's no hooded thing down there in the earth to strike out blind, kill for the sport of it . . . why then there's something else . . . something pushing up through the dark. It makes a path, dies, leaves room for something better. It's got to be that way or there's no reason, Charlie. (*DH*, 126)

This reminds one of the biblical quotation, "Unless a grain of wheat falls into the earth and dies, it remains alone, but if it dies it bears much fruit" (John 12:24). Death rather than life seems to hold the key to the mystery of a better life. Garth says "It makes a path, dies, leaves room for something better." Does he also see his death as following the same course? The audience is left to answer that question, and it is in this sense that *Dark Harvest* has spiritual depths beyond her other prairie plays.

The characterization in *Dark Harvest* is good. Garth's character has developed convincingly. He grapples with the forces of darkness in the land itself and attempts to find answers to ultimate questions. Underlying this is his effort to come to grips with his relationship to his wife, but the land overpowers even his jealousy of his brother's love for Lise. Her determination to remain with her husband because he needs her, despite her love for David, seems ironic to Garth. He philosophizes with Charlie in a passage that emphasizes his own tragedy: "Things can happen in a man's life, Charlie . . . a kind of storm . . . something he can't control, can't get his hands on. By the time he sees it coming, it's too late. And the storm takes what he believed in. Then he's useless. Like that straw waving in the wind. Finished" (*DH*, 125). He is no doubt referring here to the land, to the loss of his son, and to the failure of his marriage.

Throughout the play appears the symbol of a dead tree, struck by lightning the night their son dies. Garth refuses to cut it down. He wants it as a symbol of what he is up against—the blind forces of nature. He says it was the tree that drove him on. When at last he believes he can make it alone, beat even God, he tells David and Lise to go, in words that sharply foretell his own death: "Yes. Go . . . and tonight when you're gone . . . I'll rip out that tree . . . I'll burn it . . . it'll be a sacrifice to God . . . a sacrifice of his own desolation . . . (*DH*, 109). The tree is also a symbol of Garth himself, and this dialogue points to Garth's death. Garth is the tortured one, the victim of his own endless fight with the land, and his God, the victim of his obsessions and jealousies and furies. His is the *Dark Harvest* of the play, the title of which reflects the struggle mankind experiences in its fight for survival. The fact that there *is* a harvest implies that man's spirit cannot be destroyed. Ringwood's outlook continues to be one of hope not despair.

The three-act play format gave Gwen Pharis an opportunity to show her ability to develop character. Garth Hansen, most particularly, is fully developed. His gradual evolution from jealous husband, land-obssessed farmer, God-haunted derelict, into a man of some depth is entirely credible. His death is the only possible ending to a play with these emotional and spiritual overtones. *Dark Harvest* is much superior to *Pasque Flower* in depth of insight, characterization, and language.

The parallels between Garth Hansen and the character Abe Spalding in Frederick Philip Groves's novel *Fruits of the Earth* are uncanny. Abe Spalding, like Garth Hansen, had an obsession to conquer the land. Arriving in the prairie in Manitoba in 1900 he purchased one hundred and sixty acres as a beginning. "He was possessed by land hunger."[42] Abe dreamed of buying up all the land adjoining his farm, even that of the squatter Hall who lived in a sod hut. Hall bears a close resemblance to Al Morrow in *Dark Harvest*. Lazy and inept, he is jealous of Abe Spalding's success with the land. Eventually he turned over his title to his quarter to Abe and he left the area. Hall was "half-crazed with work and isolation."[43] Other parallel characters include Abe's wife Ruth, his sister Mary, his neighbor Nicoll, and his brother-in-law Dr. Vanbruik. In some respects Abe's city-born wife Ruth resembles the Ruth of *Still Stands the House* and Lise of *Pasque Flower* and *Dark Harvest.* All three women are averse to their husbands' obsessions with land; all three fail to change the situation and therefore withdraw into themselves; all three lose a child—Abe and Garth's wives blame their husbands for the death of their sons. But there the resemblance ceases. The Ruth of *Fruits of the Earth* is less articulate, less intelligent than Ruth and Lise of *Still Stands the House*, *Pasque Flower*, and *Dark Harvest.* From a girl of physical beauty she gradually deteriorates into a heavy, ugly, silent woman—a result of the isolation of the prairie and of Abe's neglect of her as he pursues his affair with the land. Her silent condemnation of him is always there in his conscience but he cannot change matters because, like Garth, the land has become his total absorption. "Well, he would conquer this wilderness; he would change it; he would set his own seal upon it!"[44] All real communication ceases between Abe and Ruth as it does between Garth and Lise.

Abe's sister Mary has received her share of the family farm in Ontario and spent it on a university education as Garth's brother does in *Dark Harvest.* Both Abe and Garth partly resent this education because it sets them apart, raises them in a sense above and beyond the prairie farmer. Mary is married to a doctor who has given up his practice for ethical reasons. Abe and Dr. Vanbruik gradually reach an understanding. Indeed, it is to Dr. Vanbruik that Abe goes when he needs advice. The relationship between Garth and his brother, also a doctor, bears little resemblance to this. Garth is jealous of his brother's love of Lise and he resents his sale of the land to pay for his education. Yet gradually in *Dark Harvest* this resentment begins to fade away in face of the greater confrontation between Garth and his God—that strange and mysterious force over life and death.

The only character who really understands Abe is his long-time neighbor Nicoll; the only character who divines Garth's nature is his farmhand Charlie. Nicoll is a much more fully-developed character than Charlie; the novel form allows for this more easily than a tightly written drama. Nicoll is more intelligent than Charlie but both men have a certain insight into character and both act as does the Greek chorus in emphasizing the mystery or the strange force that impels both farmers to act as they do.

In the final analysis the most powerful resemblance in *Dark*

Harvest and *Fruits of the Earth* is this uncanny likeness between Garth and Abe. These are the men of the prairie whom Ringwood and Grove have both recognized. In certain respects they may resemble Ringwood's own father, Leslie Pharis. Certain it is that they are authentic characters of the prairie who have grown in a sense out of the land and whose total concern is with the prairie, a relationship that is deeper and beyond any human relationship in their lives. Garth's immolation to the gods is total and final; Abe's is found in his acceptance of fate.

> Unless some major disaster interfered, this crop would place him at the goal of his ambitions. But could it be that no disaster was to come? He felt as though a sacrifice were needed to propitiate the fates. He caught himself casting about for something he might do to hurt himself, so as to lessen the provocation and challenge his prospect of wealth must be to whatever power had taken the place of the gods.[45]

Abe does not sacrifice himself but fate, or the gods, exact the sacrifice of his young son who dies while obeying Abe's command to drive one of the teams of horses to market. It takes Abe many years before he can accept the death of his son. By that time he has learned to see life evolving slowly but surely toward a higher order, a saner course, if a man is willing to wait.

Frederick Philip Grove and Gwen Pharis Ringwood have created mythical characters in Abe Spalding and Garth Hansen. Both leaders, respected and feared by their neighbors, Abe and Garth are heroic and tragic figures, isolated and alone both in their physical struggle with the prairie land and in their spiritual struggle to understand the meaning behind the mystery of life. They are large figures silhouetted against the prairie sky, dominating and being dominated by the earth; they are Canadian farmers with all the characteristics common to Canadians. These are the larger-than-life folk heroes of the Canadian prairie celebrated in novel and drama whose uncanny resemblance to each other makes them all the more powerful reflections of the prairie.

Gwen Pharis matured quickly as a playwright under Koch's guidance at Chapel Hill. In her two short years at the university, she had written six plays: the situation folk comedy "Chris Axelson, Blacksmith"; the play of social protest "One Man's House"; the superb folk tragedy *Still Stands the House;* the verse play *Pasque Flower,* its development into the full-length folk tragedy *Dark*

Harvest; and the short play "The Days May Be Long" on the theme of the domineering mother. The prairie plays are her finest contribution, and when she returned to the Alberta prairie in 1939 she carried with her a knowledge and experience of writing that would enhance her future creation of folk plays and serious drama.

CHAPTER 3

Robert Gard and Alberta Folklore

DURING World War II and in the years thereafter Gwen Pharis Ringwood found that she was ready and able to write independently of the drama school milieu. Between 1941 and 1952 she wrote and had produced six plays: in Goldfields, northern Saskatchewan, the folk comedy *The Courting of Marie Jenvrin* (1941), and in Edmonton, Alberta, five plays on Alberta folklore and local history: *The Jack and the Joker* (1944), *The Rainmaker* (1944), *Stampede* (1945), *A Fine Colored Easter Egg or The Drowning of Wasyl Nemitchuk* (1948), and *Widger's Way or The Face in the Mirror* (1952).

I *Northern Saskatchewan*

In Goldfields, Saskatchewan, Ringwood tried her hand independently of any critical help, at her first folk play written outside the helpful atmosphere of Chapel Hill and the Playmakers. She focused on all the qualities of the folk play which Koch had emphasized, and she developed her own combination of farce and comedy, improving this form which she had devised for "Chris Axelson, Blacksmith." In *The Courting of Marie Jenvrin* Ringwood is probably the first English Canadian playwright to introduce French Canadian culture into western Canadian plays. The protagonist, the young, vivacious, pretty French Canadian Marie Jenvrin, was modeled after a young woman with whom Ringwood made friends in Goldfields. She is a delightful French Canadian girl with whom the audience has immediate rapport. Marie Jenvrin and her fellow characters, each representative of the various ethnic groups in Goldfields, are much more individualized than are the characters in Ringwood's first play "Chris Axelson." She uses witty dialogue based not on the idiosyncrasies of immigrants learning a new language as in "Chris Axelson," but rather on comic situations. The setting is regional, the Athabasca Lake district of northern Saskatchewan. It is clear that we are now dealing with a mature writer of comedy whose touch is light but dexterous and whose ability to dramatize the quirks of human nature is original. More important is the fact that she gives first place to the human situation within the regional framework as Koch had stressed.

Of the inspiration for *The Courting of Marie Jenvrin* Gwen writes:

I was thinking that I would like to write a little play that had a kind of Valentine feeling, utilizing the new experiences and environment of the North and *The Taming of the Shrew* conflict. Babe had a wide experience of northern Canadian activities. She had cooked in a lumber camp up north and was a very interesting woman. The Werneckes were Ukrainian and represented another aspect of Canadian culture as did the French Canadian suitor, the Irish hard-rock miner, and the Catholic priest. I always felt that Dinsmore, the villain, was the weak person in the play. The plot was slight but I had fun putting all these people together and making a story about them.[1]

The Courting of Marie Jenvrin is a tightly written play combining colorful characterization with realistic comic dialogue and an amusing plot. Marie Jenvrin is a youthful, pretty French Canadian waitress, famous for her pies, who works in a primitive hotel in Yellowknife, Northwest Territories. She is a coquette, sought after by the young naive Louis Hebert, the unscrupulous middle-aged Mr. Dinsmore, and the witty Irish hard-rock miner, Michael Lorrigan. Marie is tricked into vowing that she will marry the man who can give her a Jersey cow so that she can cover her pies with whipped cream. Dinsmore immediately arranges to have a cow flown in but Michael manages at the climactic moment to get Marie out of a legal predicament. She settles for marriage with Michael. Simultaneously, he attempts to cure her of her domineering temper, maintaining that he will be the head of the household, but even as she humbles herself, we are aware that Marie Jenvrin, like the protagonist of *The Taming of the Shrew*, will triumph.

Here is comedy involving people in conflict who become real to the audience. Even such minor characters as Wernecke and his wife are developed sufficiently for us to appreciate their human qualities. The dialogue is quick, humorous, and pointed. Each character possesses individual nuances of speech fitted to his own peculiar temperament. Not influenced by polished British or American comedy, Ringwood does not use the smart one-liner but introduces the Canadian northwest by bringing situation, people, and territory together. Her humor is not satiric; she smiles indulgently at human weaknesses without minimizing them, thereby sustaining a sense of balance. The romantic touches are full of fun and planned exclusively for lighthearted entertainment. An example of this occurs in a brief interchange between Louis and Marie. Louis is declaring his undying love when Marie intimates that she loves another:

MARIE: Louis, Louis, it is no use. I will never love you—not for all the gold in Yellowknife.
LOUIS: I know—I am what they call—a dope. But I stay.
MARIE: *Tres bien.* If you must stay, you stay. But what if I tell you there is a whisper of love—just a small stirring—in my heart for someone else?
LOUIS: I will fight him.
MARIE: *C'est impossible.* Besides, he does not love me.
LOUIS: Then he is a fool with no eyes. I can fight him.
MARIE: He is twice as big as you. Anyway, perhaps I do not love him. Perhaps I hate him. Mais, j'ai malade au coeur, Louis.
LOUIS: (Solemnly.) *Moi aussi.* We French suffer, Marie.
MARIE: (With a big sigh.) *Oui, nous souffrons.* (*For a brief period these very young people suffer. Then Marie turns briskly back to her pie.*) There, it is ready for the oven. See how beautiful, Louis.
LOUIS: You are wonderful.[2]

The dialogue pivots on the one point that the French suffer, the implication being that no other race suffers as do the French. Having paused for a moment to enjoy this suffering, they then go on to more practical business.

Gwen Pharis Ringwood sent this play to Koch, who was again teaching at the Banff School of Fine Arts in Alberta; there it was given its first production in 1941, published in several anthologies, dramatized on CBC radio, and translated into Spanish. *The Courting of Marie Jenvrin* is still produced in Canadian drama festivals. A thoroughly entertaining play, it has never dated but continues to amuse Canadian audiences with its lighthearted humor and droll folk characters. An excellent folk comedy, it is dependent for its success not on its regional trappings but on the human situation with which any audience can empathize.

II *Alberta Folklore and Local History Project*

It was fortuitous that Robert Gard, director of the Alberta Folklore and Local History Project, should be in Edmonton when Gwen

Ringwood returned from Goldfields. His intense interest in grass-roots theater and his depth of research into Alberta folklore and history were the inspiration (already noted) for Ringwood's work during the decade of the forties. In 1944 he commissioned Gwen Ringwood to write four one-act plays to be paid for by a Rockefeller grant under the Alberta Folklore and Local History Project. She wrote *The Jack and the Joker, The Rainmaker,* and the full length play *Stampede.* All were produced at the Banff School of Fine Arts and published by the Extension Department of the University of Alberta.

All three plays were regional and folk comedies utilizing the early twentieth-century history of Alberta and the historical figures whose characters had not yet been explored by Canadian writers. Bob Edwards, the clever, witty, fearless editor of the famous *Calgary Eye-Opener* in *The Jack and the Joker;* Hatfield, the colorful con man and rainmaker of Medicine Hat in *The Rainmaker;* and Nigger John, the beloved Alberta black man, cowboy, and rancher who lived before the Calgary Stampede in *Stampede.* These were the kinds of characters whom Paul Green had encouraged his students to seek out and make the protagonists of their folk plays. Each is the center of a warm, human, true story set in colorful locales; each has contributed his leadership qualities to improve his individual areas; each is a folk hero and has the characteristics upon which the writer of folk comedies can enlarge and enhance, thus providing Canadians with larger-than-life heroes based on true historical records.

Robert Gard and Gwen Ringwood hold the distinction of being the first to revive interest in Bob Edwards. *The Jack and Joker* was a slight period piece on Edwards and his *Calgary Eye Opener.* Of the editor who loved to prick the bubbles of pomposity, Ringwood attempted to make a comedy out of actual incidents in Edwards's life that would reflect Alberta culture at that period of time, but the farcical comedy that she wrote on this clever, witty, but serious political thinker and his newspaper is disappointing. It fails to enlarge on the qualities of the hero; the dialogue is trite and full of clichés, and the other characters are merely stock figures in a play that is little more than an exercise in playwriting. It is true that Bob Edwards was a quiet man, but he did have a biting satirical wit in the many articles he wrote for the *Calgary Eye Opener.* It seems that Ringwood missed her opportunity to transfer this wit to incisive dialogue. His newspaper, which contained witty and sharply satiric articles, was nevertheless a serious paper when he edited it. In

Ringwood's farcical comedy Bob prevents a corrupt politician and his foolish wife from destroying his printing press and his future as an open-minded journalist. He is thoroughly honest, pulling no punches and printing the truth in his muckraking *Eye Opener*. When he opposes Dudley Carp's dishonest maneuvres for political office, Mrs. Carp forces the owner of the printing press, poverty-striken Mrs. Gudgeon, to sell out to her but at the climactic moment Edwards obtains evidence that Carp has sold useless land to Mrs. Gudgeon; thus he forces Carp to return both money and printing press. Gwen writes her comments on the construction of this play:

> Robert Gard suggested that I write a one-act play on Bob Edwards, a colorful figure in High River, Calgary. So I got out the old *Eye Openers* that Bob Edwards had edited. They were small magazines full of jokes, cartoons and brilliant and satirical political comment. The more I read of Edwards, the more I realized that it was going to be a difficult assignment because he was a very quiet man. . . . He was a lonely figure. I found it quite difficult to know how to present Bob Edwards in a play where he was to be known for his humour and wit, for the humour and wit were his writer's weapons and craft and art. In himself he was self-effacing. Although he was in the legislature, he made very few speeches and they were not fiery. Finally I took an incident that actually happened to him. I decided to place the action around this controversy. His freedom to say what he wanted was very precious to Bob Edwards. He couldn't do it without a printing press.[3]

The setting was the office of the *Sheep Creek Eye Opener;* the action was an actual incident; the time was 1904; the characters were fictitious. Ringwood tried unsuccessfully to use the slightly ribald, broad farcical comedy that appeared in Edwards's *Eye Opener*, and the characters he created, to make trenchant political remarks. She presented Edwards as he was, a quiet, considerate man who cared about ordinary people, and she placed him in a setting of farcical comedy in an attempt to evoke vivid memories of Edwards. Although it is a record of a figure who had played a great part in the early history of Alberta as a province, it lacks depth and substance. A lesser play than "Chris Axelson, Blacksmith" or "One Man's House," it is merely a trite exercise in playwriting.

J. T. McKreath, the first drama supervisor of Alberta, says *The Jack and the Joker* is nevertheless still being produced occasionally in Alberta drama festivals, and has been revised for CBC radio in Alberta. McKreath comments that Ringwood should have developed the character of Bob Edwards to a greater degree. He writes:

It is too bad that she didn't take Bob Edwards and develop him more. There she has a character, a ready-made character. Why don't we have that many gutsy characters on the Alberta scene in the way that the Americans have? There are so many American characters, not all heroic, who have been allowed to grow beyond fact into the realm of fiction and myth and who have ended up as heroes of the musical stage. Bob Edwards would have lent himself to becoming that type of hero.[4]

Ringwood lost her opportunity here to enhance and immortalize Bob Edwards. She emphasized instead light repartee as in the following dialogue which opens the play:

MRS. GUDGEON:	Good morning, Mr. Edwards.
EDWARDS:	Morning, Mrs. Gudgeon.
MRS. GUDGEON:	Have you got the paper out?
EDWARDS:	It will be out by noon.
MRS. GUDGEON:	Is the press working?
EDWARDS:	Fine. I'm going to pay for it one of these days.
MRS. GUDGEON:	I know that, sir. Mr. Edwards, the ladies are very upset about your paper.
EDWARDS:	What ladies?
MRS. GUDGEON:	The Lotos Club.
EDWARDS:	Don't they think my jokes are funny, Mrs. Gudgeon?
MRS. GUDGEON:	The jokes are funny, lad, but the ladies feel they're immoral and unrefined. They're coming to see you this morning, sir.
EDWARDS:	You keep an eye on the street and we'll hide.[5]

This dialogue is typical of the repartee throughout *The Jack and the Joker*. It fails to define Edwards's character—his quiet, self-effacing but humorous temperament, his integrity and serious purpose. It does not produce a folk hero of the stature required to immortalize him. Possibly it was Ringwood's choice of farce as a form for this play that was inadequate to her purposes. This is her first attempt at dramatizing an actual Canadian leader of heroic stature. She fails to adjust the form of her play to the requirements of his temperament and of history. She may have been intimidated by the weight of her responsibility here. Whatever the cause, the result is a superficial farce full of tired clichés. In contrast, Ringwood's next two plays—*The Rainmaker* and *Stampede*—do justice to the historical folk characters she depicts and show a marked development in her style.

The Rainmaker is a symphonic play that one might orchestrate. Ringwood thought it would make a good ballet. Impressionistic in form, it can be classified with Ringwood's poetic folk plays. Again it uses the character of a real person: Charles Hatfield, who was hired by the town of Medicine Hat, Alberta, in 1921 to bring rain to that sun-scorched soil—a land that had known only drought for four years. The play encompasses the people's reactions to Hatfield—their hopes, their cynical second thoughts, and finally their despair before the climactic moment when rain actually falls upon Medicine Hat. It is a lyric play with comic elements of that era, written ten years before the American play *The Rainmaker* by Richard Nash, which was produced in 1954. Ringwood conceived the idea for her play from Robert Gard's radio play about Hatfield, and from his book *Johnny Chinook*, in which a chapter is devoted to Hatfield the Rainmaker. Tom Kerr, who directed it several times, says of it:

> In *The Rainmaker* the strength is not just in the situation but it is in the imagery and the poetry. The structure is difficult because of the large cast, the dialogues, and monologues. In construction there are flaws because of its fragmentation and that always creates a problem unless you have a tremendously strong narrator. . . . She obviously recorded a true incident because we have prairie people who saw the play and who couldn't speak after the production because the memory was too personal. . . . The play works but it is seldom produced because the cast is so large, including a band, and it needs a lot of choreographic effects on stage. . . . I think it is a play making a good statement and recording of the times in Medicine Hat in that era.[6]

As the play opens the narrator, a farmer, Tom Arnold, in his late forties, is reminiscing on the events of twenty-four years past, Medicine Hat on 22 May 1921—the day Hatfield the Rainmaker miraculously brought rain to their arid land. The spirit of Tom's wife, long since dead, moves gently behind him, commenting quietly on his remarks. There is a sense of timelessness here, and one is reminded of the same rhythms that move through Thornton Wilder's play, *Our Town* (1938). As Tom Arnold muses on those past events, there follows a flashback to 1921 and the cast of twenty-nine people including the citizens gradually move in on the main event of the community—the possibility of Hatfield's bringing rain before midnight. Townsfolk talk to each other in front of a carnival tent erected to celebrate the event. The thirty-foot rain precipitation and attraction towers set up by Hatfield are off left, and downstage is a fairly high platform. There is a note of strained gaiety among the bystanders. Tom Arnold is there with his wife Marg who plans to leave this land of drought. Tom has pleaded with her to remain one more night, hoping that rain might be a sign that they should remain together. Rain actually comes on that climactic night to Medicine Hat and Marg agrees to stay. Unlike Thornton Wilder's stage manager and narrator who holds *Our Town* together, however, Ringwood's narrator simply opens and closes the play and is the catalyst in this slight plot. Hatfield the con man appears only in the middle of the play. He enters in flashy new clothes, bubbling with self-confidence. We are told that for ten days he has been adding "scientific" solutions to the precipitation towers' vats. Here are his first answers to questions addressed to him:

HATFIELD: Rain? Of course it will rain. My solution has been a little static, but everything's all right I tell you.
JOE: Just what I said.
HATFIELD: All we need is patience, a little patience.
SAM: That blue sky can make a man feel mighty powerless, can't it Hatfield?
HATFIELD: Not me. I refuse to feel powerless. I walk in the van of progress. It's people like you—and you, Madame—doubters, that hold up the march.
MIRANDA: I only asked you it if was going to rain.
HATFIELD: It's bound to rain, Madame, Sooner or later it's bound to rain.
MIRANDA: I see.
JOE: (As Benny asked for corroboration about the ocean so Joe turns to Hatfield) You believe in yourself, don't you, Hatfield?
HATFIELD: Eh, what's that?
JOE: You can do it, can't you? You can make it rain? You think you can?
HATFIELD: Believe in myself? My dear fellow, as Ben Franklin harnessed the lightning so Charles Hatfield has harnessed the rainfall. Science, dear fellow, pure science.[7]

Ringwood succeeds in developing the play as variations on a theme, as pearls on a string, with the people as protagonists and the drought as antagonist. The miracle of rain is the *deus ex machina*. The play is more abstract than realistic, having the effect of a piece of music or a dance. But when Tom Kerr produced it, he found that he needed that strong, outstanding character which one finds in all traditional plays (but is not necessary to the folk drama). Either Tom the narrator or Hatfield the Rainmaker would have provided him with this force behind the action, this lead character to hold the play together. Instead, Ringwood's play is a challenge to the director to develop those variations on a theme which she offers, with the people and the drought as the two leading characters. It is in the originality of this conception that the play succeeds.

There are vast possibilities for the artist who can use effectively abstract drama, impressionism in drama, and dance as a medium for drama. Several of Ringwood's plays contain these three elements. The use of abstract drama in Ringwood's works has its roots in the late nineteenth-century symbolist movement in theater. Led by Maurice Maeterlinck, the symbolist movement produced mood plays, tone-poem dramatic compositions, the use of light as a visual equivalent to music, reliance on verbal mood music, and on symbolic stage sets such as those introduced by Gordon Craig. The greatest of the English-speaking playwrights to come under symbolist influence was John Millington Synge whose *Riders to the Sea* had a strong bearing on Ringwood's work as she herself tells us. Synge's poetic language and fine sensitivity to mood and tone derive from the symbolists' influence. One can detect in several of Ringwood's plays, particularly the prairie and ethnic dramas, the effect of Synge's folk plays on her writing. One of Ringwood's contributions to western Canadian plays has been this symbolist sensibility.

Allied to this is Ringwood's use of impressionism in drama. Just as the impressionists in art relied on their own sensations, their own emotional responses to the visual world, providing thus a more lifelike interpretation of the world than the realist's, so Ringwood uses this free form in drama to string together a series of impressions in one scene after another. The total effect of this in such plays as *The Rainmaker*, "Look Behind You, Neighbor," "The Road Runs North," *The Deep Has Many Voices*, "A Remembrance of Miracles," and *Mirage*, is to stimulate the imagination of the audience to a richer perception of the theme of the play. Ringwood is improvising on this theme by offering a number of impressions—all of which combine to give a more intense image of life.

Dance is another medium used by Ringwood to create that fluidity of movement so essential to impressionism and symbolism. The dancers in *Mirage* mime the waving fields of wheat, the storms on the prairie; they are the prairie with its mysterious power. Dance provides the mood of Edson in *Look Behind You, Neighbor*, and of the Gold Rush in *The Road Runs North*. In *The Deep Has Many Voices* the use of dance mimes the confusions of youth in the counterculture period of the 1960s.

When Ringwood wrote *The Rainmaker* she was just beginning to see the possibilities provided by an original combination of abstract drama, impressionism, music, and dance. She does not use all of these in *The Rainmaker* but she does use an original impressionistic structure combining this with realistic dialogue and a sense of humor that resulted in a more lively play than an adherence to realism would have done. There are many comic moments in *The Rainmaker* as this one involving Tim, Joe, and Walt:

TIM: I remember it raining in this country once. Water come right down out of the sky.
WALT: You got to show me.
TIM: My brother plumb swooned away with the shock of that rain. Took us four hours to bring him to.
WALT: You don't say. Four hours.
TIM: We tried everything. Glass of water. Glass of wine. Whiskey. (*To Joe*). You know what finally revived him?
JOE: Couldn't guess.
TIM: Glass full of dust. Brought him right to. That was the stuff he was used to—only thing that could save him. (*R*, 3-4)

As an impressionistic play *The Rainmaker* produces a picture of the people of Medicine Hat in their final hour of drought. Because of its subject matter, dialogue, and general theme, it could have been even more successful as a musical. But in Ringwood's work we are seeing a gradual development toward musical drama which will come to fruition in a few years time. It was natural then that she would follow the rhythms inherent in *The Rainmaker* with the musically oriented *Stampede*.

Stampede was the result of a personal desire to do a big show on a large canvas with some musical background. Although not intended to emphasize totally the Stampede, Ringwood did try to make the rodeo of Calgary as theatrically interesting as Hemingway's bull fight. There is a common bond between the art of the rodeo and the art of bullfighting. Both require a certain type of choreography, a movement however swift or slow, that has been practiced, like the ballet, until it has achieved perfection. But unlike the ballet, this movement is a lightninglike flirting with death. One false step, one miscalculation of judgment means certain death. The unpredictability of the antagonist is also a frightening factor. Both the bullfight and the rodeo are expressive of a mystique that Hemingway successfully defined as a ritual of life and death.

Ringwood seeks her own definition of this mystique in *Stampede* She sees in the art of the rodeo not so much a ritual of life and death as an affirmation of community. The spirit of comraderie among the contestants, the good will expressed in the competition, the concern for fellow riders—all point to the rodeo as good fellowship and the Stampede as a community celebration. Both her absorption in the ranching era, and the publication of Robert Gard's novel *Midnight* inspired her to recreate the Calgary Stampede in this first full-length tragicomedy. The emphasis was placed on the events leading up to the Stampede and on the lives of Canadian ranchers and cowboys. The use of cowboy songs throughout the play lends a note of authenticity and of romance to *Stampede*—an early note, let us add, for in 1945 Ringwood was one of the first to dignify these old songs as an art form. *Stampede* was therefore innovative, using the old cowboy songs to explore the western mystique, making music integral to drama as Brecht and Weil had done. Ringwood recalls the writing of *Stampede* and her introduction of music into it in these words:

> I wanted a panoramic kind of play, a broad sweeping action that would recreate the early ranching days of Alberta. And I set it at the time of the first Calgary Stampede because that was one of the big festivals in the west and still is. I wanted to use music in it; we even had an orchestrated version, a kind of symphonic arrangement of the cowboy songs. . . . At that time cowboy songs were in a sort of disrepute; they were considered corny and we were trying . . . to make an artistic use of the folk song that people knew but had not treated with much respect. I also wanted to use comedy of the tenderfoot. Barney and I talked to a rodeo cowboy. . . . It was part of our myth, the myth of the cowboy. . . . Hemingway had used the bull fights. Here was something we could use and I wanted to show the risk and danger involved. . . . I remembered incidents of cowboys riding on our ranch when I was little . . . breaking horses, risking their lives, and then riding to the rodeo.[8]

In this romantic tragicomedy Ringwood uses the original cowboy music collected by John A. Lomax, a Texan, having obtained his permission to use the songs from his book *Cowboy Songs*. Many of these folk songs, after originating in Europe, became cowboy songs of the American south and west.

The time, place, and action of the play with the music, offer good dramatic opportunities for a stimulating production. The time is 1912; the place—act 1 at a camp site on a cattle trail, act 2 at a

Calgary boardinghouse, and act 3 in the enclosure behind the chutes on the last day of the first Calgary Stampede. The plot involves Shorthorn, the respected and well-loved American Foreman of Bar XY. Unknown to the other characters is the fact that Shorthorn is wanted for murder in the United States. With his cowboys he drives cattle to the Calgary Stampede. His adversary Shark suspects his secret and threatens to report him to the police. Together with Nigger John, his friend and partner, Shorthorn had planned to buy a ranch after the Calgary Stampede. At the end of the play, after saving young Bud's life, he is betrayed by Shark and forced to leave Alberta in order to escape the law. Ringwood's characters are the stereotypes of the great western stories and movies: respected leader Shorthorn, faithful partner Nigger John, mean adversary Shark, beautiful young girl Celia, her young cowboy lover Bud, the tenderfoot Larry, and a number of minor characters. The cast includes more than twenty-six.

Gwen's talent for characterization succeeds in transforming a few characters in *Stampede* into individual people. The American Shorthorn is the protagonist in the play, and his character is portrayed as a likeable man, a leader with integrity, who was involved in a murder. Audience sympathy is with Shorthorn. But the character who arouses most interest for Canadian audiences is John Ware or Nigger John, the great Alberta black man, cowboy, and rancher, who lived before the first Calgary Stampede and who therefore never really took part in this rodeo. John is no stereotype but an intelligent, kind, experienced ranch hand whose nickname is a sign of dignity, not opprobrium. His influence over the others is quiet but strong. His human qualities are underscored in the dialogue he uses, e.g., by his exclamation about stampedes: "I don't like stampedes. I hate them. I just can't see it, that's all. Raking a horse from head to flank, making an outlaw out of him, wasting him, so's people can yell."[9] He says of his horse Midnight:

> He's been hurt bad, Jim. Deeper than his skin, deeper than any spur can rake him. Midnight knows now what he always feared. He knows that man's got a mean streak in him, a queer twisted mean streak that likes to hurt and hurt deep. And most of us don't do much about crushing it down. We ought to, you know, if we don't blot it out, it'll finish us, sometime. (S, III. 4)

Although Ringwood succeeded in capturing Nigger John's human qualities, the play does not revolve around him but around the region and character of the Calgary Stampede which is Ringwood's special forte. We have seen her establish atmosphere, the spirit of a region, its mystique, in the prairie plays and in *The Rainmaker*. We see her achieve this successfully once again in *Stampede*, and we will observe this gift of hers in the plays and musicals that follow. It is true that Paul Green had encouraged his students to enrich and enlarge upon the well-known historical characters of their native countries in plays that would establish them in the imagination of a nation as great folk characters and heroes. What Ringwood does in this regard is to introduce to the Canadian people such leaders and folk heroes as Bob Edwards in *The Jack and the Joker*, Hatfield in *The Rainmaker*, and Nigger John (John Ware) in *Stampede*. The audience and readers were made aware of their authentic characters, and researchers then dug into their respective backgrounds. Today books and articles have been published on these colorful men as a result of Ringwood's dramatic introductions.

Ringwood's unusual talent lay in the establishment of the region, atmosphere, and mystique, as has been already mentioned. This is Frederick Koch's influence, a factor in her education as a playwright that will always be there implicitly in her work. Paul Green's emphasis on the folk hero is essentially American and is derivative of the American dream with its focus on the American hero and leader. Ringwood, on the contrary, is doing something Canadian with her folk plays. Her Canadian emphasis is on community, and it is the community with its differing qualities and special mystique that is unique to each area in Canada. In *Stampede* Ringwood recreates those singular qualities that make the Stampede in Calgary a community event.

The play's curious ending is a subject of interest. Shorthorn bids farewell to Nigger John. His union with Nigger John as ranch partners has been destroyed by Shark who threatens to report him to the police. One is tempted to see Shorthorn and Nigger John as symbols of America and Canada. Shorthorn returns to America. As he departs, Beanie the Barker is exploiting the Indian Chief White Calf in these words:

BEANIE: Step right up, folks. Shake hands with a genuine vanished American. Last chance. Last chance. Last chance for a souvenir—

VOICE (or WHISTLE): Yippee Ti yi—git along little dogie. . . . It's your misfortune and none of my own.

NIGGER JOHN: (Softly) Yippee ti yi, git along little dogie, they say that Wyoming will be your new home.

BEANIE: Last chance for a souvenir of the old West, folks—last chance. . . . (*S*, III. 19)

The nice blending of cowboy songs, Alberta ranch country atmosphere, and some authentic characterization make *Stampede* a colorful play. Sidney Risk directed the production at Banff in 1945 in which Bruno Gerussi, Vincent Tovell, and Ted Follows played the leading roles. It was produced also at the University of Alberta in Edmonton and in Calgary. It has not been presented often but it was revived at Banff in an anniversary celebration, and directed by Esther Nelson in 1955 as part of the University of Alberta's Department of Extension program.

Early criticisms of *Stampede* were mixed. Reactions by Elsie Park Gowan, by critics in general (recorded by Ringwood), by John Weber of Beverly Hills, by Florence James, and by Esther Nelson are worth attention. Elsie Park Gowan liked the play but she took exception to the plot. She suggested that the plot should have reflected the serious conflict in southern Alberta between the rancher and the homesteader, the saddle and the plough, the wide open spaces versus the barbed wire fenced-in farmlands. However, she makes this favorable comment on *Stampede:*

> The first scene on the prairie in the evening when the cowboys are on their way to the Calgary Stampede is beautiful, atmospheric, lovely. The second scene in the boarding house where they square dance is good theatre. The play is fine except for the plot line. Her characterization is strong. The characters are closely tied in with the atmosphere and mood; they grow out of their background.[10]

Ringwood remarked candidly that the play was not as successful in Calgary as she had hoped because the critics there felt she had overemphasized the folk elements and had missed the actual excitement inherent in the Stampede. But her play was placed at the dividing line between the culmination of the great ranching era and the beginning of the rodeo as show. It was not intended to emphasize totally the Stampede but to show the events leading up to it, the colorful lives of Canadian cowboys on the ranch.

John Weber of the William Morris Agency in Beverly Hills, California, reported on the play's adaptability for film in 1949:

. . . Miss Pharis may . . . develop *Stampede* in the form of a screenplay. . . . She should avoid tritenesses such as occur in the comedy byplay of the cowboys with the greenhorn Larry. She should also avoid such old situations as the one in which Lonesome . . . loses his roll gambling . . . audiences being as sophisticated as they are in the field of westerns . . . I do believe that the "Calgary Stampede" and the rest of the rich, fresh background possibilities *suggested* in the play and the author's notes should by all means provide at least the foundation for a very worthwhile A-western.[11]

Because Hollywood at that time had its quota of westerns, *Stampede* was never revised for film. Florence James, drama consultant for the Saskatchewan Arts Board, in a letter to Gwen, wrote this about *Stampede* in 1954:

It has, as I thought, when I saw it in Banff, very good possibilities. . . . The Stampede scene is colorful and also gives you a chance to dramatize in action all of John's [Nigger John] attitude toward the sport. It also serves believably to bring a lot of characters together, including the marshal, for the climax. You write very good, talkable dialogue, and continue to get believable colour and atmosphere into your locales without straining for effect.[12]

This is perceptive criticism with its emphasis on dialogue which is so authentic in *Stampede*. Esther Nelson who directed *Stampede* at the University of Alberta's Extension Department production in Edmonton in the summer of 1955 says this of it in a letter of 21 September 1955 to Gwen Ringwood: "The general comment seemed favorable and in some quarters enthusiastic. . . . The students . . . all responded to it. . . . Mr. Cameron liked it very much; some thought it should have gone on tour in connection with the Jubilee."[13] This response, ten years after the first production, suggests that the play is not dated and can be successfully revived.

III *Ukrainian Influences and Pure Farce*

Thus far in Ringwood's dramatic writing career, she has experimented with tragedy in the three prairie plays and "One Man's House," tragicomedy in *Stampede*, comedy in *The Courting of Marie Jenvrin* and *The Rainmaker*, and a mixture of farce and comedy in "Chris Axelson" and *The Jack and the Joker*. Now she is ready to tackle her first pure farce. Inspired by the character of the Ukrainian people in Lamont, Alberta, Ringwood knew instinctively that the use of pure farce would best bring out their strengths and weaknesses, their peculiar mixture of a colorful response to life and a brooding contemplation of misfortunes.

Farce differs from comedy in that the emphasis is on gestures and buffoonery, situation and action, rather than on character or manners. Sometimes called low comedy, it is designed to provoke laughter, not to develop into a philosophical dialogue. Usually a brief play, it is dependent also on brief comic dialogue in which the audience is more aware of the situation than are the characters on stage. Ringwood creates an excellent farce in her Ukrainian one-act play *The Drowning of Wasyl Nemitchuk or A Fine Colored Easter Egg*.

In the Ukrainian settlement of Lamont, Alberta, where the Ringwoods lived from 1946 to 1948, Gwen was fascinated by Ukrainian colorful customs. She decided, therefore, to write another play about new Canadians. Influenced by Chekhov's comedies, *The Marriage Proposal* and *The Bear*, she created the one-act farce, *The Drowning of Wasyl Nemitchuk or A Fine Colored Easter Egg* (1946), in which she recognized the similarities in the Ukrainian and Russian temperaments. All this color of middle-European life she could see in Lamont, in the church architecture, the Ukrainian dances, and the rich Ukrainian traditions such as the artistic work on Ukrainian Easter eggs. The older folk were still closely allied to these rich traditions but the younger people were fast losing them in their eagerness to espouse the new ways of Canadians. At this time also, in 1946, there occurred the great oil boom in Alberta and everyone imagined what it would be like to discover oil on one's property. All of these events moved Gwen Ringwood to write this play, of which she ways:

> I wanted very much to write a warm funny farce about the conflict between the people who envisioned great wealth from the oil and the feeling that the land was there to supply food. . . . So I wrote "A Fine Colored Easter Egg" and read it to several of our Ukrainian friends who said, "that's good and sound, especially the brooding scene" . . . where the piling of one melancholy sadness on top of another, and the long silences, punctuated by some other woe or piece of bad luck, were typical of Ukrainians.[14]

This imaginative, lighthearted farce which her Ukrainian friends assured her was ethnically correct, depicts the Ukrainian farmer

Wasyl Nemitchuk and his wife Olga who have been happily content for years in their Ukrainian way of life. But gradually Olga is tempted by the attractions of Edmonton and the lure of riches which the possible discovery of oil on their farm might bring to them. She insists on bringing in men to drill for oil and she pleads with Wasyl to give up their Ukrainian customs for what she considers a better way of life. In despair Wasyl, after leaving his clothes on the shore to indicate he had drowned, runs away to his Ukrainian bachelor cousin George who hides him when Olga appears on the scene, In the ensuing dialogue George thinks Wasyl is out of earshot. He therefore tells Olga that Wasyl has not drowned but has run off with the widow Franca. Actually George intends to have a little affair with Olga when the coast is clear. This is too much for Wasyl who appears and claims his wife. The fun for the audience is in the witty dialogue, the non sequiturs, the naiveté of the characters, and the brooding spirit of the Ukrainians. Hear Wasyl lamenting with his cousin George:

WASYL: Sit down, George. A terrible thing has happened.
GEORGE: (*Sitting meekly*) Olga is dead?
WASYL: (*Crossly*) Olga? No. Olga is alive. Olga blooms. The worse it gets the more she flourishes. (*Back to tragic tone*) George, calamity falls on Wasyl Nemitchuk.
GEORGE: Yes? Too bad, Wasyl.
WASYL: Yes. Terrible!
GEORGE: You're a good man too. I'm sorry.
WASYL: Thank you. (*They brood*)
GEORGE: Your house burned to the ground eh?—tch—tch.
WASYL: (*Indignantly*) Who said anything about my house. It stands.
GEORGE: That is one blessing then. (*Pause*) Your daughters all ruined, is that it?
WASYL: My daughters are respectable—all married!
GEORGE: Your hogs, then,—stricken?
WASYL: No! Two hundred and twenty beautiful white pigs I got.
GEORGE: Well, it's too bad, that's all, whatever it is.
WASYL: Trouble, trouble, nobody knows—up—down. Crash—bang—day and night—up down bang crash. In my brain!
GEORGE: (*Thinking he understands at last*) The doctor gives no hope?
WASYL: Doctor?
GEORGE: About your brain? The noises in your head?
WASYL: (*Angry*) What the devil are you talking about George? The noises is not in my head. The noises is on my farm. The noises is Oil. Oil, George.[15]

The repartee between the two middle-aged Ukrainians is typical of the interchanges throughout the play. The denouement occurs when the oil company discontinues its search, convinced no oil is to be found on the Nemitchuk farm, and Wasyl and Olga go back to their Ukrainian way of life.

There are some resemblances in *A Fine Colored Easter Egg* to Frederico Garcia Lorca's play *Billy Club Puppets* in which the puppet characteristics have certain affinities with the farcical Ukrainian characters in Ringwood's play. Also in Lorca's *The Shoemaker's Prodigious Wife*, the shoemaker's wife and the Ukrainian wife in *Easter Egg* seem to have come from the same mold.

Ringwood's attempt at pure farce shows mature professional skill. Describing her past comedies as "trembling on the edge of farce,"[16] she now succeeds in capturing the essence of farce in *A Fine Colored Easter Egg*. The more remote and removed she is from her material, the better able is she to disguise an attitude and express it in comic terms. She used only three characters which simplified the premiere production at the Banff School of Fine Arts in 1946. How does Ringwood create farce? Why does she do it? What does it reveal about her intent? These are the questions that come to mind when one reads *The Drowning of Wasyl Nemitchuk*. She creates farce by provoking light-hearted laughter through the clowning of Wasyl and his cousin, George, and through the comic situation of Wasyl's confrontation with his wife. Their actions and dialogue, serious to themselves but highly amusing to the audience, their doleful brooding over real or imagined misfortunes, and their quick reversal of action when situations suddenly change, are all calculated to provoke easy laughter at the foibles of humankind. Why Ringwood creates farce can be answered by reading what she has written about herself in *Stage Voices*. She finds comedy and farce more to her purpose as dramatic forms because she can then comment on the human situation from the objective position of the bystander. Ringwood sees life clearly and without bitterness. Satire is too caustic for her. Farce is playful and engenders quick laughter through the use of buffoonery and non sequiturs. Ringwood's use of farce reveals her intent—to comment on life without hurting; to observe the funny side of seemingly serious situations; to see how close comedy and tragedy are in the human situation; to avoid taking oneself or one's situation too seriously.

In writing the play, Ringwood had a strong sense of spatial relationships between the characters because of the multilevel set she had devised. It was an outdoor/indoor set with ladder and bunkbed. In the climactic scene Wasyl is sitting up on the bunkbed with his jug of wine shouting down at his wife Olga; then positions are reversed. They cannot come to a decision as to whether they should stay on the farm or go to the city. Because of the interesting set, the spatial relationship between the two was amplified. Ringwood began to hear through the pitch and tone, the music and dance, the real space between people of unlike minds. In her own mind there vibrated the pitch, inflection, and space between the voices. She says of this interesting phenomenon:

> There was real excitement in discovering that I was not riding on the lines so heavily anymore; not what they said but how they said it—vibrations in the air of the voices, the movements in space of the people. I may not have used this as effectively as I'd like to but it was a breakthrough for me of awareness.[17]

It was produced at the Banff School of Fine Arts, and adapted for CBC radio in 1946, presented in Winnipeg by Emrys Jones in 1953, and produced on CBC radio program "Prairie Playhouse" on 22 March 1956. Elsie Park Gowan says of it: "*A Fine Colored Easter Egg* works beautifully on the stage and I have seen it done successfully in the Alberta High Schools. One teacher did it with Ukrainian students and through it she generated great enthusiasm for theatre because this play was 'where they lived.' "[18] *A Fine Colored Easter Egg* was a perfect prelude to the writing of one of her most successful comedies, *Widger's Way* or *The Face in the Mirror*, which is a combination of farce, comedy, and gentle satire. The antics of Wasyl in *A Fine Colored Easter Egg* give way to capers of a much larger scope in Widger, but unlike Wasyl, Widger's character is explored and individualized.

IV *Classical Comedy Influences*

In 1951, Professor Robert Orchard, head of the Drama Department at the University of Alberta, asked Ringwood to write a comedy for the Studio Theatre, suggesting that she read for inspiration the great classical comedy, Plautus's *Pot of Gold*, and see what happened. As a result certain elements of the Plautus comedy gave Ringwood the impetus to create *Widger's Way*. She says she thoroughly enjoyed writing it: "I really was intoxicated with the writing of *Widger*. I delighted in his character because he was ultimately a man who wanted to grow but he would give and then would pull back. He seemed to me a completely Canadian character."[19] Ringwood learned to combine farce with comedy and comedy with pathos, and in this area also her work resembles the plays of Frederico Garcia Lorca. Each uses short comic dialogue in farces and each has the ability to create fully rounded characters. Proceeding from individual visions of life, Lorca and Ringwood create fantasy which becomes reality, and this reality assumes the properties of mystery. They both use traditional comic figures with ironic touches in folk plays that are lively and witty, with lighthearted resolutions often concealing some pathos.

Widger's Way, set in the Alberta prairies, is built on the age-old plot of the miser and his gold. The play opens as Widger is accosted in his farmhouse one night by a desperate stranger, Planter. With his partner Jake, they had discovered gold, fought over it, and Planter escaped with the map and the bag of gold nuggets. Jake, his murderous partner, is hot on his trail. Widger must confront these desperadoes. Planter compels Widger to hide him. When Jake arrives, Widger is forced to give Jake false directions. Planter insists that Widger hide the gold until Planter's return. After Planter leaves, Widger is tempted to keep the gold for himself. He hides it first in the old well, then up in the church bell tower, then underneath the barn, and finally in a sack of potatoes. As the play progresses a number of subplots keep the action going and the comedy at a high pitch. So frequently is the gold almost discovered that Widger lives in constant fear of losing it, of the return of the desperadoes, of being discovered by the constable. He deteriorates into a nervous shadow of his former self. When Jake finally murders Planter, Widger is suspected of the crime. As the play concludes, all the loose ends are tied satisfactorily; Jake is arrested; Widger gives the gold to the authorities; the oil company discovers oil on Widger's land and he becomes a rich man. But Widger has changed. Still cautious, he has nevertheless risked his life for his daughter Roselle, and he plans to give some of his money to her and her fiancé Peter. The play ends, as do all classical comedies, with a community celebration announcing Roselle's marriage to Peter, and Sokolander's to the widow Anastasia.

There are elements in *Widger's Way* of characters and situations from former Ringwood plays, but these are merely peripheral. Widger combines in his person a bit of Chris Axelson's naiveté, Hatfield the Rainmaker's opportunism, and Wasyl Nemitchuk's hastiness. But ultimately Widger is himself—a new character whose comic and human foibles endears him to the audience. He is also a cautious and careful Canadian farmer unwilling to get involved in other people's problems. Sokolander has affinities with Dudley B. Carp, and Anastasia with Mrs. Dorinda Carp, characters in *The Jack and the Joker.* Peter has the innocence and good will manifested in Chris Axelson's nephew; Dowser Ringgo shares, in a sense, Hatfield's optimism. The courtship of Roselle is reminiscent of Marie Jenvrin. But all of these affinities are slight beside the originality and rich comedy of *Widger's Way.*

Ringwood's view of man as seen in *Widger's Way* reminds one of novelist Joyce Cary's philosophy in *The Horse's Mouth.* Both see man as small and comic; full of inconsistencies, false hopes, and false promises; sometimes too idealistic in coping with this material world; often grasping, selfish, stubborn, and materialistic. But there is hope for man in Ringwood's observations. He will continue, down today, up tomorrow, but carrying on in his quest despite his frequent failures.

Constructed as it is in five scenes, *Widger's Way* makes use of parody and melodramatic techniques to create Ringwood's finest comedy to date. Widger, the miserly Albertan farmer, is a true native folk type conditioned by his environment of farmland and oilfields. His fellow characters reflect in comical satire the folk of that area—Planter and Jake, the unscrupulous goldminers; Sokolander, the cunning politician; Anastasia, the meddling widow; Professor Bond, geologist and opportunist, and his innocent farmland student Peter; Garrow, the slick American oil technician; Dowser Ringgo, water witch and pedlar of strange potions; and Docket, the constable. Together their personalities reflect the land, and their conversations are expressive of the folk imagination and folk idiom. Widger's mirror reveals his and their greed, cruelty, fears, and ambitions. Rich in humorous dialogue, the play expresses a way of life which Widger expounds in these words: "I've lived to myself, don't lend things, discourage children from tramping down pastures; don't borrow anything or bother anybody. They'll all remember that. That's my way. They'll say: That's Widger's Way."[20]

There is also an affinity of style and spirit in *Widger's Way* with the comedies and farces of Lorca whose use of the essential reality of fantasy, folk qualities, and lively characters, particularly in *The Shoemaker's Prodigious Wife,* is very like the comic depth in *Widger's Way.* In both comedies the protagonist develops and changes for the better. Widger's plan to marry off Roselle to old Sokolander is similar to Lorca's *The Billy Club Puppets* in which the father decides to marry Rosita to an old man. Although this is a plot often repeated in literature, the similarities in character resemblances, reactions, and ironic wit in dialogue are striking. The intense conflicts in the soul of Widger are paralleled in another of Lorca's characters, the protagonist in *The Love of Don Perlimpton.* Lorca's ability to transmute to the audience the essence of his native city Granada is paralleled in Ringwood's evocation of the prairie.

A conversation between Planter and Widger reveals the conditions of life during the drought and depression in Alberta's prairie:

PLANTER: I thik I'll stay here and be your hired man, Widger. I'll slop the hogs, make hay, fish, shoot partridge up and down the river and get drunk on Saturday on Widger's wages. A tidy life and restful.

WIDGER: Hired man to Widger? But of course you're joking. I'm not rich, you know. A poor farmer wrestling with poor land to get the meanest living! Cutworms and taxes, drought and early frost, potato blight. . . . Why Sir, you've no idea how nature contrives to keep a man's nose hugged to the grindstone. I work from dawn to dusk and at night I dream of dying in the poor house. And when I get up what do I find? A hawk has killed my chickens, the old sow's devoured all her litter, bugs ravished the potatoes, and the bull's been struck by lightning. That's how it goes with Widger. I couldn't afford you, Sir. (*WW*, Scene 1.6)

This folk comedy is full of misadventures, maddening mixtures of characters, and fast-paced action. Rich in the discovery of dinosaurs' skeletons, *triceritops*' bones, land exploitation, trial by fire—it successfully uses all the devices that farce, comedy, and satire, enhanced by melodrama, can employ to produce an entertaining play. Ringwood speaks of the setting:

I set it in the bad land, so that it gave an antique tie with things that had happened thousands of years ago. . . . It isn't really a realistic play but I was trying to do a comedy with a great deal of color and richness, moving from farce to satire to serious business with a little pathos and then moving back to comedy. All I was really trying to say was that people must grow and that Widger, when he took up the bone and hit the constable and saved his daughter while risking himself, had made his step out of his tightness to something positive. And so finally there is a possibility that he will be a member of the community.[21]

Ringwood has an instinctive feeling for the elements of good theater, for line, imagery, color, and texture. She is able to communicate well with people and therefore she can establish interrelationships between characters and between the play and the audience. When Widger's neighbors suspect him unjustly of murdering Planter they conclude that after twenty years of living near him, they do in fact know nothing of Widger. There ensues a telling dialogue between Widger and his friend, Dowser Ringgo, who acts as Greek chorus, interpreter, and wise man before the professor and the people:

WIDGER: What do we know of anyone—of anyone at all? What do you know of each other?
DOWSER: (*Diverting the mob for a moment*) There's your question, Professor. There, he's got you.
WIDGER: (*On top of the stile facing the mob*) I'm a poor man.
DOWSER: You know his bank account.
WIDGER: Over sixty.
DOWSER: You know his age.
WIDGER: A farmer.
DOWSER: Occupation.
WIDGER: With a daughter.
DOWSER: Family status.
WIDGER: I pa my taxes.
DOWSER: Property owner.
WIDGER: Vote Liberal.
DOWSER: Politics.
WIDGER: I was baptized Episcopalian.
DOWSER: Religion. And what more?
WIDGER: Why, why, that's all. That's all.
DOWSER: All—all—there you have it, Professor. Here's a poor man, over sixty, a farmer with a daughter, pays taxes, votes a respectable party and was baptized. That's all you know.
WIDGER: Oh, no. (*It is a cry*). There's more. There's much, much more!
DOWSER: (*Fast*) Yes, there's the fear and the malice and the envy. The pricking conscience and the greed, and the skeleton in the respectable closet. The little hurts to pride, the desire to know things, and the desire to own. The urge to get on and the fear of death. (*Widger looks at Dowser*) And there's the will—the thin bright spire of a man's will thrust forth from the encircling cave. (*Gently*) There's love and a need of loving.
WIDGER: (*Whispering*) Yes, Dowser.
DOWSER: Oh, there's more to a man than flesh and bones and his name on the census. What do we know of anyone at all? There's your question. (*WW*, Scene 3.25,26)

In the following scene when Widger has been taken prisoner by Docket, the constable, he sums up his own life:

I wasn't always this way. There was a time when Widger had a grasp on manhood, met the day ready to take what came. The world was his oyster, Docket, Widger's oyster. But then there were lean years and my youth was gone. And after that the times moved fast, so fast that run as I might, I found myself behind them. And the world changed. The world was a giant, Docket, waiting to crush a man. The thing to do was hide, be small and careful. The thing to do was shrink. And yet for all my care, at his own time, the Giant closes his fist on Widger. Since it's so, I'd wish myself a bigger fistful. (*WW*, Scene 4.10)

The second title given to the play, *The Face in the Mirror*, is derived from Scene 4 when the real criminal, Jake (alias Foote) interrogates Widger on the hiding place of the gold they both covet, and points out that they are brothers in their spirit of greed and cruelty:

FOOTE: Don't tell me you've not seen cruelty or greed before.
WIDGER: I've seen them on other faces, yes, but . . .
FOOTE: Is that all?
WIDGER: (*Deeply ashamed*) No. I've seen them in the mirror—looking at me, out of my own eyes.
FOOTE: We're brothers, Widger. Where's the gold? Is it in the well, Widger? (*WW*, Scene 4.17)

Widger's Way or *The Face in the Mirror* is a commentary on human weaknesses. The irony is there—witty but never harsh. In addition to the main plot of Widger, his greed for gold and need for recognition, there is the subplot of a romance between his daughter Roselle and the geology student Peter. Ringwood takes this opportunity to poke fun at the university professor, Dr. Bond, who plans to use his student's discovery to publish an article. The exploiting of students by professors, of professors by communities, is well handled. Over and above all this is Ringwood's recreation of an Albertan farm community, its people, spirit, and the land which has intrinsically developed the basic characteristics of its people.

How does Ringwood's adaptation of Plautus's comedy merely reflect Plautus, and how does it bear Plautus's stamp? *The Pot of Gold* is built around the character of a miserly old man, Euclio, who has found (by virtue of the household god) a pot of treasure buried within his house. Terrified that he may be robbed, he hides it in several different places. His fear and strange conduct is noticed by his servant and daughter. Finally he is tricked out of the pot but recovers it unexpectedly, and joyfully bestows his daughter in marriage on young Lyconides (rather than Lyconides's old uncle—an arrangement the two old men had previously made). Ringwood has used the bare skeleton of the plot but *Widger's Way* bears Plautus's unmistakeable stamp in its countless puns and quips, its jovial exuberance, its characters bordering on caricatures, its delightful extravagances, and amusing situations. Ringwood has, as we have seen, Plautus's ability to create outstanding comic characters. But what is particularly notable is this: just as Plautus adapted his comedies from the Greek dramatists but then ingeniously created typically Roman characters, dialogue, and spirit; so Ringwood uses her creative imagination to present her audiences with a comedy that is in every way Canadian—characters, dialogue, humor, situations. Euclio and Widger are two distinct personalities, each resembling the individual characteristics of his own country. It is interesting to speculate on audience reactions to both. One can be fairly certain that boisterous laughter mingled with amused recognition of human frailties in Roman audiences of some two thousand years ago is the reaction today both in the modern productions of Plautus and in those comedies that bear some resemblance to his work, of which *Widger's Way* is perhaps the best Canadian reflection.

Widger's Way has had several successful productions in the past twenty-five years. It was first produced at the University of Alberta in 1952 with Robert Orchard directing it and playing the role of Widger. Orchard also constructed the first sets out of aluminum—a clever but disastrous invention for the hands of the stage crew, as it turned out. It toured the province in 1952 and in 1955, was produced again in Williams Lake in 1959 by the Williams Lake Players Club under Ringwood's direction. In 1976 it was successfully revived at the Kawartha Summer Theatre Festival of Comedy in Lindsay, Ontario.

Ringwood's increasing interest in music which manifested itself in *The Rainmaker* and *Stampede,* her use of Alberta folklore in the same two plays, in *The Jack and the Joker, A Fine Colored Easter Egg,* and *Widger's Way,* resulted in a new direction for her. In 1952 she collaborated with a composer on a musical "The Wall" and continued on to write the books for three more musicals "Look Behind You, Neighbor," "The Road Runs North," and *Mirage.* These will be examined in the following chapter.

CHAPTER 4

The Ringwood Musicals

GIVEN Gwen Ringwood's talent for poetic rhythm, her fascination with Canadian roots, and her involvement in community life, it was natural that she should become involved in writing the books for four Canadian musicals. In 1952, with composer Bruce Haak, she collaborated on a political play with musical background for radio, "The Wall"; in 1961 she was commissioned by the town of Edson, Alberta, to create a musical based on the early days of Edson, and with composer Chet Lambertson she wrote "Look Behind You, Neighbor"; in 1968 she and composer Art Rosoman wrote the musical "The Road Runs North," based on Billy Barker and the Gold Rush days in northern British Columbia as their contribution to the British Columbia centennial celebrations; and in 1979 Ringwood was asked by the Association of Canadian Theatre History, meeting with the Learned Societies at the University of Saskatchewan, to write a play. She wrote the musical *Mirage* celebrating the development of the prairie community at Saskatoon. Three of these musical have one element in common—the founding of Canadian communities.

I "*The Wall*"

Ringwood's first musical, "The Wall," was an experiment in the use of musical accompaniment for a radio play. It used appropriate music to denote characters, to emphasize the rising action, and to highlight the climax of the play. There were no songs as in the traditional musical. Instead, music was used in the same way in which she had previously used poetry to enhance the dialogue and to suggest character traits in the dramatis personae. Elsie Park Gowan encouraged Gwen Ringwood in 1952 to write this musical for the local Edmonton radio station which had requested four plays on the international theme of cooperation and brotherly love. Deciding to try a new form, Ringwood experimented with a play having musical background and asked Bruce Haak, a young pianist and composer, to write the score. The result was "The Wall," a modest effort to convey through the use of dialogue and musical background a straightforward message on racism.

Because the dialogue was augmented by music, Ringwood created very simple lines of conversation between characters. The exchange of ideas and opinions seems to the reader to be expressed in deceptively plain language, but one must remember that the entire play is based on this musical background which changes tone and quality in accordance with each character. The radio audience was thus able to distinguish characters not only by voice but by the nuances of a musical score that paralleled and emphasized each voice. Ringwood worked very closely with the composer in order to achieve these results. What she was able to accomplish through poetry in her other plays, she now successfully effected through music with the assistance of Bruce Haak.

There is the quality of parable in "The Wall" in this short moral narrative. Indeed, the incident enacted would have little point without the moral. The wall of prejudice toward the black race is built by a white woman, and only the children can effect its destruction. They do so through harmony by means of the musical vibrations of their whistling. As the music increases in power, the wall comes crashing down. Music not only resulted in immediate aural identification of characters but also augmented the emotional impact of the parable.

The narrator, John Starborne, relates the parable. As omniscient storyteller, he assumes the qualities of a wise man, like Christ the supreme teller of parables. Starborne's name implies that he is above and beyond the earthbound characters whose story he recounts. There is kindliness but also detachment in his tone like the narrator in Thornton Wilder's *Our Town*. Starborne the boat builder, introduces in flashbacks the events of seven days creation of friendship between a black and a white boy. Starborne says: "When Mrs. Carmelodeon bought the place there wasn't any wall on the east side. There wasn't a wall anywhere, that you could see. And so on the morning of the first day, the very first day at Lake Carla, Freddy got to know Ernie."[1] There follows normal conversations between the children until, on the third day, Mrs. Carmelodeon discovers their growing friendship. Immediately she has the wall built, but this barrier presents no real problems as it fails to separate them. The two boys speak to John Starborne of a solution to their problem:

FREDDY:	Ernie and I are going to have a club, Mr. Starborne, a Secret Society. Do you want to be an honorary member?
STARBORNE:	Why, thanks, Freddy. I'd be honored.
ERNIE:	I reckon your mother's going to raise a rumpus if you belong to a club with me, Freddy.
FREDDY:	I'll talk her into it. After all, I'm her only child. (*W*, 10)

"The Wall" suggests some qualities inherent in the masque: the somewhat stiff masquelike construction, the allegorical significance, the musical accompaniment, the character of villain in Mrs. Carmelodeon (as used in the antimasque), the unity of the whole with poet or musician as leader in its preparation. The composition of "The Wall" was significant because it gave Ringwood the opportunity to experiment with music before she undertook the writing of her three major musicals, "Look Behind You, Neighbor," "The Road Runs North," and *Mirage*.

II "*Look Behind You, Neighbor*"

In 1961 Ringwood was approached for a musical by the community of Edson, Alberta, who were celebrating the fiftieth anniversary of the founding of their town. She wrote, "Look Behind You, Neighbor," in three acts, with Dr. Chet Lambertson, a professor at the University of Victoria, composing the music. Although it developed into a regional folk musical on Edson, it achieved a universal quality that made it entirely applicable to small towns anywhere. Ringwood brought 3,000 people in Edson together in a united effort to recreate their own local history, and the pride they experienced in so doing was to strengthen their belief in themselves as a community. All the resources of Edson were employed in this group project: dancing, costuming, and the formation of an Edson band. More than seventy-five local inhabitants acted in the musical. It was reported in the local newspaper, the *Edson Leader*, on 9 November 1961, that CFRN-TV had televised the major scenes for later presentation. At last Ringwood was achieving the kind of community theater for which her past experiences had been preparing her. Indeed, all her previous mentors had contributed to this work. The influences of Elizabeth Sterling Haynes, "Proff" Koch, Robert Gard, the small communities in which she had lived and worked—all these combined to produce the creator par excellence of community theater.

The use of the narrator, already a staple of Ringwood dramatic style as we have seen in previous plays, particularly *The Rainmaker* and "The Wall," is here used again in the manner of Thornton Wilder's *Our Town.* John Stewart, like Wilder's stage manager, introduces the story of Edson. He talks directly to the audience in a friendly, down-home manner, but he is not as deeply involved in the play as is Wilder's narrator. Stewart opens the musical with these words:

> Good evening, neighbors. You all know me here. Stewart's the name. John Stewart. I've lived here all my life. Tonight I'm asking you to look back to the beginnings of our town. I'm asking you to look back more than half a century. (*Chorus sings "Look Behind You, Neighbor"*). Some of you here remember when our town was young but most of us don't know about its beginnings, its history. Towns always seem to me like people—each town has a personality that sets it apart from the rest. Sometimes that personality is hard to describe. Take this town—how are we going to come down on the things that give Edson its personality?[2]

There follows a series of flashbacks highlighting the events from 1909 on: the settlers and their early activities and experiences, their coal mining, lumbering, fishing, and gardening; the opening of the Grand Trunk Pacific Railway with its consequent wild land boom and infamous real estate scandal, the closing of the brothels, the great war with the raggedy splendor of Edson men marching off to a strange land half a world away from them. The musical, touching on land development, railroad building, war, and women's rights, captured the spirit of the small town as Thornton Wilder had earlier done with his town.

J. T. McKreath, friend and director of some of Ringwood's plays, tells us about the production in these words: "I was happy to be at the premiere performance. It had a lot of energy and focus but there was no key character to push the story forward. Yet Gwen Ringwood did a fine job. There were many robust songs in it and it moved along with style."[3] McKreath's comment on the lack of a key character is a common complaint by directors of Ringwood's musicals and large-cast plays, but Ringwood is creatively developing a new style of play highlighting a series of events rather than one character to unify and solidify the whole. With this technique she is placing the challenge on the director to interpret and achieve her creative purposes. Given a good production, the results can be electrifying.

Marguerite Ahlf, Edson's local librarian and archivist, who provided Ringwood with much of the local history background for "Look Behind You, Neighbor," says: "The Edson community will always be grateful to Mrs. Ringwood whose . . . inspiration created the book which gave the long-time Edson residents a sense of pride, and the newcomers an awareness of the town's background."[4] Some excerpts from the songs will give an idea of the strength and vitality of the musical. On the scandal of the Grand Trunk Pacific Railway, from the song "Somebody Else is Gonna Get the Pie":

> Oh there's been some hanky panky down at Wolf Creek
> Oh there's been some hocus pocus down the line
> Someone tried to raise a rumpus with the railway
> But the Old Grand Trunk Pacific will not sign.
>
> Oh there's trouble, trouble, trouble,
> With the pretty Wolf Creek bubble
> And somebody's gonna get it in the eye
> For the G.T.P. won't sign its name to nothin'
> And it looks like somebody else will get the pie. (*N*, 20)

On Johnny Boniface, a Chinese gentleman and the first to build a hotel in Edson, from "Johnny's Song":

> My name is Johnny Boniface
> I've built a building in this place
> To house and feed the human race
> Whatever creed or color.
> I feel a little lonely now
> With no one to return my bow
> And no one here to eat my chow
> It couldn't be much duller.
> But tomorrow I will see
> A thousand men converge on me
> To keep me busy as can be
> I'll make a little money. (*N*, 23)

The dialogue is equally lively. In a conversation at the railway station between the young girl Melissa who has just arrived in Edson (in 1910), and Lance Delaney who has been working there, the audience recognizes the beginning of a courtship:

DELANEY: That certainly must be an interesting letter. I noticed you reading it on the train. You know what I figure? I figure you're one of these Mail Order Brides and the fellow who wrote you that letter hasn't shown up. I guess he lost his nerve.
MELISSA: Kindly keep your thoughts to yourself.
DELANEY: I didn't mean any offence. I think any man who doesn't show up after he brings a pretty girl out here to the wilderness is a downright heel.
MELISSA: (*Facing him as she stands up*) I'm not a mail order bride. I'm visiting my cousin only she must have misunderstood the date.
DELANEY: I'd better find you a hotel room. You can't sit here all night.
MELISSA: (*Moving to right*) I'm perfectly capable of looking after myself. (*Sounds of whoops and hollers off stage. Melissa shrinks a little*).
DELANEY: This will be a rough place tonight. Now you and I can go down to this Johnny's place, have a good dinner and—
MELISSA: We'll do nothing of the kind. (*She returns to bench and sits again with her back to him*). Will you please just go away.
DELANEY: I'm not going any place. I'm arrived. (*He leans over back of bench and puts a picture from his wallet in front of her face*). See that. That's me—sitting on top of that freight wagon. (*Admiringly*). You never saw anybody could drive eight horses the way I can. I've been hauling freight on the old tote road all spring. Just went to Edmonton to get me some new wagons. From now on I'll be hauling on the Grand Prairie Trunk. Good looking horses eh? I sure can handle a team. Muskeg, hills, ice, snow, mud, hail, cloudburst—don't matter to me. Just drive them through. Can't stand oxen or mules. Horses.
MELISSA: Your wife is very good looking.
DELANEY: Wife! Hah—that's Rosie; she wishes she was my wife.
MELISSA: Really?
DELANEY: Sure. She's crazy about me. Actually most women are. But I don't believe in settling down. Why wear hobbles if you can travel free! (*N*, 30)

Ringwood's talent for creating witty, lively dialogue is evidenced throughout the musical. Her sense of humor, lighting on the comic foibles of humankind, is engaging entertainment. The audience who saw the original production endorsed its validity and were enthusiastic about its local color. Desmond Bill, a writer for the *Edmonton Journal*, reviewed it in the issue of 3 November 1961. He wrote:

Fifty years of pent-up civic pride exploded on a stage here Thursday night when what was billed as a pageant depicting the town's history mushroomed into what could well be one of the best Canadian musicals in years. . . . Mrs. Ringwood and Dr. Lambertson have taken the elements of Edson's growth . . . and used them as material for some of the cleverest, most singable, tuneful new songs to be heard in a long time. "Look Behind You, Neighbor" . . . is probably the best musical written with a western Canadian locale.[5]

Produced in Edson, November 1961, and directed by Vivian Jardine, it was proclaimed by the town of Edson a total success. The following June it was revived for the duke of Edinburgh's Second Commonwealth Study Conference in Edmonton, at which representatives from every commonwealth country in the world were present. Because the musical exemplified the purpose of the conference, Edson and the musical "Look Behind You, Neighbor" became its theme. The account of the conference, published as *Conference Across the Continent,* opens with the chapter "Edson and the Conference Idea" and the words:

No one from the Conference visited Edson, Alberta. There was no reason to do so. It is just a town of 3000 people . . . the halfway stop between Edmonton . . . and Jasper . . . . Yet Edson, Alberta, became something of a symbol of what the Conference was all about. . . . "Look Behind You, Neighbor" . . . was a tale of the human consequences of industrialization as they had been seen and felt in Edson in the days when coal was mined nearby, when the Grand Trunk Pacific Railway came in and Edson was the end of steel, when it was a supply base for the Peace River district to the north. They told of Edson the speculators' paradise and of a railway town stopped in its tracks by war. It is not an extraordinary story. It could be told almost anywhere in the Commonwealth with a little change of scenery. And that was the point. This modest saga of community change, told in verse and song and vigorous movement, was produced with such elan, conviction and colour that Conference members from thirty-seven different countries and territories . . . recognized the emotions being stirred and the issues being faced. At the final chorus the audience rose in a solid body of applause and cheers. . . .[6]

Ringwood's musical recreated the history of a town. The music and dancing bound the people together, achieving a sense of solidarity, a belief in themselves and their history, a "communal spirit," a sense of a larger home where neighbors recognized their common bond in one human family. It was this quality that impressed the members of the conference and suggested Edson as the symbol of all that they were trying to accomplish. Ringwood's special gift for community theater reached a high point on that opening night performance in Edson. "Look Behind You, Neighbor" is one of Ringwood's finest achievements in community theater.

III · *"The Road Runs North"*

No one asked Ringwood to write what is to date one of her best musicals, "The Road Runs North" (1967). She and Art Rosomon, a musician, were conversing one evening on the possibility of collaborating on a musical. Billy Barker and the Gold Rush days (1861 to 1864) which opened up the whole interior of British Columbia, they agreed, was a natural subject for a centennial year. Together they planned to write and produce "The Road Runs North" in Williams Lake to celebrate British Columbia's centennial in 1967. The title was taken from an earlier work of Ringwood's, a poem written for the *Williams Lake Tribune*'s 1958 centennial issue.

It was a happy collaboration. Ringwood and Rosomon worked as a team on the story of Billy Barker who had a dream encouraging him to leave the ship on which he was a sailor and go up to northern British Columbia in search of gold. He and Judge Begbie were the only historical characters in the large cast of sixty.

The resulting musical was a combination of history, comedy, and romance with enough conflict to give it substance. It is not just the story of Billy Barker but of all those who took the road north. It tells in music and song and dialogue the drama of the Gold Rush days up the canyon and of the young engineers building the Cariboo Highway, an extraordinary feat of engineering in those days because of the sharp curves in the mountains. On Jackass Mountain, for instance, in the canyon mentioned in one of the songs, one mule jumped and went down the side of the mountain.

Ringwood wrote the book and the lyrics while Art Rosomon composed the music; together they tried to cover the wide range of people who came to the Cariboo. They used Flinn, the mule driver, Indian and Chinese, European and American miners, good-time girls, preacher, and judge. There was the widow Manders who opened a bakery, and Rosa who took her girls up to the saloons and brothels. There was Hilt Ryland who represented the fathers of those men who came for gold but stayed to become owners of the big cattle ranches. There was Hanging Judge Begbie and Jim Dorg the gambler.

Ringwood's experience with the Edson musical aided her in

writing "The Road Runs North". This new musical was more mature and had greater sweep and depth. Judge Matthew Begbie, in actual fact, had been dispatched with others to northern British Columbia by Lieutenant Governor Douglas to maintain law and order there almost at the very moment that the Gold Rush began. Hence the lawlessness and violence that occurred in conjunction with the Gold Rush in such places as Virginia City, Nevada, never happened in northern British Columbia. The historical events of those who traveled the road to northern British Columbia are faithfully portrayed in this musical.

Ringwood directed it and created the colorful "freezes" (those fixed and motionless portraits of live characters against the dramatic background of Rocky Mountains and glacier lakes which opened and closed the musical). Tom Kerr suggested some additional freezes. As in Edson, so in Williams Lake, a large segment of the community participated in the production. Sponsored by the Williams Lake Players and Glee Club, the musical was opened to all who chose to try out for parts. It was an excellent way of getting the community together and it succeeded admirably. Clive Stango, editor of the local newspaper, played the role of the gambler villain. He said this of the musical and of Ringwood's effect on the Williams Lake community:

> "The Road Runs North" was a large production reminding one of the musical *Oklahoma*. The set was excellent giving one an impression of different plateaus in a mountainous region. The music and the variation of scenes added immeasurably to the whole. What continued to amaze me was Gwen's ability to get so much out of amateur performers. She would take people with apparently no acting ability and train them successfully. Her impact on Williams Lake, her expertise, and dedication, changed the character of the place. She gave people a new interest in theater. The effect was cumulative and hard to estimate. She threw a large rock in a small pond and the ripples have continued. She established a standard that people tried to emulate.[7]

Clive Stangoe's comments are important in showing Ringwood's gift for bringing a community together in a united effort through theater activities. Produced in Williams Lake in 1967, for the centennial celebration of British Columbia, "The Road Runs North" enjoyed a successful run of ten days. More than one hundred people were directly involved either as actors, stage crew, glee club, choir members, or musicians in the orchestra. When the musical opened, the stage looked like a portrait of nineteenth-century costumed people, a period piece of the old west, and as Billy Barker stepped forward and introduced them, each one came to life. Other freezes, effectively created, broke into life with rollicking songs.

Ringwood brought her characters up the Cariboo Trail to the gold-mining town where they settled. She included a storm and an accident whereby Hilt meets the Indian girl he eventually marries. The audience enjoyed the songs, whose titles suggest their colorful content: "The Mother Lode Song," "The Mule Song," "Somewhere She Waits," "Sufficient Unto the Day," "Take a Chance," "Billy Barker," "Gold in the Canyons," "The Song of Lo Chen," "Song of the Royal Engineers," "Somewhere I'll Find a Place," "Blue Clay," "Easy Come-Easy Go," "I'm a High Class Gal." Among the songs from "The Road Runs North" is "The Mother Lode Song":

Somewhere she waits
By a rock or a stream
She's a flame and a star
She's a witch and a dream
She's brightness and beauty
A queen that you toast
Who turns to a phantom
A glittering ghost.

We look for the Mother Lode.
We look for the Mother Lode.

She'll strip you of kin
Leave you friendless, alone.
She'll drink of your blood
And she'll gnaw at your bone.
She's a bawd and a hag
Yet she's bountiful, kind,
She's a worm in the heart
And a fire in the mind.

We look for the Mother Lode
We look for the Mother Lode.[8]

"The Mule Song" ends each of the six verses with the refrain "His best friend is a mule." One of the verses is as follows:

A horse or a bull or an ox can pull
Wagons across a plain
But a mule's sturdy back is made to pack
Over Cariboo terrain.

The song ends with the punch lines:

The devil waits below Hell's gate
He's laughing at his prey
But through that spot that God forgot
My mules will make their way.

(*RR*, I.1.12)

"Gold in the Canyons" is a ballad, of which the first stanza gives the tempo:

In Cariboo country gold nuggets abound
There's gold in the gravel, there's gold in the ground,
With gold in our pockets and gold in our poke
We'll be rich forever and never go broke.

(*RR*, I.1.19)

The scene when Billy Barker strikes gold is effective. He and his men have been digging for months with no results, and now that their money is gone, the men insist on stopping. They take a vote and it is four to three (Billy's vote carried it) to continue five more feet only. They are already fifty feet down.

BARKER: I'll go down and shovel. Come on—
(*He goes down. The seven partners and Hilt sing*):
Blue clay and the bedrock pitching
Cow's tongue. Black sand in the pan
Down, dig down, it's bedrock pitching.
Down, dig down to the golden sand.

BARKER: (*Shouting . . . from the diggings*) Hey Dexter! Dexter! There's something here. My God, man, I've struck it! Gold. Gold. Gold. . . . Pull up the bucket. It's a strike! I tell you, it's a strike!

DEXTER: He's out of his head. He's gone crazy.

BARKER: (*Coming up from the shaft*) No, no, I'm not crazy. Look, we've hit the old stream bed. We've struck it, boys. That's gold.

DEXTER: He's right.
BARKER: Fifty-two feet and she's lying there—right under my shovel. (*They all show great excitement as they examine the nuggets*).
ANDERSON: We've got it. Gold! We've got it!
DEXTER: It's strike! Strike on the Barker I!
BARKER: (*Wildly excited, showing the others*) Gold! I've found gold! Gold! Gold!
GEORGE: Look at it! Look at that nugget!
GABEL: We'll have a party.
ANDERSON: We'll go on a spree.
WALKER: Richfield, here we come!
BARKER: Who's crazy now? I told you—blue clay and the bedrock pitching. Gold! Gold! Gold!—We're rich!
GABEL: New field. New field in Cariboo.
BARKER: Yeah, new town—there'll be a new town here. Billy Barker's town.
ANDERSON: We'll call it Barkerville—after you, Billy.
BARKER: Barkerville. Yahee! Oh, I'm English Bill—Never worked and never will—Stay away girls—or I'll tousle your curls.
(*The Miners sing "Blue Clay and the Bedrock Pitching"*)
(*RR*, I.6.68-70)

In act 2, scene 1 "The Heyday of Barkerville, The Lucky Strike Saloon, June 15, 1963," everyone is rich. Billy Barker, having staked a lot of miners, has left for Victoria. The Hurdy Gurdy Girls have arrived as entertainers, and on this same day Billy returns with a wife, Elizabeth. But Billy and Elizabeth are wild spenders. Finally, his money gone, Billy opens Barker II mine, then Barker III, but he never strikes it rich again. His wife leaves him, and in ill health he is forced to work as a chef. In the closing dialogue of the play he says: "Barkerville. Hah! I leave something here anyway—my name. Rosa, you said 'it will all be the same in a hundred years.' That's wrong. A man's life must count for something. It's got to. Billy Barker may be gone. Billy Barker's town may be gone, but the future . . . the future will know we were here once, Rosa. The future will know" (*RR*, II.3.113).

This final effect of "The Road Runs North" is typically Canadian. It ends on a note of mitigated sadness. Billy Barker was a hero, but in the Canadian sense; he leaves a name but he dies poor. This is the typical nonheroic cast of Canada's heroes. Yet the overall effect of "The Road" is one of triumph. All those people involved in the Gold Rush were united in a common purpose. The discovery of gold, apparently climaxing the musical, is really subordinated to the founding of a community at Barkerville. Ultimately it is not the discovery of material wealth, not the creation of a Canadian hero, but the miracle of founding a community that is celebrated in "The Road Runs North" and indeed in all Ringwood's musicals and large-cast plays.

IV *Mirage*

In 1979 when Ringwood was commissioned to write a musical for production at the Learned Societies meeting at the University of Saskatchewan, she chose the subject of the development of the prairie community in Saskatoon. She returned to "The Road Runs North" for the character of Hilt Ryland, the miner who went to the Cariboo for gold and remained to settle the land; and to *Widger's Way* for the character of Dowser Ringgo, the water diviner. Both these characters are necessary to her purpose in *Mirage* for both are idealistic men, contributing each in his own unique way, to the development of the prairie community. Dowser Ringgo is not only the water diviner but he is a seer, a philosopher, a man who observes and understands life in all its forms. Ringwood needs Dowser Ringgo for he is the interpreter of the mirage. Hilt Ryland is the prospector turned farmer and it is his progeny who people the prairie land of Saskatchewan. On these two characters depends the success of *Mirage*.

Music and poetry both inform the play; original music by Gary Walsh and Steven Bengston; poetry by Gwen Ringwood recited by Dowser Ringgo and others, and lyrics sung by the group. Of special value is the prologue, rich in metaphor, which begins and ends the play. One stanza is of particular beauty:

> What gods I know
> Rose in plumes of dust at high bright noon,
> Or flattened themselves on the long shadows
> Of morning and of evening on the prairie.
> Phantoms in drifting snow howled with the blizzard,
> Etched mandalas on the window panes
> In the stillness of late dawn when it seemed
> The world would crack apart with cold.[9]

The refrain "They were no easy gods" is the initial line of three of the seven verses of this lyric poem. Singing of pioneer hardships, the poet speaks of "the gods" as mysterious life-giving forces taking shape in buffalo, bird, lynx, crocus, golden rod, dust-cone, crying out "Hunt us down, for without us you are forever homeless."

The lyrics written by Ringwood for the music composed by Gary Walsh include "The Home Waltz," "The Rollicking Polka," and "Jeanne Ryland's Strathspey." Steven Bengston composed both the music and the lyrics for "Let's All Meet in Moose Jaw," "Ain't That Enough," and the theme song "Prairie Song."

Additional songs by Ringwood include "The Ploughman's Song" in scene 3, "The Harvest Song" in the Wheat Fantasy scene 4, and "The Train Song" in scene 5 as John leaves with wheat samples for the Toronto Exhibition in 1913. All of these lyrics have a prairie color and feeling that is indefinable. In "The Ploughman's Song" Ringwood writes:

> Grass is turned under in a long straight furrow
> Grass turned under as the horses plod
> Pleating the earth into black straight furrows
> Plowing the prairie, turning the sod.
>
> (*M*, I.3.14)

And in the Wheat Fantasy scene the eight verse "Harvest Song" describes the grass lands, the stookers, the threshing team, the bundle wagons, the separator, the elevator, and the night train that transports the precious grain to the east. The fifth and sixth verses are particularly colorful:

> Pick up the stooks for the separator's waiting,
> With a mouth as wide as a giant's maw
> Pitch those bundles while the fly wheel's turning
> Keep on pitching though your hands are raw.
>
> (*M*, I.4.16)
>
> Golden kernels flew to the wheat bin
> Wheat wagon races down the long straight trail
> Races to the elevator, races to the box cars,
> Races to the train that's waiting on the rail.
>
> (*M*, I.4.17)

"The Train Song" is merely a "Clickety, clackety, chug, chug" as the cast mime a train in scene 5.

Ringwood's dialogue throughout the musical is realistic and

humorous as she depicts the pioneers in their early struggles with the land. When Jeanne and John Ryland first come to Saskatchewan they hire Dowser Ringgo to witch a well for them:

DOWSER: We'll see what we have here. If you're lucky we'll tap some underground stream or pool not too far down.
JEANNE: That's all you need. That forked stick?
DOWSER: That's all. See how I hold it, loosely in my hands, young lady. No pressure. I wait for the willow stick to find the earth's secret. Without water there's no joy in this new holding. It's not here. Nor here. I look for some pool or running stream, some cool and silent pool below the ground.
JEANNE: John, it's . . . it's twisting in his hand. The willow bends.
DOWSER: Yes, see how the wand bends, twists, just there . . . that means water . . . that divines water. You're in luck, John Ryland. Here you are. (*M*, I.2.12)

In the final scenes of the musical Laura, a daughter of the third generation of Rylands, recites two poems, one to her hippy friend Wilson and one she has composed for her grandmother Jeanne Ryland. To Wilson she reads the poem she has written for her little brother Hilt:

Prayer for the Innocents

God rest you child and animal and bird
And all the innocents who walk the earth
This is my prayer, that you may long endure
And find a time for living and for birth.

(*M*, II.8.68)

Three verses follow petitioning the seasons to help the child escape "the shattered air and blasted earth," to find paths away from "the spreading wasteland," and ending with the lament "Without you Earth is a lost and lonesome place."

The second poem, called "Circle Song," again celebrates the earth:

Through sun, moon, star, rain
The small earth turns and turns again
While summer, autumn, winter, spring
To wind and sky their banners fling.

Day and dark take turn about.
Tide's in. Tide's out.
Water, rock and salt and fire
Merge in motion, form, desire.

And beast and flower, bird and tree
Forsake the star-fish and the sea,
While man with hand and memory blest
Begins his restless, hungry quest.

And birth and death their changes ring
To summer, autumn, winter, spring.
While the small earth turns, and turns again
Through sun, moon, star, rain.

(*M*, II.9.72)

Both of these poems emphasize the smallness of the earth in the immense space of the universe; and the parallel of the prairie girl Laura, caught in the great spaces of the west, marks the kind of perspective given to those who dwell on the prairie.

Mirage is a re-presentation of the spirit of Ringwood's early prairie plays in the form of a musical and multimedia production. It is dependent on a miraculous melding of poetry, song, chanting, sound track, dance, and slides projected on a huge screen depicting the broad sweep of prairie sky and horizon with a mirage of grain elevators in the distance. There are no properties; instead the actors mime as do James Reaney's N.D.W.T. company in *The Donnellys*. There is indeed a close affinity with the Reaney style in this play. The sweep of the action over three generations of Rylands, the choreographed movement of the cast, their rhythmic chanting and miming, the elements of expressionism and fantasy, the development of history in a romanticized epic structure without recourse to the documentary form of drama, invites immediate comparison with the Reaney style. Both playwrights are engaged in recreating a vision of life. For their separate purposes they use all the elements of poetry and rhythm to bring to bear on the audience a sharing in that vision. Many factors are used conjointly to achieve their ends. The miracle occurs only when all these factors meld together in unity.

Of *Mirage* one can observe that almost all the elements unite to achieve a wholeness. The symbol of the mirage with its multifaceted layers of meaning works beautifully in the play: the simple mirage on the horizon, the mirage of life-giving spirits, the mirage as vision for the future, the mirage as memory of the past, the mirage as dream and unreality and necessity. The mirage *is* the play. Its deep-seated meanings tease our minds and set us personally off on quests during the performance. What fails to work is the symbol of the medicine bag—a lovely symbol of an Indian's life, paralleled in the end by Grandma Jeanne's flour sack of mementos and Hilt's realization that a man's life is epitomized in his collection of mementos. The medicine bag is a fine symbol but it fails to grow out of the play as it should. Instead it appears to have been tacked on, an afterthought. In all of Ringwood's many uses of symbolism throughout her plays, this is the only symbol that apparently fails to belong essentially to the play.

Mirage depicts three generations of Rylands, living through the pioneer struggle with the land, the depression, the march to Regina, two World Wars, women's liberation, the western Canadian political scene, the relationship of white man and Indian, the hippie movement of the late sixties, the Vietnam War, and opportunistic American land developers in the west. Ringwood may have tried to encompass too much of history in one play. Yet the overall reaction was favorable, probably because the director, Tom Kerr, and Gwen Ringwood worked together to present a smooth-flowing production that never faltered in its movement to recreate the Saskatchewan prairie. Once again the emphasis is on the land rather than individual characters—the land as it contributes to the development of community. The union of Indian and white man is underlined in this play. In "The Road Runs North" Hilt Ryland had married an Indian girl during the Godl Rush. In *Mirage* we are given the saga of the Ryland family in three generations. Grandmother Jeanne Ryland, of Scottish ancestry, was obsessed by the mysterious significance of the medicine bag which she had found buried in the earth. Young Jeanne White Calf, an Indian from the north, had obviously inherited her name Jeanne from an early Ryland woman. The name White Calf was taken from Ringwood's Blackfoot Indian acquaintance, Chief Two Gun White Calf. Throughout *Mirage* the Ryland women of each generation are assisted by friendly members of the White Calf family. This continued association of Rylands and Indians is mysterious and leads one to conjecture on the possibilities of an eventual assimilation of both races.

Ringwood's four musicals reveal her gifted talent for combining music and poetry, dance and film, miming and choreography into a unified whole. Her ability to work with large casts is another strong point in her use of theater. Her originality is discerned in her freedom to produce large-cast plays and musicals without dependence on any one leading character to give solidity and direction to her plays. Like Chekhov, she can offer a variety of characters, all equally prominent, and a many-faceted chain of events through which her play moves. Essentially it is the land and the community growing out of the land that is her initial and final focus.

CHAPTER 5

The Plays of Social Protest

THE focus of Ringwood's present work is social injustice. Although always singularly conscious of world ills, and in particular of Canada's problems, Ringwood is more articulate today in defining them in her drama and in censuring a society when it fails to alleviate suffering. Protest is most effectively used by the artist who can write with detached objectivity. In the theater it is the playwright who does not have "an ax to grind," one who is not consciously proselytizing, nor committed to an ideology, who is free to recreate the human situation through art. Thus a people who have read about a problem in the newspapers, heard it on radio, and observed it first hand on television news programs, can then see it on stage, transformed by art. Art takes that living vital reality and commits that reality to memory; art assists in the total absorption of that reality into the very being of the beholder. It is this progression from life through art into the subconscious mind of an audience that constitutes the most subtle and effective means of protest.

Ringwood's immediate concerns today are with the plight of the Indian in Canada, with the rootlessness and confusions of youth, and with the sufferings of the elderly. All are victims of a society and a way of life that seem to be beyond control. Ringwood looks at these problems clearly. She creates realistic characters caught in the mesh of societal indifference, government agency's powerlessness, family self-centeredness. She then allows these characters the freedom to react realistically to their sufferings. The Indian as victim in her plays *Lament for Harmonica* (1959) and *The Stranger* (1971) becomes the Indian as seer who joins forces with another victim, the retired white woman, in "The Lodge" (1975). The problems of youth and society in the sixties are strikingly manifested in "The Deep has Many Voices" (1968) and in "A Remembrance of Miracles" (1975).

The techniques used by Ringwood vary with the essential needs of each play. All five plays are poetic and romantic in quality but each is written in a different dramatic form. *Lament for Harmonica* is a serious confrontation play; *The Stranger* uses the form of Greek tragedy; *The Deep Has Many Voices* is a multimedia production using surrealism and expressionism; "A Remembrance of Miracles" is a modern morality play; "The Lodge" is a Chekovian style of drama. A study of each play should reveal how the form grew naturally out of the subject, both enhancing and shaping its essence.

I *Indian Problem Plays*

The Indian's close assimilation to the land, and the symbolism of his rituals and customs, suggests the poetic quality of the Indian way of life. Ringwood is very sensitive to this, and she therefore chooses poetic drama to express the Indian as victim and seer in her plays *Lament for Harmonica* and *The Stranger*. Ringwood's interest in the Indian people and their problems began in early childhood when she could see the Blood Reserve Indian encampments and tepees on the banks of the St. Mary's River which bordered the Pharis farm. In Browning, Montana, before she was eighteen years old and while working as bookkeeper on the Blackfoot Indian Reservation (as previously mentioned), she made acquaintance with both the Metis and the Blackfoot Indians. One of her closest friends was Cora Welch, half-Indian, half-Irish. Gwen's feeling for the Indians and their problems was thus strengthened considerably. She became friendly with an older Indian Chief, Two-Gun White Calf, whose profile, she was told, had been used as a model for the face on the American nickel. A reading of the Wismer Collection of Blackfoot Indian Studies gave her an understanding of the Blackfoot mythology, which she found, she says, as rich as Greek or Norse mythology. At Chapel Hill she attempted to dramatize these ancient Indian rituals in a play about an educated Blackfoot, but her professors found the play unsuccessful. Returning to Alberta and Saskatchewan, she met members of Indian tribes, but Ringwood worked again with them only when she and her husband moved to Williams Lake. Then she offered her services as a Friday afternoon teacher of drama, language arts, and creative writing, with the Sisters who staffed the Cariboo Indian School at Saint Joseph's Mission outside Williams Lake. There she came in contact with the Carrier, Chilcotin, and Shushwap Indian children whom she grew to love. She helped them edit Indian folklore and produce children's plays. In her musical "The Road Runs North" she invited some twenty Indians from Sugar Cane, Soda Creek, and Alkali to participate, and they were exceedingly proud of their roles. Ringwood was one of the first English Canadian playwrights to introduce the social-conscience play, concentrating on the Indian and his problems, when she wrote *Lament for Harmonica or Maya* in 1959. John Coulter had written *Riel* nine years earlier but its focus was historical and political rather than sociological. Gwen's concern was to depict the response of the Indian to his problems in a white society.

The one-act play, *Lament for Harmonica* portrays the life of a Shushwap Indian girl. Ringwood probes the inner depths of the Indian's conscience in an effort to view her on her native ground and folkways, and to articulate her confusion in a white man's world. Maya in *Lament for Harmonica* and Jana in *The Stranger* are similar in spirit to Lorca's character *Yerma* in the play of that name. Yerma is a symbol of the peasant, living out her personal conflict in violence, as do Maya and Jana. The forces to which all three characters submit themselves are forces struggling within their souls. Life and death are at stake. All three women possess their people's generic character as they are led by fate to death. They are, in fact, destroyed by destiny. Like Lorca, Ringwood is deeply concerned for her people. She says of her abiding concern for the Indian:

> I'd always been aware of Indians as people, as an exotic part of our population because they have a rich tradition of ritual, myth, image, particularly visual images. Always lingering on the edge of my consciousness was a concern for Indians . . . to see them no longer as ragged outsiders on the edge of our town, ignored in our society. Certainly they're not being ignored now but it's past time for us to accept the fact that they have a great deal to teach us, that without the Indians we would never have been able to map the west.[1]

In *Lament for Harmonica* Ringwood dramatizes the effects of an Indian girl's involvement in a white society, her arraignment of that society, and her final tragedy when she destroys her Indian lover and intrinsically her own identity.

There are many images in this play germinal to the Indian people. Josephina, Maya's grandmother, mentions Indian signs of death—

the whiskey-jack which flew around the fire three times on the morning that Maya's son died, the black lizard which crossed her path and went under the old church. References are made to the Indian war songs, potlatch songs, dog dance, chicken dance, and wolf mask. Maya speaks of Indians singing. She says, "How deep the frost lies on the golden heart while Time, the ape, sits grinning at the wheel."[2] She refers to herself, "I'm an Indian, stretched on a plain as barren as a burnt-out star" (*L*, 139). Her grandmother, who hopes to take Maya away to Alkali, exclaims, "We'll go into the woods and mountains, fish for salmon, hunt berries and trail the young deer, like in the old days. That will heal you" (*L*, 139).

Lament for Harmonica won first prize in 1959 in the Ottawa Little Theatre Competition. It was produced on CBC-TV "Shoestring Theatre" in Montreal in 1960, published by the Ottawa Little Theatre Series and in *Ten Canadian Short Plays*, and produced on CBC radio in 1979.

Ringwood's second Indian play, *The Stranger*, was written for the opening of the new Gwen Pharis Ringwood Outdoor Theatre at Boitanio Park, Williams Lake, in 1971. She had long thought that the *Medea* story with the following events could have been the story of an Indian woman: the betrayal of Jason, the terrible anger which the betrayal engendered in Medea, the desire for vengence that causes Medea to kill her two children and destroy Jason's lover. Ringwood took this story as a basis for *The Stranger*, but she uses only the name Jason, from the Greek play, and his character is not fully developed.

Ringwood places the play in the Chilcotin and Shushwap country. Jana, the Chilcotin Indian girl, journeys to the strange Shushwap land to join her lover, the white man Jason. She has left her father and her people. With Jana is her infant son fathered by Jason, and she is accompanied by her old aunt and an elderly man. They travel in a wagon while Jana rides a fine palomino stallion beside them through the country, across the Fraser River and into Shushwap ranch land. Upon arrival Jana discovers that Jason plans to marry his white woman employer, Barbara, the owner of the ranch. Jason tells Jana that their love affair is over but he would like to have their son; he wishes to educate him as a white man and give him those opportunities he would never have if he grew up as an Indian. Out of this situation Jana plans her revenge. Jason's abandonment of Jana and his yielding to Barbara is symbolized in Barbara's gelding of Jana's stallion. Ringwood also used the traditional Greek chorus with a group of Indian women who temporarily camp on the ranch while their men work in the hay fields. This chorus not only presents dire forebodings but it also does what all Greek choruses do—it heals. There are a number of Indian rituals used in the play: the drums; the playing of *La Hel,* a gambling game often used at funerals; and the old ritual of killing the salmon. Ringwood compares the dialogue used in *Lament for Harmonica or Maya* with the language used in *The Stranger.* She says:

> *The Stranger* is not a realistic play but a sort of poetic realism, I suppose. And maybe I was much closer all the way through to Indian speech and rhythms than I was in *Maya* particularly in the main characters. . . . Once more I did not want to write a documentary about the white people's treatment of Indians but rather a tragedy of a truly fine and spirited woman who happened to be Indian, who had suffered betrayal and had failed to make a bridge between the two worlds.[3]

A reading of the dialogue from the confrontation scenes in both plays will give the reader an opportunity for comparison. In *Maya* or *Lament for Harmonica,* Allan, the white man, who is now married to a white woman, is drawn irresistably back to Maya whom he loves:

> ALLAN: I thought of you all the time after I left. I wanted to come back, meant to come back, and then—
> MAYA: Then you got married.
> ALLAN: You knew about that?
> MAYA: I read it in the papers. I can read, you know. My grandmother doesn't read but I read well. That's progress.
> ALLAN: I've never forgot those days in the mountains. Have you?
> MAYA: No. Each morning was a promise. Each night when I put my arms around you I felt we were one flesh, one hope. (*L,* 143)

Allan tries to prevail upon Maya to go away with him for a few days. She refuses. Her Indian lover returns and in the ensuing conflict between the two men, Maya preserves Allan's life by killing Gilbert. As the full realization of what she has done dawns upon her, she sends Allan away and holds her Indian lover in her arms: "He's dead, Grandmother. he won't ride anymore; he won't jump on the black bronc, tighten his knees against the twisting flanks or take first money in the chutes on Sunday. He's dead and I killed him. I killed you, (*whisper*) Gilbert. I, Maya (*pause*) I wanted something. I don't know. I thought to be something different" (*L*, 146).

The confrontation scene between Jana and Jason in *The Stranger* is quite different. It occurs immediately after Jason discovers that Jana has killed his intended bride, Barbara. Jana appears on a rock above the clearing holding their child in an Indian basket:

JANA: Yes. She's dead, Jason. She died from the gift I sent her. Your white whore dies from the twisting pain I sent her. And you suffer now!

JASON: (*Low*) You . . . killed her? Murdered her . . . Jana, no!

JANA: Yes, I killed her—like a rat—
You think you suffer now, Jason. Oh, no,—
I will show you how to suffer.
You will know pain and where you walk or run or cry out in bad dreams, your pain runs with you.
So, you would use me and throw me down.
No, Jason, no!
A flower lies bruised under your feet,
Or a wild tree, ripped from its roots,
Will die and make no sound,
But flesh and blood cry out!

I will show you how to suffer, Jason.
Here is your son, sleeping. Sleeping.
See your son.

(*A knife flashes in her hand above the basket and comes down swiftly.*)

He sleeps forever Jason. I have killed our son.
Now you suffer.

Live, Jason. Live for a hundred years and remember Jana.
Then I am paid back. Then I am satisfied.

JASON: (*Cries out*) . . . (*Low to a terrible loud cry*) Oh . . .

JANA: And for the rest.
I came to this place with the old man and the old woman.
Gilbert will take them home.
But this man, Jason Carr, made me and my son homeless.
He would pay me off like a whore on the street.
His word was a hooded snake.
There is no honor in him.
He thought to throw me down.
Suffer, Jason! Suffer!
Then I am paid back.[4]

An examination of the dialogue in *Maya* and *The Stranger* reveals a marked difference. Maya, except in her very last speech, talks realistically in prose. There is satire and a few figures of speech. But Maya's character is revealed through the educated, straightforward, sharp, concise language of the intelligent Indian girl who has been destroyed by white society, its customs and mores. We see her, painfully clear to us, as a member of that ragged group of Indians on the fringes of the white man's society. The dialogue written by Ringwood is necessary to this type of realism. It works. Through it is created the ordinary Indian girl in contemporary Canadian life whom we will not easily forget.

Jana is a totally different character from Maya. Because Ringwood used the conventions of Greek tragedy and poetic dialogue in *The Stranger*, Jana is raised to the regal position of Indian princess. She is royalty and she speaks like royalty. Although Ringwood does not sufficiently develop the overpowering conflict between Jana's love and her spirit of revenge, she does develop a royal personage through whom we see the background of the Indian race, its nobility, its courage, its principles, rituals, and customs. Contrasted with this is the reprehensible vision of the despised Indian in today's society. "A man of sorrows and acquainted with infirmity," the biblical image of Christ informs the vision. In *The Stranger* Ringwood has created a tragedy, for she uses a woman of stature, an Indian whose language indicates royalty; in *Lament For Harmonica or Maya* she has presented a serious social conflict, a picture of the ordinary exploited Indian in a country controlled by white men. Yet *Maya* also has its own inherent poetry because of the poetry of the Indian way of life. The austerity of the low-keyed prose is poetic in the images it creates rather than in its rythmn. Although both women kill members of their own race in defiance of the white man, there are deeper and more classical reverberations in *The Stranger* than in *Maya*. Nevertheless, both one-act plays are significant contributions to the Indian drama being written in Canada. Bruce Thompson, reviewing it for the *Williams Lake Tribune*, praised it in these words:

> *The Stranger* was like a classical Greek tragedy, transplanted into the Cariboo. The play started with Alphonse's drum involving the chorus in a ritualistic chant of the four seasons with vivid imagery of a wild water's rushing over "the roots of the willow" and "sage bloom and blaze of the

poplar" establishing a poetic, dance-like quality to the play. . . . The performance provided the audience with an immensely rich evening's entertainment.[5]

The use of *Medea* gave Ringwood a strong story line and the choruses provided her with the opportunity to dwell on the seasons, Indian life, and Indian fatalism. The drumming, the sense of strength, the Indian voice, contributed to what Aristotle called a heightened sense of language, in order to reach the essence of her message. Thus she had more freedom through the use of poetic language in *The Stranger* than she had in her prose dialogue in *Lament for Harmonica or Maya*. She had more scope with time because the classical tone in which *The Stranger* was written raised it above the here and now to a universal experience. The plays *Lament for Harmonica* and *The Stranger* constitute the first two of a trilogy of Indian tragedies. The third, still in the exploratory stage, is called tentatively "The Furies."

II *Youth and Old Age*

Related to the Indian plays in their artistic exposition of contemporary problems are the plays Ringwood has recently written on the confusions and mistakes of youth in the sixties—*The Deep Has Many Voices* (1971) and "A Remembrance of Miracles" (1975)—and on the loneliness and confusion of retired people in "The Lodge" (1977).

Again, these plays have certain affinities with Lorca's dramas. The concept of human fatality emphasized in Lorca's work is subtly expressed in these serious Ringwood plays. In climactic situations and moments of dramatic intensity, Lorca and Ringwood both resort to verse. This is seen particularly in Ringwood's *The Deep Has Many Voices*. Lorca's *Blood Wedding* incorporates live persons into his own poetic mythology; Ringwood's "A Remembrance of Miracles" fuses actual events with poetic and dramatic elements to emphasize the realities of life.

The Deep Has Many Voices is a multimedia poetic drama using surrealism and expressionism. It includes a large cast of more than twenty characters. This play was also written for the opening of the Gwen Pharis Ringwood Theatre. The theme is one she had used before in *A Fine Colored Easter Egg* and will be using again in "The Lodge": that we are put on this earth to change the world, to make it better. In *The Deep Has Many Voices* she deals with several levels of consciousness, using the concept of people trying to reach

each other and being unable to do so. This subject was aided immeasurably by the form of a multimedia production.

The focus is on Melissa and her interaction with other young people in the revolutionary mood of the sixties. Melissa realizes that high-school education has failed her on many levels. Ringwood then takes Melissa on a journey—a small pilgrim's progress. She passes through a village where she meets and questions the villagers. She moves from a rock music group, to a drug scene, to traditional religious services of Catholics and Protestants, to Eastern mysticism, and on to contemporary free-lance evangelism. A scene of masked dancers contributes to her bewilderment; she is utterly confused by the bombardment of differing values. The play ends with the end of Melissa's pilgrimage, her union with Willy Thannis, son of a Greek carpenter, and their quest for a better, more compassionate, way of life. They set out to change the world.

The opening scene reveals the elderly women, Sarah and Maria, uttering lines of poetry describing spring and using colors, savoring color as one would savor food. Judith enters with branches of blossoms. One becomes aware of their strong biblical names which give another spiritual dimension to the play. The dialogue contains a semi-mystical tone which continues throughout. Judith speaks:

JUDITH: No sun this morning. Good morning, Maria, Sarah. I found these at the edge of the forest. Perhaps they'll entice the sun.

SARAH: You didn't go into the deep woods, Judith?

JUDITH: No. No. I wanted to . . . I heard the sound . . . I thought I heard—

MARIA: You were wise to stay at the edge of the forest. The forest swallows people.

JUDITH: Sometimes it pulls you. . . .

SARAH: I heard that if you go deep into the woods, you find a mirror. You look down and down into a deep well that is a mirror and you see yourself and all the barnacles fall from you, and you see yourself the way you could be. (*Pause*) (*Her reflective mood is displaced by impatience.*) Who'd want that?

MARIA: Too late, Too late.[6]

Elderly Jonathan utters strong words in the introductory scenes on the shortness of life. He says to Melissa:

JONATHAN: (*Lost in memory*) Spring and the sweet pine. Oh long-drowned ecstasy and the sun-drowned flesh spilling its seed, star-bursting comet curving to ocean. It's hard to remember spring, Melissa.

MELISSA: Was it a good life, Jonathan?

JONATHAN: Hard to remember spring. (*A sound of muffled drums and the boom of guns.*) Survive . . . that's it . . . survive! Kill or be killed. We learn that early. Kill or be killed. So you killed that other to survive. Cain and Abel. That's how it was, is, has to be . . . kill or be killed. (*D*, 7)

Other characters also contribute to the vision of life and death. Steve, a youthful westerner, describes a young moose trapped in the headlights of his car. The symbolism of youth trapped in a world we have made, and the enigmatic feeling of timelessness sweeps over the audience. Miriam, a middle-aged beautiful woman, dances. It is clear that she is in despair. She questions time and place and life. She brings mankind together as brothers in her apocalyptic vision that is in spirit reminiscent of Thomas Wolfe's *Look Homeward, Angel.*

MIRIAM: Oh willow, wait. O willow, weep for me.

MELISSA: What does she look for, Judith?

JUDITH: She stands at the window, hunting the destination, stands idly pin-pricking at the turning globe. Journeys not taken, journeys yet to take.

MIRIAM: Inide and outside. Oh my child, my husband, oh my friends, see how I run to where you stood, run with my arms out, coming, coming, this time not too late. And all you dead, all you beloved dead, listen . . . I remember how you smiled and spoke and that your words somewhere still ripple in the quivering air. (*D*, 19)

Miriam recalls the events of her own life and that of the world about her, the holocaust of the Jewish people, the Kennedys, Gandhi, the events of a planet's life—more than her mind can bear. This sense of timelessness brings all these events together as though happening in the here and now:

When I was nine I dreamed of the Apocalypse with fire-rimmed saucers floating down to claim the blest and save them from the vultures. I was chosen for the resurrection and yet I woke up crying. I think now I would choose to stay on the riven planet, choose to view the Apocalypse from here rather than catapult to glory. Yes, better to die on this small beloved earth than take part in some unearthly glory. One could perhaps shelter a flower, shelter a single seed of some small flower, salvage something. I'd like that.

(*To Melissa*) So you see, dear child, all those half truths, the good intentions, domestic virtues, all those singalongs were not enough . . . statistically summed up they amount to nothing. There must be some other road if I can find it.

(*Turning away from them all*) Oh my world, see how I run back now, run with my arms out, coming, coming, this time not too late. (*D*, 20)

Ringwood seems to be suggesting that man must be free to see and hear and feel and help those around him. The semi-mystical poetic dialogue places this drama outside the realm of realism, in a surrealistic and expressionistic mode. Throughout the play Melissa hears trumpets in the forest, the deep calling to her to abandon all and enter the mystery of life. At the end of the play she and Willy go forth into the deep as the old man Jonathan calls after them, "The deep has many voices, so they say" (*D*, 29).

The production was theatrically exciting partly because it involved projected slide images of Cretan and Greek art and of great religious paintings on a background screen, chanting, and a musical accompaniment. The dynamic beat of the rock music, the soft intonation of the rosary by Catholics, the shouting of the evangelist, the rhythmic chant of the Hare Krishnas, the trumpets, Beethoven's music—all resound as the young couple leave on their quest. An excerpt from Bruce Thompson's review of the play in the *Williams Lake Tribune* describes the effect it had on the audience: *The Deep Has Many Voices* bombarded the audience with a wide spectrum of sensory experiences extending from a dance scene, complete with rock music and a light show, to a mimed fight between Cain and Abel, with the players' shadows providing a grotesque backdrop."[7] Tom Kerr commented on its orchestration of language and images, its kaleidoscope of different types of situations and people, its abstract images, analogies, and symbols. He says:

It is a very strong theatrical piece. There isn't any great star but, like all Gwen's work, it needs a very strong ear to orchestrate because Gwen is a poet. That's what makes her such a good playwright. *The Deep Has Many Voices* is full of beautiful poetry. . . . It reminds me of the work of Dylan Thomas because it has revelations of the town and hints about intriguing things in each character's life. . . . To me Gwen Ringwood is at her strongest when she does plays like *The Deep Has Many Voices*.[8]

Tom Kerr has pointed out the secret of directing successfully a Ringwood play when he says "it needs a strong ear to orchestrate." The audience must be made to hear the music in her rhythmic language because the meaning is conveyed as much by tone and rhythm as it is by words.

A metaphysical and morality play, *The Deep Has Many Voices* expresses the confusion of choices and values that young people of each generation confront when they do not know whether to follow parents or peers. It is a cataclysmic experience in which Ringwood shows her belief in and identification with the humanism and idealism of the young. Touching on major events in world history, the play attempts to surround all of life and look ahead to a future escape from false ideologies, human weaknesses, and violations of God's laws that trapped man in the past. Melissa is called upon to change the world.

The Deep Has Many Voices requires an intelligent and creative production if one is to appreciate and observe the unity in its many and varied facets. To the reader it may appear disjointed and unfocused, lacking in a firm plot. What is apparent to the reader, however, is the rich poetry informing the drama throughout and giving meaning to the play as a whole.

Four years later Gwen created another play on the problems of contemporary society, "A Remembrance of Miracles" (1975). It was conceived as a woman's play for the women's project at the Playwrights Co-op in Toronto and written with a certain amount of passion and excitement. The play's theme is the force of community bigotry producing hysteria and violence. Three events influenced the creation of this play: a newspaper editor friend made favorable comments on the introduction of a family-life project in his town and as a result he suffered at the hands of a bigoted community; a hospital controversy in a local community which could have been settled amicably grew instead into a furious debate out of all proportion to the original issue; a magazine article documenting a battle fought in a southern state community over family-life education resulted in the death of two people.

Ringwood decided to create a young woman, a high school teacher, and embroil her in this type of conflict. The play centers on Merrill Adams who is accused of perverting her students by reading poetry with sexual allusions. A student, Jodie, who had been secretly raped as a child and therefore has problems accepting her own sexuality, stirs up her parents and the townspeople against Miss

Adams. Verna Gliddens, a candidate for political office, uses the conflict unfairly to support her own election campaign, and is responsible for the ensuing violence. From the legitimate use of great literature, the attention of the townspeople is directed to Merrill's former life in a commune, her extramarital relationship, her loss of the baby which is mistakenly taken by her enemies as an abortion, and her publication of a short story based on these events.

Among those who support her are newspaper editor Steve Harding; a student Paul Rae; the narrator Bert Penny and his wife Opal who is head of the school board; and the Reverend Andrew Ainsley, minister and member of the school board. Constructed in seventeen short vignettes, the play opens with Merrill addressing a letter on the situation to her narrow-minded mother, followed by narrator Bert Penny telling the audience how the hysteria developed. There follows a series of flashbacks: the classroom scene with students reading love poetry from major poets; Jodie's hysterical reporting of this to her parents; the meeting of the school board and Verna Glidden's use of the issue to support her political campaign on television. There follows a television call-in show exhibiting the ignorance of local parents; the explosion of a time-bomb in the high school; the physical attack on student Paul Rae for supporting Merrill; another board meeting; a parents' meeting culminating in the public burning of precious library books; and the final courtroom scene. The denouement occurs when young Jodie, at last facing her own problem honestly, realizes Merrill is innocent and refuses to testify against her. Merrill is acquitted but leaves town to avoid further disturbances.

Introducing many scenes are recitations of appropriate poems to musical accompaniment. These poems underline the theme and suggest the traditional Greek chorus. In one scene the newspaper editor Steve Harding interrogates Merrill:

STEVE: Please don't be nervous. I'm not a witch hunter. We're getting a lot of calls at the paper—on both sides. I'm afraid you've raised some dicey issues. I'd like to hear your side of the story.

MERRILL: Come in. Sit down, please.

STEVE: Thanks.

MERRILL: What do you want to know?

STEVE: Facts mostly. Do you often read selections from poetry and prose to your Grade X class?

MERRILL: Yes. I feel it starts the class off with something that—well, expands the consciousness.

STEVE: I understand you've read excerpts from Henry Miller, Ginsberg, Purdy, Birney, D. H. Lawrence, Cummings, Plath. Isn't that pretty strong stuff for Grade X?

MERRILL: The things I've read don't all have to do with sex Mr. Harding. I've read about bears and cats and sharks and Hiroshima and Dachau and God. I read things that seem meaningful to me—to them—to our time.

STEVE: In what way meaningful?

MERRILL: Just that—meaning for the individual. Poetry transmutes ordinary experience into a, well, a celebration of life. Cummings calls it "a remembrance of miracles." When I was the age my students are now, poetry meant a lot to me. I want my students to remember miracles. . . . The miracle of . . . everything. Of just being alive.[9]

In the dialogue there are many thought-provoking statements on education, on poetry, on censorship, and on life. Several contemporary devices are used for the play's technical development such as television, the radio "call-in" show, and the court scene. The set is an abstract one with playing areas where light shifts from one area to the other. "A Remembrance of Miracles" was produced on radio in January 1978 and was well received, especially by teachers. This play has the potential for powerful drama. It could have emphasized the forces of evil against the forces of good with a sweep of action as in *Antigone,* and the central character an Antigone figure rather than a victim. What Ringwood achieves is a topical play with strong emotional conflicts, a confrontation play on community bigotry, hatred, and near violence. Her plot line is solidly constructed and mounts naturally to the desired climax of hysteria.

Although the protagonist is a victim, rather than an Antigone figure, Merrill is a fully-rounded character for whom the audience has sympathy and compassion. Steve and Paul are two other believable characters. The remainder of the cast are mere stereotypes. A firm plot line holds the play together. Only Jodie, who plays an important role, seems artificial and unconvincing. But for the most part the characters and their dialogue provide food for thought on a timely and explosive issue. Merrill's words toward the end of the play serve well to sum it up. Merrill is asked in court why she reads poetry to her class and she replies: "I wanted them to see that language . . . can try to express what's at the very core of the heart. Poets give the essence of themselves; they spend themselves trying to say how it is for them. That's why I read poetry to my class. All art celebrates the miracle of life—no matter how ugly or twisted or ordinary the subject, if it's the true artist's subject, it's a celebration of the miracle of life. I wanted my students to remember that miracle."[10]

Another recent Ringwood play is "The Lodge" (1975). A serious drama on contemporary middle-class Canadian life, "The Lodge" brings together a group of people whose life-styles and value systems, revealed through family confrontations, are endemic to society in the seventies. In style this play has affinities with Chekhov's *Cherry Orchard,* Lillian Hellman's *Autumn Garden,* and Tennessee Williams's *Cat on a Hot Tin Roof.* It also shares some close affinities with Lorca's tragedies *Blood Wedding* and *The House of Bernarda Alba.* Lorca's penchant for poetic signs and symbols; his use of lyric passages to express the essence of his drama; his creation of simple, symbolic, leading characters; his integration of music to assist the poetry in his plays; his ability to grasp the substance and voice of the earth and express it lyrically; his obsession with life and death—are all here in "The Lodge," which focuses on a family reunion, a birthday party for Jasmine Daravalley, the grandmother and head of this selfish clan, which quickly deteriorates into a spectacle of greed as each member endeavors to acquire Jasmine's land and estate.

Jasmine, an artist, gathers three generations of her family together for a reunion before she leaves for Africa to pursue her career. Unaware of her future plans, the family squabble over her property, as they secretly plan to get power of attorney, control of her land, and authority to commit this seventy-year-old woman to a home for the elderly. At the climactic moment Jasmine overhears these plans and reveals to her selfish family that the estate on which they based their hopes is nonexistent: the family home has burned to the ground, the land has been sold to the government, and the money used to endow a school in East Africa. The only property left is valuable land at Soda Springs; this, Jasmine had originally intended to divide among her family, but having discovered their avarice, she decides instead to will it to the Indian tribe who inhabit that area, with the provision that it be kept in its present state for fifty years from the date of will.

A full-length play, "The Lodge" is constructed of three scenes. Scene 1 introduces the various members of the family to the audience as they arrive at Wilderness Lodge which is owned by Jasmine's granddaughter Shelley and her husband Allan. This scene reveals the conflicts between members of the family. Scene 2 exposes individual weaknesses and fears at mysterious Soda Springs at night, high in the mountains where the family members gather. Scene 3 returns to Wilderness Lodge and dramatizes the final confrontation between Jasmine and the family.

There are a variety of characters in "The Lodge." The most fully developed is Jasmine, the grandmother: artistic, sensitive, unpredictable, a woman of sound principles and good judgment; still beautiful in a fragile way, she is the only "free" character (in the Henry James sense), in the play. The others exercise degrees of freedom, but Jasmine is the sounding board on which all the rest are measured. They may be classified in two groups: those who have varying degrees of freedom, and those who are imprisoned by their own narrow attachments. The partially free characters who bear some resemblance to Jasmine are her artistic, sensitive, granddaughter Shelley who yet lacks the maturity to fully understand her young husband Allan; her impractical, idealistic grandnephew Robin, a remnant of the counterculture generation of the sixties who demands Jasmine's land for use as a commune; her gentle, sensitive, middle-aged daughter Connie, devoted to bird-watching and bird preservation, but intimidated and bullied by her husband, a retired army major; and her grandson Quentin who never appears in the play, but whose work in East Africa has obviously been an inspiration to Jasmine. Other characters, related only by similar ideals and values to Jasmine, are the Indian Chief Jimmy Lashaway, his granddaughter Marybelle, and Shelley's husband Allan.

At the opposite end of the spectrum are those members of the family who are bound by materialism, greed, and a total indifference to others. These include Jasmine's narrow, mean-minded, covetous daughter Alice whose machinations to put her mother away as senile make her the leader; her husband Eardley, an enterprising, scheming opportunist; and Connie's husband Roland, a retired army major whose sole pleasure is killing birds and wild animals for sport. These oddly assorted characters are brought together in Wilderness Lodge to reveal through conversation, contention, and confession, their philosophies of life, their self-centered motivations, and shocking disregard for one another.

The dominant symbol in this play is the wild animal, the cougar, whose natural beauty and freedom is destroyed by Roland. In a sense the cougar represents Jasmine who is hunted and stalked by the family and whose freedom is in jeopardy. At the moment that the cougar is discovered and wounded in the woods, Jasmine is discovered after overhearing her family's cruel plans to commit her to a home for the elderly. As Allan puts the cougar out of its misery, so Jasmine feels free to deal directly with the family.

Lorca's poetic language in his tragedy *Blood Wedding* abounds in symbols drawn from nature: the thistle, carnation, rose, star, moon, blood, water, bull, horse, wasteland. Ringwood's work, already illustrated, is full of like symbols.

Other Ringwood images include the horses depicted with broken legs on Shelley's batiks symbolizing the wanton destruction of wildlife in the wilderness; the lodge, itself a wilderness, where the family wander in confusion, capitulating to selfish desires; Soda Springs, a symbol of nature's mysteries, which Jasmine seeks to understand and interpret. Only at Soda Springs, as in a church or sanctuary, do the individual members of the family explore the depths of their real selves. This soul-searching takes place in a timeless atmosphere reminiscent of the forest in *The Deep Has Many Voices*. But in "The Lodge" the characters actually reach the center of the mysterious sanctuary. All achieve a degree of truth there but not all are changed by it. Jasmine and the Indian Chief Jimmy Lashaway arrive first at Soda Springs. It is night. Great slabs of glacial rock encircle the clearing around the mysterious hot spring from which arise mists that swirl and change shape.

JIMMY: There it is.
JASMINE: (*Kneeling.*) It's the same. The very same.
JIMMY: It's not big, is it?
JASMINE: No, not big.
JIMMY: Just a small hole in the ground with the soda water bubbling up.
JASMINE: It's warm. It's like touching the heart of the earth.
JIMMY: In the old days, the Indians used to come here before the fall hunt. They would sing and dance. It was a ceremony.
JASMINE: Yes. A visit to the Oracle.
JIMMY: My grandfather came here when he was a boy. He told me he came here a boy, but he was a man when he went down to the people. I brought Marybelle here when she was twelve. Three years ago she came here and stayed two nights alone. She never told me how it was but she was changed.
JASMINE: How?
JIMMY: She was proud again, like when she was little. In the old way. She quit running around. She studied. She knew she was an Indian. She was glad. I think so. You want a drink from the spring now?
JASMINE: We should make a ceremony.

JIMMY: Sing and dance? (*Chuckling.*) That old tree would think it's funny, two old people singing and dancing underneath the moon.
JASMINE: We could make a wish.
JIMMY: At our age?
JASMINE: I still have some wishes.
JIMMY: Yeah, I have some too.
JASMINE: So we'll drink the soda water and we'll make a wish.
JIMMY: I'll dip for you. There. (*He does so.*)
JASMINE: (*Taking the cup.*) I wish not to be helpless. I wish to die before I'm helpless. . . . Please God let me go on painting. Another chance. Another chance to—.[11]

Jasmine and Jimmy appear as at a sacrificial banquet, drinking the sacred draught and uttering wishes and prayers to Deity. Jimmy begs that future generations of Indians will continue to worship at Soda Springs. Here in this semi-mystical environment the audience becomes aware of the depth of the family emotions, symbolized by the hot springs bubbling up from the earth's core. Greed and fear, lust and love, are revealed in each family member's wish-making over the sacred spring. Eardley wishes to own Soda Springs for lucrative purposes; Roland to kill the cougar; Robin to have Allan's wife; Connie to bridge the gap between herself and her husband; Allan to reach his wife Shelley; and Shelley to know the meaning of love. This is similar in spirit to Lorca's *Blood Wedding* in the mysterious atmosphere in which Lorca's characters (and Ringwood's too) are converted into forces fusing with nature and gaining thereby a human and poetic significance.

There are several confrontations during the Soda Springs episode. Particularly disturbing is Robin's challenge of Shelley which is, in fact, a challenge of the entire hippy generation:

ROBIN: How could you walk away from everything we had together?
SHELLEY: Spain wasn't real, Robin. The whole Europe thing wasn't real.
ROBIN: Don't tell me that. Laughing and swimming and working together, being together. It was real.
SHELLEY: We were high on pot and wine and the excitement of getting away from home. We didn't really see Spain. We saw each other, and people like us . . . the young travellers.
ROBIN: We planned to go on . . . to join Quentin. To do what he's done—teach, serve, change things.
SHELLEY: We talked a lot. I guess I got tired of talk. I . . . I got homesick. . . .

ROBIN: So you end up in a hunting lodge with a husband who doesn't have a clue. You call that freedom? (*Lo*, II.48)

It is in the confrontation scenes that Ringwood defines the confusions of youth and the problems of mature people. Setting, dialogue, and theme give unity to this play. The setting, reminiscent of Chekhov's plays, is the environment of Chimney Lake in northern British Columbia where a family assemble who are rootless and strange to the environment. There is authenticity to this setting, to the Indian characters, and particularly to the atmosphere of Soda Springs. The symbols grow naturally out of this setting, and the dialogue is realistic. Jasmine's final words are prophetic. To Alice she exclaims, "Maybe I'm setting you free, Alice. All of you" (*Lo*, III.72). To the family she says, "It's too late for you to nurture the land and too late for it to heal you. Sooner or later you'd spoil what's there, defile the mystery. And when the mystery is gone, the land would become your enemy" (*Lo*, III.72). There is more than one theme in "The Lodge": the end of the counterculture revolution; the obsession with material wealth; land, wildlife, and family preservation; the right to dignity and independence for the elderly; the quest for life's essential meaning.

A comparison can be made between "The Lodge" and Lorca's *The House of Bernarda Alba*. Both plays are dominated by a single character although that character differs in each play. But the contention and violence, the starkness and intensity of Lorca's play has its counterpart in "The Lodge." The dramatic tension resulting from a clash of wills in each play suggests a tragic sense of life. Both Lorca and Ringwood possess a deep understanding of their country's generic character and the ability to infuse their plays with the unique spirit of their people.

"The Lodge" was given a workshop reading at the New Play Centre in Vancouver and it placed second in their Women's Play Competition. It was produced by the West Vancouver Little Theatre in October 1977. Pamela Hawthorne, director of the New Play Centre, said of it: "I felt the strength of the play lay in two areas: the general thematic idea and the older generation. . . . Jasmine is a catalyst—she set it all up."[12] It is the character of Jasmine around whom the play revolves and in whom is established its unity and power.

Ringwood's plays of social protest succeed in their intentions. She knows how protest is most effectively and artistically made. Hence she presents striking characters, vivid scenes, and poetic dialogue. Her characters are victims of society's indifference—the Indian, youth, the elderly. A deep note of compassion runs through all five plays. It is impossible to read or see these plays without being moved to suffer with these victims and to protest the conditions that led to their tragic circumstances.

CHAPTER 6

The Children's Plays

OCCASIONALLY there has occurred a hiatus in Ringwood's literary career. When this happened she filled it by writing for children. Her stage plays and numerous radio plays for the young, written over the years, deserve some consideration because they offer new insights into Ringwood's versatility.

The magic of play impulse in children is well understood by Ringwood. In her children's plays she seems to have explored the creative, qualitative, interpretative, and psychological possibilities in drama for the young. The creative aspect sparks the play impulses of children so that they participate vicariously in the adventures of the characters; the qualitative aspects—characters, dialogue, plot, staging, dance, music, pantomime—give structure and richness to children's drama; the interpretative aspects allow children to reflect upon past experiences and grow in sympathetic understanding of the world and its people; the psychological aspects permit them to deal with their difficulties by seeing characters with similar problems.

A gift for visual images, a good story line, a sense of humor, and a love of children are also prerequisites for the successful children's dramatist. Ringwood possesses these qualities, and she obviously enjoys writing children's plays for child actors. Her own children inspired some of these plays and acted in them. The plays fall naturally into four categories: early stage plays, educational radio plays, adaptations of children's stories, and a multicultural theme play.

I *Early Stage Plays*

Three stage plays for children and young people were written in the early period of Ringwood's career: *The Dragons of Kent* (1935), *Red Flags of Evening* (1940), and *Saturday Night* (1940). *The*

Dragons of Kent is a well-developed children's play; the other two are merely exercises for drama workshops.

In *The Dragons of Kent* (1935) Ringwood reverses the roles of St. George and the dragon. The present descendant of the original dragon is a dragon scholar and researcher as well as a vegetarian. His thesis is that the dragon put St. George to flight by breathing fire and flame. The present descendant of St. George, with three Oxford dons, challenges the dragon to battle. Unable to breathe fire and flame, due to his vegetarian diet, he has recourse to his meat-eating dragon son who successfully routs St. George's descendant, whereupon the three Oxford dons admit the truth of his assertions and award the dragon scholar an honorary degree. The play concludes with the singing of an old dragon folksong. Without moralizing, the play laughs at human foibles. Easily produced in one act and one set, *The Dragons of Kent* is irresistible to children's imaginations. First directed by Elizabeth Sterling Haynes at the Banff School of Fine Arts in 1935, and by Leslie Pharis at Magrath School in 1936, it has since had several successful school productions.

Saturday Night (1940) and *Red Flag of Evening* (1940) are exercises for junior-high-school students. The first one treats of the conflict between children and parents over who gets the family car on Saturday night; the second play, set in the early 1900's, deals with the perennial suitor who never pops the question. Humorously written in the tradition of Calderon's short Spanish plays, they are approximately fifteen minutes in length, with established characters, a conflict, and a resolution, easily staged for workshop productions.

II *Educational Radio Plays*

Ringwood is a knowledgeable radio-script writer accentuating only those features of character portrayal, dialogue, and story line which will captivate the ear and imagination. In 1936 Sheila Marriot, director of CKUA educational radio station, Edmonton, commissioned Gwen Pharis and Elsie Park Gowan to write twelve plays each for the program *New Lamps for Old*. Ringwood's plays highlighted various historical figures but unfortunately the scripts have since been lost.

"The Fight Against the Invisible" (1945), commissioned by CBC for the *Science on the March* series, is a stimulating radio play designed to engage the imagination and ear of the child. The setting is Delft, Holland, and the story is the discovery of microbes by

Antony Loewenhoek, furthered in a later period by Louis Pasteur and Robert Koch, and related in the twentieth century to the contagion brought by gophers to Alberta. A narrator and a young lad make the transitions in time easy and natural.

Five plays were written for the CBC *Health Highways for Children* series (1951). These scripts were to radio what *Sesame Street* is to television today. They were based on Fred Allen's format for *Allen's Alley* and included rhymes and songs, little stories and plays, and a fable for the wise child. The cast of characters starring the cowboy Big Bill Raymond from Brazeau, and the school nurse Miss Lily Belle, remained the same throughout the five plays. Each play demanded some form of audience participation. The titles are self-explanatory: "Frontier to Farmland" stresses Alberta prairie farms, soil erosion, and necessary rotation of crops; "Ten Hours a Night" emphasizes proper sleep, using a wise and a foolish grizzly bear; "Beware the Germ," "Stand Tall," "A Fuss About Food," and "Stop and Think" complete the group. They were broadcast from CBC Vancouver to the four western provinces. Ringwood also wrote a radio play which has not been produced, "The Potato Puppet Twins," a delightful program of fables and rhymes, presenting Tommy and Petunia who also invite audience participation.

Ringwood's three radio plays on student writing include one for the *Creative Writing* series "Books Alive" (1951); and two for *The Adventures with Books* series: "The Play's the Thing" (1954) and "A Polished Performance" (1954). In "Books Alive" she takes the children on a train ride through the west looking for storytellers. Everyone she meets offers a story, and Ringwood suggests how these stories can be written appropriately. She ends by reading a story actually written by a child. "The Play's the Thing" (1954) introduces Mr. Young, a schoolteacher, and his students, who discuss playwriting. The play they eventually write together is then enacted. "A Polished Performance" (1954) is a challenge to students to write a letter emphasizing style and polish in a prize-winning contest. All these educational programs were written with lively dialogue and colorful characters.

"The Bells of England" (1953), commissioned by Doris Berry Gauntlet, director of radio school scripts for the Department of Education, was designed to celebrate the coronation of Queen Elizabeth II. It employs the ancient custom of bell ringing in England in an effort to involve young Canadians in the long history of the monarchy. A Canadian boy goes to England with his family for the coronation, meets the church bell ringer, and eventually finds himself ringing the Peter bell for the coronation. Produced on a coast-to-coast broadcast it succeeded in its original intent.

III *Christmas Plays and Adaptations*

"So Gracious the Time" was originally written as a short Christmas story read on CBC radio in 1954, then dramatized and produced on stage in Edmonton for a Christmas entertainment, and finally adapted as a radio play on a Christmas coast-to-coast program. Set in the woods beyond Edmonton it tells the meaning of Christmas through the eyes of a six-year-old girl whose parents give up a planned Christmas trip to Edmonton in order to care for a poor pregnant Indian woman and her husband. The newborn babe arrives on Christmas day. A poignant story, it succeeds because the plot line is firm and the characters, both Indian and white, are realistically created.

In 1959 Ringwood adapted the story of *Heidi* for serialized CBC radio production, directed by Esse Ljungh. Her ability to bring regional places to the imagination of children made the *Heidi* series a success.

"The Three Wishes" (1965) was adapted for the Williams Lake Players Club for the Christmas show and directed by Gwen Ringwood who also took the role of narrator. The traditional story of the wishes of three poor children and their grandfather is told with charm and simplicity, and the play involves a parade, a clown, and a cow. The variety of characters and the lively dialogue made "The Three Wishes" a success.

"The Lion and the Mouse" was adapted for stage in 1964, when Ringwood, who was giving a course on writing to college students, suggested adapting a fairy tale as an excellent way to learn to write dialogue. The line of action is already there; the student has only to introduce conflict. Ringwood adapted "The Lion and the Mouse" as an example to the students of this type of writing and she succeeded in producing charming animals and rhythmic dialogue.

In 1965 she adapted another fairy tale for stage, *The Sleeping Beauty*, specifically for the Indian children at St. Joseph's Mission. They requested it and the adaptation worked surprisingly well. Ringwood translated it into Indian terms using an Indian chief and his daughter, a crow, a goose, a loon, and a coyote. Indian masks, drums, and dances were also used. Choruses were written with an ear to Indian speech. The setting was the natural rock surroundings of the Cariboo. For "The Basket Weaving Song" Ringwood wrote both lyrics and music. Many Indian customs with Chilcotin background were woven into the play. The Indians who performed in this play were ideal because of their familiarity with ritual, their proud demeanor, their authentic dancing, and the rich, resonant tones of their voices. Presented at the Williams Lake adjudicated drama festival, it was given high marks.

The Golden Goose (1973) was adapted by Ringwood for another college course in creative playwriting at Cariboo College in Williams Lake. Written simply as an acting exercise, it has not been produced.

IV *Multicultural Theme Play*

In *The Magic Carpets of Antonio Angelini* (1976) carpets are used as symbols for the rich cultures of various countries; and the main character, Antonio, is a seller of carpets. Antonio tells the story of each rug so that the rugs are stylized versions of the stories. Songs, mimes, and dances enact the stories and thus bring an added dimension to the play. *The Magic Carpets* is a comedy that a director could adapt to his own particular conditions. Each of the six characters has a rich role to play. The theme is simply that wherever we come from we all have a story, we all have a name. *The Magic Carpets of Antonio Angelini* is one of Ringwood's finest children's plays. It won first prize at the Ontario Multicultural Theatre Association's National Playwriting Competition in 1976 and Ringwood was brought to Winnipeg to assist in its production.

Ringwood's plays for children, both stage and radio productions, employ many of the qualities best suited for children's drama. A study of these plays is a stimulating pursuit; a production of any one of them is a rewarding experience. Particularly enjoyable is *The Magic Carpets.* As the play opens Maria is looking for her husband Antonio who sells carpets. With her donkey Samothracia she meets Thor Orlakson, the self-proclaimed Masked Marvel who attempts to steal her donkey. Samothracia bunts him around so he gives up, very discouraged, as it is his first robbery. Thor is from the Icelandic settlement in Gimby, Manitoba. Out of work because the fishing industry is closed down at Gimby due to pollution, Thor has decided to become a robber. At this point Antonio comes along singing:

> Rugs, Rugs, Beautiful Rugs.
> Softer than kisses, warmer than hugs.
> Rugs, Rugs, Gorgeous to see.
> Hand made Canadian. Buy them from me.[1]

Thor decides to hide and to attempt at the right moment to steal a rug. Antonio pulls the cart of rugs on stage while continuing to sing:

> Beautiful hand made rugs for sale.
> Prayer rugs, sleeping rugs, Little Babies' Creeping rugs.
> Thick rugs, thin rugs; walking out and in rugs.
> Magic carpets, flying carpets. Weave yourself a dream carpet.
> (*MC*, 4)

This opening is designed to stir the imaginations of children as they think of all the different uses of colorful rugs. Meanwhile Antonio puts up his sign proclaiming a story in every carpet. He hears snoring behind the rock and discovers Thor whom he asks to guard the rugs while he looks for his wife, as he sings up and down the scale, Samothraciamaria. He meets Jacques who wants to sell him a carpet woven with the story of LaSalle leaving Quebec. Antonio buys it and then teaches Thor his song:

> Rugs! Rugs! Gorgeous to see.
> Hand made Original. Buy them from me.
> Whatever the pattern, the story you seek.
> Ukrainian, Eskimo, German or Greek.
> Wherever we came from, whenever we came.
> We all have a history, we all have a name.
> Rugs. Rugs. Gorgeous to see.
> Magical carpets. Buy them from me. (*MC*, 7)

Antonio continues to teach Thor to sing his songs, showing that Canada is an amalgam of many people from many lands.

> Anglais or Francais, whatever vous pensez.
> From London or Nancy, whatever you fancy.
> Chinese or Punjabi; Fine rugs are my hobby.
> Old English medallion; West Indies; Italian.
> For floor, wall, or ceiling, from Madras or Darjeeling.
> A tartan that's Clanish; A Basque rug; a Spanish.
> A Shuswap, a Sioux rug; Portuguese blue rug.
> A Kilkenny tower; a Japanese flower;
> Dutch and Moravian; Rich Scandinavian;
> Finnish, Bavarian, Tibetan, Hungarian. (*MC*, 8)

Maria returns to discover that Antonio has bought a new rug with the money they had saved to purchase a license for their donkey.

She is despondent, saying that no one will buy their rugs; everyone wants wall-to-wall today! Antonio consoles her with the reminder that they still have the magic carpets which will take them all over the world. But fearful that the police will take their donkey, Antonio asks Jacques to warn him of their approach by making the sound of wild geese. The audience is asked to chime in. While the police look for the wild geese, Antonio will have time to hide the donkey. Soon a policeman appears. Jacques begins the sound of the wild geese. Antonio, forgetting it is the signal, joins the policeman in searching for the geese. Ringwood knows how to bring laughter to children. The policeman inquires Antonio's name and when he hears it he maintains that Antonio is not a Canadian but a foreigner. When Antonio insists he was born in Sudbury, Ontario, the policeman tries to Anglicize his name to Tony Angel. Angelo then displays his rugs, and, as he tells each rug's story, dancers and singers enrich the tales—Indian, East Indian, Eskimo, Ukrainian, French Canadian, Italian (the story of Maria and Angelo). The officer purchases the French-Canadian carpet, thus giving Antonio the money to buy a license for the donkey, his rug business, and the cart. The play ends happily with Thor returning to his home in Manitoba, Jacques inviting Angelo and his wife to his aunt's home, and the officer promising to bring the mayor to purchase a carpet.

In this play Ringwood has fulfilled the needs of children. *The Magic Carpets* gives them the opportunity to participate in the play, by singing and making the noises of loons, coyotes, and geese. They also enter into the adventures of the characters and are encouraged to express their emotions audibly. Dancing, singing, pantomime, and good staging are calculated to appeal to the imagination and play impulses of children. The experiences of Antonio and Maria and the Masked Marvel allow the children to reflect upon their own past experiences and to grow in sympathetic understanding of the world, of Canada, and of its people. The problems in *The Magic Carpets* give children an opportunity to reflect upon their own problems. These are the qualities needed for a successful children's play, and Ringwood has fulfilled them admirably.

CHAPTER 7

Novels and Short Stories

ALTHOUGH Ringwood's novels and short stories are few in comparison to the number of plays she has written, they are nonetheless significant in quality. Her talents for a lyric interpretation of life, for creating unique and fully rounded characters, and for natural dialogue, are ideally suited to the novel. Her sense of theater, her ability to create a single effect, and, in the prairie plays, to work with a few key characters, are appropriate skills for writing short stories. Ringwood has written two novels, *Younger Brother* and "Pascal." She has several short stories to her credit, including "Get Along Little Dogie," "Home Base," "The Last Fifteen Minutes," "The Little Ghost," "Little Joe and the Mounties," and "Some People's Grandfathers."

I *Novels*

Younger Brother was created at the instigation of Robert Gard who was editing the Home Place Book Series and wanted a novel about southern Alberta. It was written in 1958 and published the following year, not by the Home Place Book Series publishers, but by Longmans, Green of New York. It was given two printings. Gard suggested that Ringwood take materials that were a part of her life and use them as fiction but to give them the regional background of home. He said in a letter to Gwen Ringwood: "You used to tell me . . . about experiences that you and your brothers had had in which the whole region, the feeling of the prairie life, played such a part and developed such deep emotional attitudes. Can't something of this be transferred into fiction?"[1] Ringwood followed his advice. Much incidental material is memory material such as the dogs running the sheep, the horses' panic in icy river water, cattle rustling, and the general picture of southern Alberta. The background lends a sense of reality and immediacy to the story. Since the theme is the evolution of a boy's life from childhood to young manhood, Gwen Pharis's brothers and their collective experiences were used.

Younger Brother is the story of a boy poised on that precarious edge between childhood and manhood. Fourteen-year-old Brandt Merrill is experiencing the tragic loss of his brother Jules whose recent death overseas in the Canadian Airforce (during World War II) has made a deep impact on Brandt's sensitive nature. The novel is concerned with Brandt's need to accept Jules's death, and his search for answers to his questions on life and death, and on life after death. This is the deeper level of the story, the undercurrent throughout the novel. The plot revolves around the stealing of cattle in the area near Brandt's father's farm in the prairie of southern Alberta. Because Brandt's parents have gone east for two weeks, Brandt feels accountable for the farm although his father has hired a mature young farmhand Hank Symes to be responsible. Brandt admires Hank—his courage, independence, easy attitude toward life; he despises Hank's buddy Mike Broder for his cruelty, dishonesty, and brutal nature. *Younger Brother* takes us through the events of two weeks in the life of Brandt Merrill. Brandt's affinity for the land and his need to travel back over the old trails he had often taken with Jules leads him to the Sink Hole, to the discovery there of the hides of the stolen cattle, and eventually to the realization that the cattle thieves are Hank and Mike. Because Brandt's Indian friend Andy Running Wolf is suspected as the culprit, Brandt feels that he must disclose the truth to the police. When Mike becomes aware of this, he pursues Brandt to the top of the cliff and attempts to kill him. Hank defends Brandt and in the ensuing fight both men roll over the cliff to their deaths. As the story ends and Brandt is faced with the loss of his friend Hank, he goes down into the ravine, to the great old poplar and there in the heart of nature he finds his peace.

Younger Brother is similar to Marjorie Kinnan Rawlings's powerful novel *The Yearling* in its sensitive handling of a child's rapport with nature; its poignant descriptions of the land, sky, water, and wildlife; and its youthful questioning of life and death. Ringwood's introduction, setting, plot, characterization, and dialogue blend easily into a unified whole. The language is rich in the use of figures of speech, metaphor, and rhythm. A feeling of timelessness—a phenomenon we have observed in several of her plays—pervades this novel. The introductory sentence focuses immediately on the relationship between young Brandt and the man Hank. "Brandt

Merrill walked away from the bunkhouse, fighting back tears of anger and humiliation. At that moment he hated Hank Symes."[2] Hank had forgotten his promise to explore the river and go fishing with Brandt. Unconsciously Brandt was putting Hank in the place of his lost brother; this tenuous relationship runs through the entire book and accounts for Brandt's tragic sense of loss at Hank's death—the second tragedy in Brandt's young life.

The setting presents the reader with a vivid picture of the variety of wildlife on the prairie. Through Brandt's eyes we see the sparkling water, the peninsulas and sand bars of the river separating the Merrill farm from the Blood Indian Reservation. With Brandt on his small black mare Babe, we ride through the prairie observing gophers, coyotes, deer, snakes, badgers, porcupines, wheeling hawks, and geese in flight. We see the dew on grass and bushes, the strawberry patch, the gold poplar leaves, the wild cherries, the rose leaves and crimson hawes, the goldenrod, and black-eyed Susan. We ride down through the deep mysterious coulee with its underground stream rising above ground through twisting roots and lichen, exotic fronds of fern, wild ladyslipper, brilliant moss, trumpets of tiger lilies. Then down into a deep ravine and in the gorge we behold the three tall pines rising from the bottom of the cavern and below them standing alone in the ravine, the majestic poplar lifting its massive arms to the light. Within this setting of coulee and ravine, ranch and farmland, we watch Brandt bringing in the cattle, protecting the sheep, tracking down stolen steers, driving the truck, running the mower, milking the cows, and feeding the calves and pigs. He is beginning to do a man's work now. For recreation he hunts for prairie chickens and rabbits; he explores caves and waterfalls; he swims in the cool river water, fishes along its bank, and fords it on horseback to visit his friend Andy Running Wolf on the reservation.

The way in which these details function to aid the intent of the novel—how, in fact, Ringwood's material works—is to transpose it, through the imagination of the reader, into a living picture in which the reader experiences vicariously life on the prairie. Through Brandt's senses the reader feels the impact of prairie wind and rain, heat and drought, storm and blinding snow; observes prairie grass and flowers, grain elevator and horizon, coulee and ravine; hears the sounds of prairie animals and birds, river and stream, farm machinery and farm activities. Such is Ringwood's gift that the reader, to whom the prairie may be totally foreign, becomes vividly aware of its very essence. Transferring the reader thus into the life stream of the prairie, Ringwood is then able to develop characters out of this environment, whose personalities and life-styles echo the prairie out of which they came. The natural reactions of these people to the situations in which they find themselves is then entirely credible to the reader.

The plot is moved forward by reference to a number of past and present events. Some of these are Brandt's recollections of the past, such as the first Model T Ford races on Dominion Day in 1936 in which Hank and Jules had participated; the night that Jules had an appendix attack and young Brandt was unable to overcome his fear of the dark in order to saddle the horse and go for help; the day on the river ice when Brandt, his father, and Andy Running Wolf tried to cope with the horses' panic as one horse plunged through the cracking ice into the freezing water. Other events occur in the present and involve Brandt, Hank, and Mike killing wild dogs who were running the sheep over the cliff; Hank saving Brandt's life when Brandt had gone down the side of the cliff to rescue a lamb; Brandt secretly observing Mike and Hank's midnight burial of stolen cattle hides in the Old Sink Hole. All these events are held together by a firm plot line and by the persistent questions in Brandt's mind on life and death, on past and present activities, and particularly on the stolen cattle.

The characterizations are realistic. Brandt is a believable fourteen year old, sensitive, idealistic, questioning, silent, lost in his griefs, longing to emulate the best in Hank. An enigmatic character, Hank is strong, masculine, independent, easygoing, inclined to take risks, seemingly indifferent to others, yet kind and understanding of Brandt. The other characters are merely stereotypes: the villain Mike Broder, the awkward young cook Helga, the slow-witted farmhand Ollie, the middle-aged farmers Sam and Orv, and the Indian Andy Running Wolf. The character of Jules pervades the book. We see him through Brandt's eyes—a hero and a loving brother. Brandt's need to live up to his memory urges him on but the reader realizes that Brandt's character, in formation now, might eventually surpass that of Jules in manhood.

The dialogue is natural and suitable to the various characters involved. The rhythms and nuances of the spoken word are faithfully recorded so that each character is given his own voice. Brandt tells the story and we see everything through his eyes. The episode of the wild dogs running the sheep is an example of Ringwood's use of dialogue. Brandt, Hank, and Mike had surrounded the sheep and were shooting off the wild dogs. Brandt's faithful dog Tansy was helping but at a climatic moment,. Mike who hated Brandt, turned his gun on Tansy:

Broder stood with the revolver in his hand. He looked huge in the moonlight; his grin was wide, terrifying as he laughed soundlessly.

"Got them both straight between the eyes. Did you see that?" he shouted at Brandt.

Then his arm went up, and Brandt could see him aiming to shoot again. Broder's arm was a straight line to the gun and the gun was on Tansy who was racing toward Brandt.

"No! No! That's my dog. That's Tansy!" Brandt screamed. Then to the collie, "The sheep Tansy, get the sheep! After the sheep, Tansy!"

Tansy had been well trained. She obeyed. She turned back, started after the milling flock.

Broder fired. The revolver made a small sound for a pistol. Brandt held his breath, let it out in a long sigh of relief. Tansy had run out of range.

Brandt rushed at Broder, tried to smash at his face. "You meant to shoot Tansy. You wanted to shoot her!" he screamed. Broder's arm flew out, his elbow hit Brandt in the stomach, sending him flying off to the ground, doubled up with the wind knocked out of him. "Keep your shirt on, kid," Broder said. "I didn't know it was your dog."

"You knew . . . you heard me . . . you didn't care!" Brandt finally got it out. He was almost sobbing with anger and pain.

"Don't you call me a liar." Broder was grinning down at him. "I play for keeps. Come on, I'll help you up."

"Don't touch me." Brandt jerked away from Broder's hand, got up, picked up his gun and started toward the corral. (*Y*, 158-59)

Much of the descriptive language used by Ringwood in *Younger Brother* is that poetic prose we have begun to associate with the Ringwood style. In her descriptions of the prairie she uses figures of speech, imagery, metaphor, simile, and symbol naturally and easily. Here is her description of a poplar tree as seen through Brandt's eyes:

As he recrossed the coulee, Brandt noticed a single poplar ablaze with leaves of so bright an orange that the tree seemed to quiver with a consuming fire. He half expected that the small earth-bound tree might break apart before his eyes under the burden of this unearthly beauty. He wished his mother could have seen the poplar just as it was, that instant—a burning bush circled by holy ground. (*Y*, 141)

The biblical image of Moses and the burning bush with its mystical connotations of the divine presence is recalled in Ringwood's image of the orange poplar quivering with a consuming fire. Frequently throughout *Younger Brother* nature is seen imbued with mystery; the prairie becomes a kind of sanctuary, an Eden impregnated with the voice and presence of the mysterious source of life. Another use of metaphor is the comparison made between the untimely death of the bay gelding and that of Brandt's brother Jules. Brandt's contemplation of death suggests memories of that magnificent horse which had galloped up the steep slope, stood poised and triumphant on top of the cliff, and then was killed as the ground broke away.

> One moment he stood so, mane flying, nostrils quivering. . . . his flanks gleamed copper, the muscles rippled under his hide. Then the chain started. . . . The overhanging bank gave way and the bay gelding swayed, toppled and went crashing down. The shrill whinney had hung in the drowsy air. Then came silence. To be cut down in his youth without warning, to be drunk with spring and the daffodil sun and to go crashing down! (*Y*, 66-67)

Note the violence of the language used by Ringwood here. Indeed, there is much violence in both of Ringwood's novels. What is she attempting to do with this violence? It would seem that the violence is in some way related to the prairie as well as to senseless war. Man's awful confrontation with the violence of nature on the prairie is paralleled or even echoed by the violence within himself; man's deep prejudices and frustrations, his inordinate anger and blind fury breaking out and venting itself upon the innocent, is Ringwood's vision begotten of the holocaust and of the wanton death and destruction of World War II. Her two brothers were destroyed in that war like the magnificent bay gelding cut down in its youth. Although Ringwood is writing in the tradition of the western novel, she is using it as a means of making a serious statement about life: "And Jules, born inland, knowing only the sweep of the prairie, the clear, sweet water of the river, had gone down in an arc of flame over the bitter ocean, the unfamiliar sea" (*Y*, 66-67).

Time is suspended in this novel, in the middle of the Alberta prairie, during World War II. Life here is detached from a war a whole continent away. Brandt's blending with the earth as he lay beside the river, feeling the sun on his back, has a timeless quality about it, that same sense of timelessness that pervaded *The Deep*

Has Many Voices and "The Lodge." Ringwood describes Brandt's union with the earth:

> Brandt became lost in the mystery of the earth itself. He could feel the bubbling, boiling lava at the earth's core, feel the hot molten mass struggling to escape deep below. He could imagine too how it was when the planet itself was rocked free of the sun, a swirling vortex of white heat, thrown out and out into the void, until it began to circle the sun.
>
> Lying there on the sand, the boy could see in his mind torrents of rain fall on the cooling lava, see cracks and fissures split the gray surface of the lifeless planet. In his mind he watched the shapeless fog roll up from the valleys, saw white steam shoot from the rifts in the white-hot rock.
>
> And then the miracle! There in the salt slime, something moved!
>
> For a moment Brandt was overpowered with the wonder of earth itself. For a moment he became the earth, his ego, his flesh, bone, sinew gone, and he was a part of that empty planet, part of the rock and the sleeping lava and the steaming water, part of the slime where some particle had moved. He, who had never seen the ocean, was one with the salt sea, one, too, with the first living cell. (*Y*, 96-97)

Note again the sense of violent movement described by Ringwood at the earth's core; note that the first living cell comes forth from that violence. We are here once again at the core of the Ringwood vision—that we are part of the earth and indeed of the violence of this planet.

The climax of the novel is another scene of violence, but after Hank's death Brandt seeks the solace of the great poplar tree standing alone in the deepest part of the ravine. The polarities in man and in nature—violence and serenity—are here strikingly realized. Brandt seeks peace. The roar of the river reaches Brandt as a strong and timeless voice, and he embraces the huge trunk so deeply rooted in the earth but with its branches in the sky so that "it held in its trunk some property of healing, some balm drawn from the earth and sky" (*Y*, 212). As Brandt merged with the tree, time and thought were suspended until he felt comforted and able to accept Jules and Hank's deaths. The prairie had provided him with the solace he needed. This blending with nature is typically Canadian. Realism and violence are subsumed by romanticism.

Younger Brother is a successful novel because Ringwood has control of her symbolism, imagery, and use of metaphor. Although her descriptions in themselves are superb, giving the reader a rich experience of the prairie, there is deeper than this a grasp of the essence of the very earth itself and of man's vital union with the earth, its rhythms and changes, its violence and peace. Added to this are the realistic details of a family, so like her own. Many of Brandt's experiences are recreations of actual events on the Pharis farm in Magrath. Of special importance to them was the giant poplar in the deep ravine. Gwen and her brothers penetrated this ravine and became aware therein of the mysteries of life and death. Once in a magical moment they had flung out a challenge to God just as Brandt does in *Younger Brother*. Brandt recalled Jules and his sister crying out, "God, if you be God, let this tree fall upon us" (*Y*, 65). And they felt a deep sense of disappointment when the challenge went unanswered. Gwen referred to the mystery of the ravine, the fact that Greek myths all took place in a ravine, that the Oracle spoke in a ravine. She would like children especially to understand that they each develop a personal body of myths through their experiences.

Younger Brother was later adapted and dramatized as a serial for CBC radio in 1960. Ringwood chose not to do the adaptation herself. It was written as a series of thirteen episodes by George Salverson, and directed by G. Kristjanson, who was at that time drama producer for CBC radio in Winnepeg. He says of it, "I . . . recall *Younger Brother* as being a warm, human story with a prairie setting."[3] Emily Crow Selden said of Gwen and the novel, "How well you managed the novel form . . . like an old hand! Your descriptions I liked especially. The character of Brandt came across very clearly, and through him, that of the older brother."[4]

Ringwood's second novel "Pascal," as yet unpublished, was begun in 1970, twelve years after *Younger Brother*. She improves on the techniques used in the earlier novel while continuing to strengthen her style as a poetic novelist. Ringwood uses vivid imagery and she ranges backward and forward in time. She possesses a deep appreciation of nature but always in juxtaposition with man. Both in *Younger Brother* and in "Pascal" the earth is used to reveal character.

"Pascal" treats of the struggles of a young Chilcotin Indian to survive and develop as an artist in a white man's world. A sensitive and perceptive picture of the complexities of Indian life in northern British Columbia, "Pascal" uses the theme of an Indian's attempt to walk that precarious and narrow bridge between the white and the Indian way of life. Within the confusions of his struggle Pascal realizes finally that he wants simply to be regarded as a human being, but at this point neither the white nor the Indian world will accept him.

The plot follows the events in Pascal's life from winter until the early summer Stampede. As truckdriver for a logging company and part-time ranch hand, Pascal moves easily within the white world. Having already impressed the American millionaire ranch owners, George and Mary Rand, with his abilities at handling horses, Pascal is invited back to their British Columbia ranch to break in a new stallion and offered the position of ranch manager. A brief infatuation with the wealthy divorcee Lynnette Gordon is followed by a serious interest in Kathy Selwyn, the young daughter of the local doctor. Unaware of his devotion, Kathy becomes engaged to a white man. In despair Pascal returns to his own Indian people only to be rebuffed by Sarita whose affections he had previously slighted. The novel ends in violence as Sarita is raped by three white men and Pascal is killed in his attempts to punish the rapists.

But this is not the conventional story of Indian misfortunes with white people. Although the plot may sound familiar, the story is told in distinctive poetic prose that makes it unique. Set against the panoramic background of the Fraser valley and ranchland, the characters are viewed in relation to this rich region of forest and plains. Through symbolism and imagery the plot and characters develop. The author keeps a sure hand on the text with a lightness of touch, a juxtaposition of landscape and character, and a movement backward and forward in time. A long passage at the opening of "Pascal" serves as a good example:

> The young man, Louie Pascal, more Indian than white, smiled as he drove the logging truck around the first bend of the long descent from the Chilcotin plateau to the Fraser river.
>
> A thousand feet below, the old angry river narrowed to a swift, sullen channel between its own ice boundaries. Shadows lay on the river but halfway up the far bank the February sun turned the spruce trees to shimmering green. Above the trees, a great square of granite, flecked with quartz and mica, blazed in the afternoon light. High, shining, and alone, the rock stood sentinel above the valley.
>
> "The Everlasting Rock"—the phrase slipped into his mind, bringing to Louie Pascal memories of the Mission chapel where each Easter to triumphant swell of song the Rock was split asunder. Small, bony knees bent to the hard wood as the priest offered the antique chalice. Prayers borne on incense rose to the blue-robed white Madonna smiling her stiff, plaster smile above the young brown faces that twisted fiercely around the

Latin responses. "Ave Maria, Mater Dolorosa, Ora Pro Nobis" . . . the sounds and smells and feel of the chapel were vivid in his memory. He remembered too his longing to run away from the Mission school, fly back to the Indian hillside, back to a time, a place when unfettered feet ran with the wind towards the western horizon, ran towards the rim of the world.[5]

At this point Louis Pascal is swinging his truck down a serpentine sheet of ice in twenty-three switchbacks to the bank of the river and the bridge. He is on the dangerous slope before he knows it. This time he makes it but we realize that next time it may be a different outcome. His memories of the past get in the way of his close attention to present reality. Ringwood is using this experience to prefigure Pascal's future. As an Indian he will walk the precarious path between the Indian and the white man's world, and it will be his past that will govern the outcome of his life. This opening passage, therefore, offers the reader insights into Louie Pascal's life and character and also suggests the author's intentions and techniques in achieving her ends. We discover that Louie Pascal is a twenty-four-year-old, intelligent, fearless Indian with excellent coordination, and a vivid imagination, totally absorbed in his own thoughts. Brought up and educated by priests and nuns in a Catholic mission school, he missed the freedom of the Indians, rejected mission confinement, and at sixteen, moved swiftly out of it into the while world. Despite his partially white ancestry, Pascal is wholly Indian in temperament and character. Pascal's preoccupation with the mission school and religion, triggered off by the sight of the huge granite rock, may be Ringwood's device whereby she sets the action of the play against Pascal's white and Indian background in landscape that suggests both. Ringwood achieves this by symbolism drawn naturally from the landscape, by juxtaposing landscape and character, and by ranging back and forth in time. She will continue to use these stylistic devices throughout the novel.

Gradually we are introduced through Pascal to a large cast of white and Indian characters who congregate in the hotel, the beer parlor, and on the streets of the town. The white people are more stereotyped than the Indians. They include George and Mary Rand, Lynnette Gordon, Kathy Selwyn, Dr. Selwyn, Chris Allen, Tom Ellison, and Tannis Moreno. Only Mary Calderon never appears, but her postcards from Greece awaken Pascal's interest in art. These white people form a backdrop, a shadowy white world against which Pascal and his Indian people play out their destiny. Only Tannis

Moreno, the artist, and Dr. Selwyn approach fully rounded white characters. The Indians, on the contrary, are rich three-dimensional characters—Pascal, Sarita, Theresa, Caroline, Gabriel, and Charlie Mercy. Their dialogue reflects the flat tones and implacable character of the Indians. But under the influence of liquor those tones turn to rich, loud, colorful volubility.

Ringwood moves the action forward with a lively description of events on the ranch, in town, and on the reserve. One of her most striking scenes, full of variety and interest, is the beer parlor, that great leveler of whites and Indians. Through Pascal's eyes and ears we see and hear both races drinking and arguing. The pride and the degradation of the Indian is clearly emphasized here. At the Sitko Ranch we observe at first hand Pascal breaking in the stallion Cherokee Star. There we also witness the branding and castration of newborn calves. We move with Pascal and Sarita to the Indian reserve and see the poverty and lack of dignity to which the Indian is reduced. We follow the white people and the Indians to the stampede and share with them the exciting events of this annual show. We are present at the lavish white celebrations of the stampede in town, and then view the raucous Indian party at their encampment on the edge of town. Always there is the comparison unobtrusively made through symbol and image between the Indian and white world. We see it all through Pascal's eyes.

Indian rituals, old Indian customs, songs, dances, and legends are woven into the story. Pascal's recollections of his grandfather Johnny Andrew, chief of the Chilcotin Tribe, comes swiftly to his mind on many occasions. As Pascal observes the dynamiting of the old bridge, he recalls salmon fishing and the ceremonial knife used by his grandfather in the ritual of returning to the river the bones and entrails of the first salmon caught, with the injunction, "Go and tell your fellows that you have been treated with respect" (*Pa,* 3). He remembers the story of the bear who is quick to resent an insult, of the landlocked sea monster, of the owl who spoke in Indian tongue and foretold death (*Pa,* 90). He reflects, as he sees Caroline's sick baby, on her baby moccasins with holes cut in the soles so that death the messenger would see them and not take the child. No one with faulty moccasins could make that long journey to the spirit world (*Pa,* 112). Pascal dreams of the great riderless phantom horse outside the broken wooden cemetery fence. The Chilcotin earth seemed to drain the land of its white significance, giving it back to the Indians. Intermingled with his memories of Indian symbols are the Christian symbols he has learned at the white mission school. When Pascal places the old Indian wagon wheel against the great rock he is amazed to see that the spokes form a rough wooden cross—a Christian symbol and a symbol of the passing of the Indian way of life.

The poetic device of the refrain is frequently used in recurrent dreams, in imagery, and in repetition of phrases. Pascal's repeated dream of murdering an unknown person is finally revealed to be his own Indian boyhood. The image of the narrow bridge resolves itself into Pascal's realization that he is precariously walking it and that he is in the middle, neither Indian nor white. The repetition of Henry Miller's novel title *Remember to Remember* becomes in Pascal's mind the refrain "Remember to remember to remember" his Chilcotin heritage. His grandfather's words are reiterated, "Go back to the old ways. Live and think like an Indian. The old ways are best" (*Pa,* 33).

"Pascal" is also a portrait of the artist as a young Indian; his contemplation of nature and his attempts to recreate what he sees of living nature on canvas; his introduction to abstract art and his excitement in the new form; and finally his wild and angry painting because, as he replies to his teacher, "All Indians are wild and angry inside" (*Pa,* 141). Even in his dreams Pascal paints—the copper stallion as king of the world, the moose, beaver, wolf, fox, bear, a mask of animals from Indian myths, the golden cougar, the old coyote, the rabbit, weasel, and wild mountain sheep; the young doe dying who reminds him of Sarita. Wherever he goes Pascal leaves his paintings on the walls of stalls and sheds and caves, on paper and canvas. He is a symbol of the Indian as creator and as victim. "In the dream Pascal felt like God creating a world in which each form stood for the seed locked in the genes of each shape and variation" (*Pa,* 187). But inevitably in his dreams white hands destroyed it all.

Time is used by Ringwood again and again to encompass within the moment, past, present, and future events. A young buck whom Pascal held at gunshot and then decided not to kill is described as they face each other: "He found himself locked in that reciprocal look as if tied invisibly to the young buck by some mindless recognition of something shared" (*Pa,* 43). And the sight of the stallion mating the bay mare reminds Pascal and the others: "Each one felt himself briefly without existence, except as a part of some continuing force, felt himself devoid of personality, of species, felt himself existing only as a seed tossed briefly on the flood of time" (*Pa,* 76). Ringwood does not use the stream-of-consciousness technique but she brings the reader easily into the mind of the character through interior monologues. We share Pascal's thoughts, his memories of the past, his mounting fears for the future. We see the vivid symbols constantly appearing to Pascal as, for example, the young doe mesmerized by the headlights of Pascal's truck and held immobile. In the doe Pascal sees Sarita hypnotized by the glamor of the white world and her future destruction at their hands.

Figures of speech—imagery, metaphor, simile, personification—are used abundantly but unobtrusively. They arise naturally within dialogue or description. Many examples can be offered to show Ringwood's poetic style. Pascal's fellow artists, white middle-aged women clustered around a projector, suddenly turn together and stare at Pascal "like a covey of grouse huddled together on the roadside" (*Pa,* 125). When Pascal enters the mill with its sawdust burner, white hot screen and orange red sparks flying straight up, he sees it as "a fantastic surrealist world of fire and shadows" (*Pa,* 10). An old man describes the Fraser River to Pascal as "Always different. Greedy as a wild cat, gentle as a kitten. Sullen. That's what she is today. Sullen" (*Pa,* 121). Of a colorful abstract painting he had done, the picture seemed to Pascal like "a window opening on another magical country where treasures spilled out in burning splendor" (*Pa,* 143). Pascal's Indian friends realize that he is trying to fit into both the Indian and white world. Rojan Jim says, "You putting salt in both pastures?" Pascal retorts "What's wrong with that?" Rojan Jim shrugged. "Nothing wrong except it hasn't worked in three hundred years. Time to quit kidding yourself" (*Pa,* 215).

"Pascal" is Ringwood's expression in terms of character, landscape, and story, of all she had discovered of Indian life. Her understanding of the Indian in the Cariboo is profound, and she is able to share his response to life as she moves the reader also to identify with him. The Indian's rapport with nature, his confusion in a white world, his explosive anger at injustices done his race, are all depicted in "Pascal." The hero, although romantically conceived, destroys any possible illusions the reader may have about Indian and white relations. "Pascal" transcends its British Columbia setting; it could be a story about any submerged population group attempting integration. It reflects the conflicts of contemporary life and reveals the vital issues. Ringwood's poetic style is personal and contributes to the intensity of her vision. Pascal's dying words, "I need light, more light" (*Pa*, 242) are symbolic of his struggle and of Ringwood's too, to find meaning behind the mystery of existence. This is in fact the essence of many of her plays and of *Younger Brother* and "Pascal." It is unfortunate that "Pascal" has never found a publisher.

II *Short Stories*

Ringwood's short stories are very different from her novels. She used the novel form, as we have seen, to reveal the violence in nature and in life, and to make a serious statement about life. Her short stories, on the contrary, are brief vignettes of personal experiences. Some of these are merely humorous tales; others are thought-provoking examples of prejudice and selfishness. None of them are concerned with violence nor are they making strong, powerful statements about life. They are interesting to read from the point of good short-story technique and because of their entertainment value.

Many of Ringwood's short stories grew out of actual experiences. She learned how artistically to transform experience into fiction. An example of this is her first published short story "The Little Ghost" (1945). Gwen and a young married woman, whose husband was also overseas in the war, decided together to rent a cabin near a lake for their children during a short period in the summer. While there they met and were shocked at the indifference of an ignorant foster mother toward seven half-starved little waifs for whom the woman was receiving government aid. Gwen fashioned from this encounter "The Little Ghost," a short story about one of these children, Kristie, who yearns to be adopted by the loving mother whom she meets at the lake. The mother's inability to take Kristie leaves a deep, guilty, and unforgettable picture of the waif in her mind. Gwen sent this story to Robert Weaver who helped her to see some of the ways in which experience can be transmuted into fiction. Weaver published "The Little Ghost" in *Canadian Short Stories*, and it was eventually read on CBC radio as well as published in other anthologies.

"Get Along Little Dogie" (1947), her second published short story, is a delightful tale of Shorthorn the cowboy who plans to punish a new tenderfoot because he refuses to drink canned milk. The plot is brought to a humorous climax when the cowboy discovers the new tenderfoot to be a baby. "Home Base" (1962) is a baseball narrative inspired by the stories of Ring Lardner and James

Thurber. Dr. Hugh Atwood, a close friends of the Ringwoods, helped with baseball details. "The Last Fifteen Minutes" (1963), using an actual experience, is a comic story on a wealthy man's endurance of a long sermon in church and his decision not to endow that religious institution. One of her most sensitive short stories, "Some People's Grandfathers," was written in 1963 and has been included in several anthologies since then. It is a poignant and true tale of an old Indian trapper and his eleven-year-old grandson who saves his grandfather's life when a moose attacks him. Another humorous Indian story, "Little Joe and the Mounties," was written in 1966 and published in the *Family Herald*. It is a short suspenseful story of the stampede and how Little Joe saves Bobcat Charlie from the Mounties. Ringwood's depiction of Indians is very realistic. Her latest short story, "Restez, Michelle, Don't Go," read on CBC radio in Vancouver during 1977, is a timely reminder of the French separatist movement. Told in the first person, it is an actual story of an English Canadian playwright caught in the midst of a French Canadian production of her play and unable to understand the comments, changes, and directions given totally in French. Eventually director and actors bend to her problem and speak English for her sake. The incident induces some sobering thoughts on English Canadian responsibility for bilingualism.

The predominant characteristic of all Gwen Ringwood's short stories is their preoccupation with children. Her characters usually include children who possess more wisdom than the adults ("Some People's Grandfathers" and "Little Joe and the Mounties"). The action is often observed through the eyes of the child, as in the above two stories and in "The Snow Princess" and "So Gracious the Time." Frequently the story belongs to the adult who has failed a child ("The Little Ghost" and "Supermarket"), or who finally realizes that the child is in control of the situation ("Home Base"), or who needs a child's moral support ("The Last Fifteen Minutes"), or who is stymied by a child ("Get Along Little Dogie"), or who is trying to save a child's life ("The Will of the People"). Occasionally Ringwood's stories concern adults who are acting like children. There is the adult who has never grown up ("Mr. Finnburley and the Nesting Swallow"); the adult forced by nature and events to assume the role of the wondering, questioning, despairing child ("Portrait of a Woman" and "Clock Time"); elderly people herded together like children ("Excursion"); and adults forced like children to learn a lesson ("Restez, Michelle, Don't Go" and "Mr. Gunderson and the President of the Republic"). This preoccupation with children controls the treatment of her material, so that Ringwood's short stories are told with clarity and simplicity, as though to an audience of children. Certainly some of her stories were written for children but even these are of interest to the adult reader.

Using the artistic analyses and directives of a modern master of the short story, Frank O'Connor (in *The Lonely Voice*), we may judge how well Ringwood's work meets current standards. Speaking of realistic art in the fashioning of a short story, O'Connor says, "Any realistic art is a marriage between the importance of the material and the importance of the artistic treatment."[6] Obviously Ringwood sees her material, children and children of an older growth, as important. Then she endeavors to fashion an appropriate treatment of this material. Her opening sentences usually introduce us immediately to the two most important characters in the short story and their relationship to each other. Take, for example, the opening sentences of one of her most successful short stories, "Some People's Grandfathers":

> The boy and the old man started out early to look at the trapline. They took some bread and dried salmon to eat along the trail.
>
> The boy, Sammy Joe, wanted to go fishing with the other Indians but he had no choice. Whenever his grandfather, Old Joe, went anywhere Sammy Joe was expected to go along.
>
> "The old man don't see so good," Peter Jacob would say to his son. "You go with him. Watch he don't fall over the cliff." Since the trail to the trapline went nowhere near a cliff, Sammy Joe thought this a very stupid admonition. He looked at his father every time to see if Peter Jacob was making a joke but Peter's face remained flat as a stone.
>
> If Old Joe acted like some grandfathers, I wouldn't mind, Sammy Joe told himself. Some people's grandfathers made jokes and told stories and gave their grandsons cigarettes to smoke. But not Old Joe! When he talked, he ordered. "Get this. Do that. Have respect." When he wasn't ordering, Old Joe stomped along in silence.[7]

Here we learn immediately about the personalities of the two most important characters. We realize it is to be a story of Indian trapping and a sense of suspense indicates that the climax will probably be a meeting with a wild animal. Will Sammy Joe show more wisdom than Old Joe? Since Old Joe carried the gun and refused to let Sammy Joe use it, the actual meeting with a huge moose proves too much for eighty-year-old Joe who fires but fails to kill the moose.

The moose charges grandfather, lifts him high in the air, and drops him sprawling on the ground. The action then concerns Sammy Joe who by various ruses captivates the moose's attention so that he does not finish the job on Old Joe. Finally the moose, having lost much blood attempting to charge Sammy Joe, drops to the ground dead. The story ends with a return to the tribe, a celebration, and an acknowledgment from grandfather that Sammy Joe is "Some Man." The following spring when Old Joe and Sammy Joe resume their inspection of the traplines, Old Joe says to Sammy: "You better carry the gun. We might see something."[8] Obviously the child has proved himself ready to take on manhood, a theme Gwen pursues in many of her stories.

O'Connor also suggests that the short story genre may often be associated with submerged population groups remote from the community: "The short story remains by its very nature remote from the community—romantic, individualistic, and intransigent."[9] Ringwood's short stories are concerned with such people as Indians, immigrants, Quebecois separatists, solitary and lonely people, orphans, the elderly, farmers and ranch hands in isolated places. Often these people are unable to speak for themselves. From our comfortable outside position we look in at their problems and eccentricities. Ringwood inspires our sympathy and understanding without forcing us to take sides. Unlike the novel, this detachment in the reader's response is the essence of short story writing.

One of the talents required of short story writers is a good sense of theater. "The storyteller," says O'Connor, "differs from the novelist in this: he must be much more of a writer, much more of an artist—perhaps I should add . . . more of a dramatist."[10] Style and technical control are important in developing a short story; as in a play there must be an element of immediacy and a coherent action. At the end, again as in drama, everything must have changed It is, like the play, a piece of artistic organization following a definite pattern. Ringwood's short stories, like her plays, are tightly knit and artistically developed. She rarely chooses to write in the first person ("Home Base" and "Restez, Michelle, Don't Go" are exceptions), but she fashions the story through the eyes of one character, usually a child, or an adult with childlike qualities, or a grownup with a deep understanding of children. Through this character's simplicity or naiveté we see the action develop and we observe the other characters. The action is enhanced dramatically by dialogue typical of each character.

Nothing extraneous enters into the development of Ringwood's short stories. An exception here is in the short story "Get Along Little Dogie" where the action is interrupted by a rather long digression on Shorthorn's background which adds little to the story but rather impedes its progress. In most of her stories she acquaints the reader with background material unobtrusively through dialogue and action or through interior monologues. "Little Joe and the Mounties" is an example of this. A good portion of the story is told through a combination of Little Joe's interior monologues and a description of the action. For example, his ruminations on Bobcat Charlie, the protagonist in the story set at the stampede:

"Hey, Bobcat! Bobcat!" called Little Joe. No answer. Little Joe paused. Yeah, it was Bobcat all right. But his shirt wasn't snow white any more. And he wasn't sure and easy the way he had moved in the shutes this afternoon. He was untidy and unsteady and drunk.

Dumb Bobcat! He'll probably have a hangover when he rides tomorrow. Likely, he'll make a big fool of himself at the dance tonight too. Little Joe didn't want to go to the creek now. He didn't want to talk to drunk old Bobcat who was mumbling like he didn't have any sense.[11]

This monologue is interrupted by the Mounties' car driving past in search of drunken men. Little Joe goes into action immediately, pushing Bobcat Charlie under water in the creek, effectively hiding him from the Mounties. Bobcat retaliates by pushing Little Joe under. When they return to the Indian camp, wet and sodden, Bobcat claims he had saved Little Joe's life. The story ends with the words: "Little Joe hunted his mind for a phrase he'd heard a white kid use. At last he remembered it. 'In a pig's eye,' Little Joe whispered to himself. 'In a pig's eye he did.' "[12] "Little Joe and the Mounties" is not a profound story but simply a vignette of Indian life at the Stampede.

A more serious story and one with strong bearing on the treatment of foster children is "The Little Ghost." Ringwood uses description, interior monologue, and dialogue to express the theme of human loneliness, sad in itself, but doubly tragic in the life of a small defenceless child. "The Little Ghost" is a dramatic story based on memory. The young married woman Kathy Preston, with four children of her own, will always be haunted by the memory of three-year-old Kristie whom she had left to the indifferent cruelty of Kristie's foster mother. "Kristie stood looking back at her, and standing so was as terribly alone as if she had been lost in a parched and limitless desert. When Kathy waved, the tiny face crumpled in despair. Kristie was crying, soundlessly, crying as one betrayed."[13] The single effect that Ringwood has designed for this short story is compassion for homeless children such as Kristie. Ringwood achieves it through the foster mother's cruel references to the foster children who are present and listening to her; through the vivid descriptions of the seven listless, underfed, and crippled children; and particularly through the feeling the reader gets of soft little bodies, in passages such as this:

> Kristie's tiny arms crept around Kathy's neck and her little body settled without resistance against Kathy's shoulder. Kathy could feel the small bones under the child's soft flesh. And Kristie snuggled closer and closer to her as if driven by a fierce physical need for shelter and warmth. As they walked Kathy told her nursery rhymes, crooned and repeated the child's name "Kristie, Kristie, dear little Kristie darling."[14]

Ringwood possesses a quality which is lacking in some short-story writers, that is heart. She loves her characters and suffers with each in his loneliness, lack of understanding, and inability to assimilate with his community. It is this quality which informs her short stories with a poignancy and delicacy that, like a small voice, persists in being heard.

CHAPTER 8

Fragments

RINGWOOD's place in theater is unique. Unlike most playwrights who seek to live and work in the big city centers of theater—New York, London, Dublin, Toronto—Ringwood chooses to remain within the confines of a small community in the west where theater is not seen as something apart from life but *is* life. Ringwood wants people to see that life can be art also. All her life she has been writing, and that writing (whether it be plays, novels, short stories, lectures, essays, poetry, dramatic sketches, and evenings of entertainment) has been directed toward defining life in western Canadian communities. Even her nondramatic works, her poetry, her editing, and her "Coffeehouses" have had that one goal. An examination of these works or literary fragments, from this point of view, should be helpful in understanding the whole Ringwood canon.

I *Nondramatic Works*

Ringwood's essays and articles are written on a wide variety of topics including: "Alberta is My Birthright," "Some Tall Tales from the Alberta Hills," "Some Memories of the Theatre in Alberta," "The Adjudicator Says . . . ," "Drama in the Open," and "The Carolina Playmakers 1919-39."

Her series of university lectures was given on radio station CKUA in Edmonton in the fall of 1939 as a radio correspondence course for the Department of Extension at the University of Alberta. Entitled "So You Want To Be An Actor," these lectures were directed toward the art of theater which she had learned at the University of North Carolina and earlier in her association with Elizabeth Haynes and the Prairie Theatre. They focused the attention of the student on prairie theater as an interpretation of western Canadian life.

Equally important from this point of view were her many lectures given during the past forty years. Mention should be made of "The

Frogs, the Chairs, the Cherry Orchard, and Laura Secord" presented at the Dominion Drama Festival in Vancouver in 1964, and of her speech "Women and The Theatrical Tradition" offered at the Conference of Inter-American Women Writers at the University of Ottawa in 1978. Her speech for the Dominion Drama Festival is typical of those she had made at festivals since the mid-1930s, encouraging young people to see theater as life and to work for perfection. Her recent speech at the Conference of Inter-American women writers when she faced a distinguished audience of women authors from Latin America, Mexico, the United States, and Canada, was a powerful plea to women dramatists to use theater to express life in the varied communities from which they came.

Perhaps Ringwood's finest essay to date on her own work is that contained in the volume *Stage Voices*.[1] In this work she examines her reasons for writing drama, her conception of a good play, the influences on her work, her manner of creating a drama, her inspirations, subjects, style, characterization, and her future plans for writing.

Ringwood's workshops consisted of lectures mainly on theater, fine arts, and education. Some intriguing titles are "The Well Adjusted Parent," "Elizabeth Haynes and the Prairie Theatre," "Rumination While Browsing through Roget's Thesauraus," and "Joan Baird: Homemaker." These are only a scattering of titles from a store of lectures given by Ringwood over the past forty years. They are evidence of her interests, her clarity of thought, her education, and sense of humor.

"Notes to Myself" consists of a series of personal anecdotes, reveries, philosophical thoughts, lists to remember, people to think about, descriptions of the moon, plans for plays, short stories, diaries, and symbols. Perhaps more than anything else these "Notes to Myself" reveal the real woman—the sensitive, honest artist struggling with words and ideas, people and events. They form the basis for some of her plays and short stories.

II *Poetry*

The unique talent that emerges in all her works is Ringwood's gift for poetry. Her plays are full of poetic dialogue; her novels and other prose works are resonant with poetic rhythms. Yet she has accomplished very little in the way of pure poetry. Rather she is a poetic dramatist and a poetic novelist. She has created some verse written for its own sake including occasional published poems such as "The Road," "The Cariboo Trail," "Oh Canada My Country," "Afterwords"; there are some unpublished poems—love poetry for Barney overseas, verses for her children, rhymes for the grandchildren, ballads, and poetic Christmas greetings. All have the quality of imagery and wit, of rhythm and song that marks her writing, but they are almost without exception inferior to the poetry in her plays and novels. This is her singing gift—to enrich her works with poetry that is an inseparable part of drama and fiction.

Her "Fragments" consist of some twenty-three pages of fragments of thought written in poetry, prose, and drama on such varied topics as a room at night, a chance meeting, a hunting trip, people high on pot. Composed for the most part in free verse, they are used when needed in her plays and prose works.

III *Indian Folklore*

Ringwood's editing of folklore for the Indians at St. Joseph's Mission had primarily the goal of making the Indian Community aware of its rich heritage. Chilcotin, Shuswap, and Carrier Indian tales formed the basis of the two books, both entitled *My Heart is Glad*, which were the result of an experimental program in speech arts for grades 7 and 8 children in 1964-1965. The students contributed stories, songs, legends, and descriptions of the Cariboo. With the help of these pupils Ringwood also drew up an Indian-English dictionary. All of this work including her adaptation of *The Sleeping Beauty* and original Indian drawings were combined in the two-volume work edited by Ringwood and Sister Germaine, and mimeographed and bound at the *Williams Lake Tribune*. Based on tales handed down from generation to generation, they form a valuable contribution to Indian culture in the Cariboo.

IV *Coffeehouses*

During the decade of the 1960s Ringwood became increasingly involved in community affairs. She therefore created her popular short community plays "Encounters." Such plays had been a tradition in Spanish literature. Calderon and Benavente had both written short comedies with two or three characters. Ringwood had read these and found the structure ideal for her "Coffeehouses." One of Benavente's comedies, "No Smoking," caught Ringwood's attention. More than just a skit or sketch, it is a penetrating study of contemporary society exposing vices and follies with smiling irony. She used this as a model for her satiric sketches on political and social issues in Williams Lake. Ringwood produced as many as twelve in an evening, through the Williams Lake Players Club. These "Coffeehouses" became a social event for the gathering of the townspeople. There was music and refreshments. "Encounters" highlighted people and events in Williams Lake as well as larger problems affecting people everywhere. They became highly successful, drawing large audiences to the Williams Lake Arts Workshop. One playlet explored the possibility of the Cariboo seceding from Confederation because Williams Lake had applied for money to build a new hospital and the Social Credit party had failed to help them. This playlet set up the Cariboo as a little republic of its own, another Monaco with gambling casinos to support it. "Elizabeth Bailer" was a satire on Elizabeth Taylor's television show in England. A third play dealt with the suspicions of Canadians when some Russians flew to Canada. Once their true reason (to buy wheat) is revealed, all suspicions vanish—the moment they become your market, they become your friends! The contrast in this play between the two societies is very marked. These "Coffeehouses," continuing for several years during the sixties, succeeded in being timely and humorous comments on life in Williams Lake. In 1970 Ringwood was teaching a large acting class in Williams Lake and, deciding to prepare a performance for them, she asked the Players Club to sponsor it as a "Coffeehouse." It was produced in the basement of St. Peter's Anglican Church, and the results of this group of "Encounters" were mixed. Those who had been to the early "Coffeehouses" were appalled at the bitterness of the social comments in this series of plays. The actors presented each short play in quick succession with merely a few chords of a guitar between plays. They were dressed in black leotards and turtleneck black sweaters. The sunnier, comic aspects of the early "Coffeehouses" had disappeared entirely. Among the new little plays was "Wail Winds Wail" which opens on the aftermath of a dinner party when couples who had complained of their children joining protestors' marches suddenly see them on television in a police shoot-out where one daughter is wounded. "ZZZZZZ" is set in 1990 when children discover a book edited in 1970 with pictures of all the traditional animals, birds, fish and insects now extinct! The children practice moon walks for daddy's vacation and are greeted by a huge swarm of bees, a mutation, returning to earth. "Compensation Will Be Paid" is concerned with the testing of poison gas in which a child dies and the company trouble-shooter says comfortingly,

"Compensation will be paid." In "Seal Hunt" baby seals talk about the vindictiveness of the animal, man. "Strictly Confidential" is an interview of two neighbors by a representative of International Credit Card Ltd. The interviews are conducted separately and both ladies later discover that they have been interviewed about each other. "The Thing To Do is Integrate" is an encounter between the Indians and the white men in which the Indians are refused a loan to build a fishing lodge even though they have the land and collateral. The white men tell them the thing to do is integrate with other Canadians! This last group of "Coffeehouse" sketches is far removed from the earlier, humorous playlets. The tone now is one of strong social protest and resembles in spirit her later plays of social conflict. "Encounters" can be defined as satiric sketches making incisive points on political and social problems in Williams Lake. Here, indeed, theater is life for the community.

Ringwood also wrote dramatic sketches as light entertainments when long-time residents were moving away from the Williams Lake community. So strong a bond had grown among them, due to Ringwood's musicals, plays, and "Coffeehouses," that a dramatic farewell of some sort was essential. These sketches consisted of parodies on well-known tunes joined with a comic history of the person or family and their involvement in the community. It was a gentle kind of humorous "roast" as a last farewell.

Ringwood also designed floor shows for various organizations in Williams Lake. One was an artful little comedy on Canada's initial trade agreement with Japan when Williams Lake sends the town council off on this trade mission. Instead of selling their wares, the trade council returns with a group of geisha girls whom Japan has cleverly sold to Williams Lake. Humorous floor shows such as this were designed for many organizations in the Cariboo.

For the past forty years Gwen Pharis Ringwood has been and is still actively engaged in writing. The output of stage plays, radio programs, musicals, children's plays, novels, short stories, poetry, essays, coffeehouses, sketches, floor shows, drama workshops, lectures, and articles, reveal an energetic and creative woman for whom theater is life, and life is art, and art is the total dedication of one's talents to community.

CHAPTER 9

Conclusion

GWEN Pharis Ringwood is a serious artist consciously aware of her craft, who has sustained and developed and changed her style, her themes, and her vision of life gradually over the forty years of her creative writing. What remains a constant in this development is her sensitivity to poetry, her talent for characterization, and her deep emotional response to life.

It is this passion for life in all its manifest forms that motivates and informs all her work. Robert Gard remarked, "Her whole obsession is with life."[1] Vivien Cowan said, "She's extremely serious about everything concerned with life—which of course is the basis of her writing."[2] And Doris Gauntlett wrote that she has ". . . compassionate insight into the lives of those around her, sharpened by humorous honesty turned toward herself; a large spirit."[3] Gwen herself uses in her conversation such terms as "surrounding things" and "fitting into one's own skin" to define the life-giving forces in and around her. In her lecture, "So You Want To Be An Actor," delivered on CKUA radio in Alberta in 1940, she said: "It is time for us to try to interpret the life we know and love to the rest of the world, unless we are content to go down as a people who were blind and inarticulate and afraid, a people who had nothing to say."[4] Ringwood followed her own advice, interpreting the life around her in artistic forms that indicate a gradual development in style, theme, characterization, and personal vision.

Ringwood's initial style, derived from Frederick Koch, was the traditional folk play as seen in her first dramas at Chapel Hill: "Chris Axelson, Blacksmith," "One Man's House," *Still Stands the House, Pasque Flower*, and *Dark Harvest*. In this early period of her work she experimented with comedy, farce, tragicomedy, and tragedy. During these two years of experimentation she discovered that her most comfortable medium in the folk play was a combination of farce and comedy. Hence the second period, her work in

Alberta, was one in which she consistently used an interesting blend of farce and comedy, refining and developing it in the farcical comedies: *The Courting of Marie Jenvrin, The Jack and the Joker,* and *The Rainmaker.* She experimented with pure farce in *A Fine Colored Easter Egg,* and culminated this comic period in her writing with the mature and successful farcical comedy *Widger's Way.* This second period in her writing also saw the introduction of music into her comedy *Stampede.* This feeling for rhythm moved her naturally into the third period of her creativity when she wrote her musicals incorporating comedy and farce in an awareness of western Canadian history in the musicals "Look Behind You, Neighbor," "The Road Runs North," and "Mirage." In the fourth and present phase of her work her style has changed from comedy to the style she had earlier abandoned—tragic drama. Eschewing the folk elements of her initial period, she now experiments with various forms of tragedy, including a serious confrontation play in *Lament For Harmonica,* a use of Greek tragedy in *The Stranger,* surrealism and expressionism in *The Deep Has Many Voices,* a modern morality play in "A Remembrance of Miracles," and a Chekhovian style in "The Lodge." During the past forty years, she has thus moved from folk plays to farcical comedy. to large scale musicals, culminating today in experimental plays of social protest.

Her use of symbolism remains a constant in her work. From the first superb use of it in *Still Stands the House,* her symbols drawn usually from nature, from animals and plants, have supported and strengthened her style and theme. This is most clearly seen in the use of hyacinths and the unborn colt in *Still Stands the House,* the fragile blue flower in *Pasque Flower,* and the wheat field and the dead tree in *Dark Harvest.* Other animals include Midnight the horse in *Stampede,* the gelded Palomino stallion in *The Stranger,* the moose hypnotized in the car's headlights in *The Deep Has Many Voices,* the doe mesmerized by the truck's headlights in the novel "Pascal," the golden cougar and the broken legs of the batik horses in "The Lodge." The symbols of the giant tree and the sink hole are mythmaking in the novel *Younger Brother.* Ringwood uses many other symbols in her works but those drawn from nature seem to be her dominant symbols.

Ringwood uses poetry and poetic figures of speech, particularly metaphor, simile, and personification, most notably in *Still Stands the House, Pasque Flower, Dark Harvest, The Stranger, The Deep Has Many Voices, Younger Brother,* and "Pascal." All of Ringwood's works contain poetry or poetic prose to some degree. Even her titles are to a large extent metaphors supporting the theme, for example, "One Man's House," *Still Stands the House, Pasque Flower, Dark Harvest, The Jack and the Joker, A Fine Colored Easter Egg,* "The Wall," *The Deep Has Many Voices,* and "A Remembrance of Miracles."

Ringwood's deep emotional response to life is demonstrated most powerfully through her use of language. She is definitely a poet giving voice to her vision of life through symbol, metaphor, simile, rhythm, and the blending of vowels and consonants into dialogue that has the persuasive power of music. Because of this gift her plays become metaphors of western Canadian life. That she often combines music with dialogue reveals the enrichment she sees in a musical reinforcement of her poetic images. Her poetry catches the attention of the reader and playgoer to the extent that some of her poetic lines have become oft-repeated sayings as already illustrated in this book. Her plays use the rhythms of Canadian speech which differ slightly from American cadences and are very different from British speech patterns. The magic of words captures the reader and playgoer. Another talent is a visual gift for description. She is therefore able to produce an orchestration of language and images. Although she has used this gift in large panoramic dramas and historical musicals, she is at her best in developing subtle shades of feeling in plays that explore the emotions of a few characters only.

In theme her early plays dealt with the isolation and suffering of prairie people and immigrants in western Canada, followed by wry observations on such western Canadians as goldminers, newspaper editors, rainmakers, immigrants, farmers, and cowboys. Ringwood gently exposed human follies and foibles. The musicals examined prejudice in "The Wall" and life in Edson and the Cariboo. Her present period of writing is marked by serious attention to the exploitation of Indians, the violence and confusion of young people, and the self-interest and greed of contemporary society. As Ringwood moves away from the themes imposed by the land on her characters, she confronts human weakness and malice in its barefaced culpability.

Underlying the surface theme in each of her works is the deeper theme that we are put on this earth to improve conditions, to make life better for others. From her earliest plays, e.g. "Chris Axelson, Blacksmith" (1938), to her latest plays, e.g. "The Lodge" (1975), this idea is apparent. Chris enriches the life of his nephew and his neighbors by considering them first. Ruth looks to the future happiness of her child in *Still Stands the House*. Lisa forfeits her own chances in favor of the happiness of her husband in *Pasque Flower* and he immolates himself for her in *Dark Harvest*. Marie Jenvrin celebrates life as does the community in *The Rainmaker*, "Look Behind You, Neighbor," "Mirage," and "The Road Runs North." Bob Edwards preserves truth as his contribution to the enrichment of life in *The Jack and the Joker* and John Ware offers salutory advice on life in *Stampede*. Widger wishes "to be a bigger fistfull" of life, and Wasyl seeks real values. The children in "The Wall" destroy bigotry. Maya, Jana, and Merrill are seeking a better life although their quests end in tragedy. Melissa sums up in her person the search of all the Ringwood characters, and Jasmine admonishes her family that it is too late for the land to enrich them. We have come full circle here. Ringwood begins and ends with the land as an enriching factor in preserving and improving life.

In characterization Ringwood has chiefly created female protagonists. One notes the gradual emancipation of women in the roles she assigns them. Originally a traditionalist, Ringwood created her women willingly subordinated to their spouses, bearing the traditional burdens of household and children without any thought of individual careers. Ruth in *Still Stands the House* and Lisa in *Pasque Flower* and *Dark Harvest* are subservient to their husbands, quietly accepting their roles as wives and mothers. But Marie Jenvrin is the exception. She works with one aim in mind—to marry, love, and dominate her husband. The ladies in *The Jack and the Joker* are offensively superior gossip-mongers. Margaret in *The Rainmaker* is easily moved to return to her husband when rain falls on Medicine Hat. Celia in *Stampede* is the stereotyped young romantic in love. Olga in *A Fine Colored Easter Egg* urges her husband, in traditional style, to capitulate to up-to-date and expensive ways of living. Roselle and the widow Anastasia in *Widger's Way* seek romance and husbands. Mrs. Carmelodeon in "The Wall" is a narrow-minded and bigoted snob. The ladies in the musicals "Look Behind You, Neighbor" and "The Road Runs North" are stereotyped camp followers, husband-seekers, faithful wives, and good mothers. It is only in the present period of her work that Gwen uses what Elsie Park Gowan had long ago urged her to employ—women's liberation. Ringwood today changes her stance in the present and fourth period of her work, creating the characters *Maya* and *Jana*, independent women fearlessly defining their positions in the face of ignorance and opposition; Melissa, a woman with a strong sense of herself as a person seeking the answer to the mystery of life; Merrill, a career woman unsuccessfully defending herself against a bigoted and small-minded community; Laura in "Mirage" leaving with Wilson for the north, without her parents' approval; Jasmine the artist forthrightly confronting her family's selfishness and greed. These women in Ringwood's last six plays are far removed from the old-fashioned concept of women portrayed in her earlier works. Her present protagonists are three-dimensional people struggling with the problems of contemporary life.

Ringwood's personal vision of life has remained constant through the years but her position has radically changed from silent onlooker to articulate critic. Always aware of the world problems of poverty, war, and the enslavement of peoples, she was, in the past, unable to voice her pain but took refuge instead in comedy and gentle satire. Her folk plays were written before the end of the depression and during World War II. She found herself too deeply and emotionally involved in those tragedies to be able ruthlessly and dispassionately to confront the evils they engendered. Although in "One Man's House" she decries social injustice, and in "The Wall" narrow-minded prejudice, these are isolated examples in plays of indifferent quality. It is not until her present period of writing that she seems to be able to attack evil in straightforward manner. Her ability to cope literally with evil in tragic tones which was early evidenced in *Still Stands the House*, once again is manifested in the plays of this present period.

In reviewing the body of her work one is impressed with her insights on human relationships, human conflicts, and human comedy in daily life. Her characterizations of Canadians in the early folk plays, in the Alberta comedies, the musicals, and the present serious dramas, are fine contributions to Canadian literature. Her best work is equal to and in some instances surpasses that of the more prominent Canadian playwrights today. Her language is evocative of the prairie and ranch country of western Canada. To theater in the west she has contributed forty years of dedicated work not only in her own playwriting and directing but also in helping others to realize their creative abilities.

Underlying all her work is the affirmation of man having some control over his destiny, some responsibility for changing the world, making it a better place in which to live. She espouses a philosophy which asserts that human beings can make some choices toward the good. The mystery of life challenges her, and although she has no positive answers on the existence of God she is drawn toward the mysteries of earth, of things that well up from the earth. Her plays include such images as dinosaurs, oil, soda springs, deep forests, and the mysteries they symbolically imply. Through image and word she often uses classical Greek references and Greek choruses, comic and tragic Spanish forms, Irish peasant styles as fitting receptacles to hold her quest for truth. In the final analysis Ringwood is defining those small steps towards growth, growing up, expanding to fit the mold in which a person is cast—the ideal. She is interested in the steps people take "to become a bigger fistful," toward the assertion of the dignity of being human.

Still productive, Gwen Pharis Ringwood is struggling to cope with her own strengths and weaknesses—to find the medium that will today give artistic expression to her vision of life. The international scope of her present political and social concerns is forcing her to seek the form that is best adapted to her particular temperament and talent. The strength of *Still Stands the House* is just that extraordinary combination of form and language, of characterization and symbol, that constituted her total métier forty years ago. Today she seeks this miracle once again. Like Melissa in *The Deep Has Many Voices*, she is on a quest. Whether she achieves her goal, one thing is certain: as she says of Melissa, the search is all. Recently Gwen Pharis Ringwood wrote: "Somewhere just beyond one's fingertips there always seems to lie the subject, the theme, the people who will say something pertinent and relevant to the human situation, if one can find it and say it all simply and dramatically and honestly."[5]

Notes and References

Preface

1. Personal interview with Gwen Pharis Ringwood, 17 May 1976.

Chapter One

1. Gwen Pharis Ringwood, letter to Robert Gard, 1952.
2. Ringwood, letter to Robert Gard.
3. Gwen Pharis Ringwood, "She Demanded Greatness," *Remember Elizabeth*, Memorial program, ed. University of Alberta Drama Department (Edmonton: University of Alberta Press, 1974), p. 5.
4. Gwen Pharis Ringwood, MS (subsequent references to MS are to those in the Ringwood Archives, University of Calgary Library, Calgary, Alberta).
5. Personal interview with Clive Stangoe, 18 May 1976.
6. Emily Carr, *Hundreds and Thousands, The Journals of Emily Carr* (Toronto: Clarke Irwin, 1966), pp. 6-7, as quoted by Peter Mellen in *The Group of Seven* (Toronto: McClelland and Stewart Limited, 1970), p. 168.
7. Peter Mellen, *The Group of Seven* (Toronto: McClelland and Stewart Limited, 1970), p. 183.
8. Frederick H. Koch, "American Drama in the Making: A Commencement Address Delivered at the University of North Dakota on June 11, 1935," *Carolina Play-Book* (1936), pp. 79-80.
9. Koch, p. 82.
10. Samuel Selden, *Frederick Henry Koch: Pioneer Playmaker* (Chapel Hill: University of North Carolina Press, 1954), pp. 60-61.
11. Paul Green, "Presence by the River," in *Pioneering a People's Theatre*, ed. Archibald Henderson (Chapel Hill: University of North Carolina Press, 1945), p. 65.

12 Paul Green, *Dramatic Heritage* (New York: Samuel French, 1953), p. 50.

13. Archibald Henderson, ed., *Pioneering a People's Theatre* (Chapel Hill; University of North Carolina Press, 1945), pp. v-vi.

Chapter Two

1. Letter received from Emily Crow Selden, 17 June 1976.
2. Personal interview with Emily Crow Selden, 13 June 1977.
3. Personal interview with Elizabeth Lay Green, 16 June 1977.
4. Letter received from Samuel Selden, 16 June 1976.
5. Personal interview with Gwen Pharis Ringwood, 16 May 1976.
6. Letter received from John Parker, 25 June 1976.
7. Personal interview with John Parker, 15 June 1977.
8. Gwen Pharis, "Sandy," *Carolina Play-Book* 10, no. 4 (December, 1937).
9. Gwen Pharis, "Chris Axelson, Blacksmith," pp. 4-5; hereafter cited as *A*.
10. George Broderson, "Gwen Pharis—Canadian Dramatist," *Manitoba Arts Review*, no. 4 (Spring 1944) 14.
11. Personal interview with Gwen Pharis Ringwood, 17 May 1976.
12. Gwen Pharis Ringwood, "One Man's House," MS, University of North Carolina, Chapel Hill, p. 20; hereafter cited as *O*.
13. Personal interview with Gwen Pharis Ringwood, 16 May 1976.
14. Ibid.
15. Personal interview with Gwen Pharis Ringwood, 17 May 1976.
16. Ringwood, personal interview.
17. Letter received from Emily Crow Selden, 17 June 1976.
18. Gwen Pharis Ringwood, *Still Stands the House* (New York: Samuel French, 1939), pp. 10, 11; hereafter cited as *SS*.
19. Ringwood, personal interview.
20. Margaret Atwood, *Survival* (Toronto: House of Anansi Press, 1972), pp. 33, 20.
21. Frederick Philip Grove, *Settlers of the Marsh*, New Canadian Library, no. 50, ed. Malcolm Ross (1925; reprint ed., Toronto: McClelland and Stewart, 1966).
22. Sinclair Ross, *As For Me And My House*, New Canadian Library, no. 51, ed. Malcolm Ross (Toronto: McClelland & Stewart, 1941).
23. Sheila Watson, *The Double Hook*, New Canadian Library, no. 54, ed. Malcolm Ross (Toronto: McClelland and Stewart, 1966), p. 127.
24. Ibid., p. 134.
25. Atwood, p. 245.
26. Ibid.
27. Personal interview with Emily Crow Selden, 17 June 1976.
28. Personal interview with Elsie Park Gowan, 12 May 1977.
29. Personal interview with Walter Kaasa, 13 May 1977.
30. Kaasa, personal interview.
31. Personal interview with Tom Kerr, 16 May 1977.
32. Gwen Pharis, "Preface to *Still Stands the House*, in *American Folk Plays*, ed. Frederick H. Koch (New York: Appleton Century, 1939), p. 392.

33. Gwen Pharis, Program, "Pasque Flower," premiere performance, Chapel Hill, North Carolina, 2-4 March 1939.
34. Personal interview with John Parker, 15 June 1977.
35. Gwen Pharis, *Pasque Flower, Carolina Play-Book*, 12, no. 1 (March 1939), 13; hereafter cited as *P*.
36. Anton Wagner, "Gwen Pharis Ringwood Rediscovered," *Canadian Theatre Review*, no. 5 (1975), 64.
37. George Broderson, "Gwen Pharis—Canadian Dramatist," *Manitoba Arts Review*, no. 4 (1944), 4.
38. Personal interview with Gwen Pharis Ringwood, 17 May 1976.
39. Ringwood, personal interview.
40. Gwen Pharis Ringwood, "Dark Harvest," *Canadian Theatre Review*, no. 5 (1975), 108.
41. *Dark Harvest*, p. 109; hereafter cited as *DH*.
42. Frederick Philip Grove, *Fruits of the Earth* (Toronto: J. M. Dent, 1933), p. 4.
43. Ibid., p. 10.
44. Ibid., p. 11.
45. Ibid., p. 113.

Chapter Three

1. Personal interview with Gwen Ringwood, 17 May 1976.
2. Gwen Pharis Ringwood, *The Courting of Marie Jenvrin* (Toronto: Samuel French, 1951), pp. 11-12.
3. Personal interview with Gwen Pharis Ringwood, 17 May 1976.
4. Personal interview with J. T. McCreath, 13 May 1977.
5. Gwen Pharis Ringwood, *The Jack and The Joker* (Edmonton: University of Alberta, Department of Extension, 1944), p. 2.
6. Personal interview with Tom Kerr, 16 May 1977.
7. Gwen Pharis Ringwood, *The Rainmaker* (Toronto: Playwrights Co-op., 1975), pp. 10-11; hereafter cited as *R*.
8. Personal interview with Gwen Pharis Ringwood, 17 May 1976.
9. Gwen Pharis Ringwood, *Stampede* (Edmonton: University of Alberta, Department of Extension, 1945), p. 6; hereafter cited as *S*.
10. Personal interview with Elsie Park Gowan, 12 May 1977.
11. John Weber, letter to Blake Owensmith, 28 March 1949.
12. Mrs. Florence James, letter to Gwen Pharis Ringwood, 13 April 1954.
13. Esther Nelson, letter to Gwen Pharis Ringwood, 21 September 1955.
14. Personal interview with Gwen Pharis Ringwood, 17 May 1976.
15. Gwen Pharis Ringwood, *A Fine Colored Easter Egg*, In *Prairie Plays*. (Edmonton: NeWest Publishers, 1980), pp. 8-9.
16. Personal interview with Gwen Pharis Ringwood, 17 May 1976.
17. Ibid.
18. Personal interview with Elsie Park Gowan, 12 May 1977.
19. Personal interview with Gwen Pharis Ringwood, 25 May 1977.

20. Gwen Pharis Ringwood, *Widger's Way* or *The Face in the Mirror* (Toronto: Playwrights Co-op, 1976), Scene 3, p. 22; hereafter cited as *WW*.

21. Personal interview with Gwen Pharis Ringwood, 25 May 1977.

Chapter Four

1. Gwen Ringwood, "The Wall," MS, p. 3; hereafter cited as *W*.

2. Gwen Pharis Ringwood, "Look Behind You, Neighbor," MS, p. 2; hereafter cited as *N*.

3. Personal interview with J. T. McCreath, 13 May 1977.

4. Letter received from Marguerite Ahlf, 27 July 1976.

5. Desmond Bill, "Edson Pageant Explodes into Top Grade Musical" [review of "Look Behind You, Neighbor"], *Edmonton Journal*, 3 November 1961.

6. *Conference Across a Continent: An account of H.R.H. The Duke of Edinburgh's Second Commonwealth Study Conference on the Human Consequences of the Changing Industrial Environment in the Commonwealth and Empire, May 13-June 6, 1962* (Toronto: Macmillan of Canada, 1963), pp. 1-2.

7. Personal interview with Clive Stango, 18 May 1976.

8. Gwen Ringwood and Art Rosomon, "The Road Runs North," MS, I. Scene 2. p. 34; hereafter cited as *RR*.

9. Gwen Ringwood, "Mirage," MS, p. 2; hereafter cited as *M*.

Chapter Five

1. Personal interview with Gwen Pharis Ringwood, 17 May 1976.

2. Gwen Pharis Ringwood, *Lament for Harmonica or Maya*, in *Ten Canadian Short Plays*, ed. John Stevens (New York: Dell, 1975), p. 143; hereafter cited as *L*.

3. Ringwood, personal interview.

4. Gwen Pharis Ringwood, *The Stranger, Canadian Drama* 5, no. 2 (1979), p. 279.

5. Bruce Thompson, review of *The Stranger, Williams Lake Tribune*, 23 June 1971.

6. Gwen Ringwood, "The Deep Has Many Voices," MS, p. 2; hereafter cited as *D*.

7. Bruce Thompson, review of "The Deep Has Many Voices," *Williams Lake Tribune*, 23 June 1971.

8. Personal interview with Tom Kerr, 16 May 1977.

9. Gwen Ringwood, "A Remembrance of Miracles," MS, Scene 10, pp. 21-22.

10. Ibid., pp. 46-47.

11. Gwen Ringwood, "The Lodge," MS, Scene 2, pp. 36-38; hereafter cited as *Lo*.

12. Pamela Hawthorne, letter to Gwen Pharis Ringwood, 31 March 1976.

Chapter Six

1. Gwen Pharis Ringwood, *The Magic Carpets of Antonio Angelini* (Toronto: Playwrights Co-op, 1979); hereafter cited as *MC*.

Chapter Seven

1. Robert Gard, letter to Gwen Pharis Ringwood, 27 November 1956.
2. Gwen Pharis Ringwood, *Younger Brother* (New York: Longmans, Green, 1959), p. 1; hereafter cited as *Y*.
3. Letter received from G. Kristjanson, 1 September 1976.
4. Emily Crow Seldon, letter to Gwen Pharis Ringwood, 19 October 1959.
5. Gwen Pharis Ringwood, "Pascal," MS; hereafter cited as *Pa*.
6. Frank O'Connor, *The Lonely Voice* (Cleveland: World Publishing Company, 1963), p. 217.
7. Gwen Pharis Ringwood, "Some People's Grandfathers," *Family Herald*, no. 3, 31 January 1963, 44.
8. Ibid., p. 47.
9. O'Connor, p. 21.
10. Ibid., pp. 23-24.
11. Gwen Pharis Ringwood, "Little Joe and the Mounties," *Family Herald*, no. 8, 14 April 1966, p. 79.
12. Ibid., p. 80.
13. Gwen Pharis Ringwood, "The Little Ghost," in *Canadian Short Stories*, ed. Robert Weaver and Helen James (Toronto: Oxford University Press, 1952).
14. Ibid., p. 10.

Chapter Eight

1. Gwen Ringwood, ["A Playwright Talks About Her Life And Work"], *Stage Voices* ed. Geraldine Anthony (New York: Doubleday, 1978) pp. 90-105.

Chapter Nine

1. Letter received from Robert Gard, 15 June 1976.
2. Letter received from Vivien Cowan, 15 July 1976.
3. Letter received from Doris Gauntlett, 7 July 1976.
4. Gwen Pharis Ringwood, "So You Want to be an Actor," *CKUA Radio Correspondence Course* (Edmonton: Department of Extension, University of Alberta, 1940-1941), p. 1.
5. Letter received from Gwen Pharis Ringwood, 15 October 1978.

Selected Bibliography

PRIMARY SOURCES

The following list includes works both published and unpublished. Ringwood's works are at the University of Calgary Library Archives, Calgary, Alberta. A significant number of the plays are also in the Drama Collection, Metro Library, Toronto, Ontario.

1. Plays

"Chris Axelson, Blacksmith." MS University of North Carolina, Chapel Hill, 1938.

"Christmas, 1943." MS University Women's Club, Edmonton, 1943.

The Courting of Marie Jenvrin. 1941. Toronto: Samuel French, 1951. Also in: *Carolina Play-Book*, 14 no. 4 (December 1941), 101-16; *The Best One-Act Plays of 1942*, edited by Margaret Mayorga (New York: Dodd Mead, 1943); *Canadian School Plays*, ser. 1, edited by E. M. Jones (Toronto: Ryerson Press, 1948); *International Folk Plays*, edited by Samuel Selden (Chapel Hill: University of North Carolina Press, 1949); *Adventures in Reading*, edited by J. M. Ross and B. J. Thompson (New York: Harcourt Brace, 1952); *Canada on Stage*, edited by Stanley Richards (Toronto: Clarke Irwin, 1960); CBC Edmonton, 1941.

Dark Harvest. In *Nelson's Collegiate Classics*, edited by George L. Broderson. Toronto: Thomas Nelson & Sons, 1945. Also in *Canadian Theatre Review*, no. 5 (Winter 1975), 70-128; CBC Toronto, 1945 and 12 September 1951.

"The Days May Be Long." *TS*. Chapel Hill, 1938.

The Deep Has Many Voices. In *Canadian Drama*, 6, no. 2 (1980).

The Drowning of Wasyl Nemitchuk or A Fine Colored Easter Egg. In *Prairie Plays*. Series No. 3 Edmonton: NeWest Publishers, 1980. CBC Edmonton, 1946. *Prairie Playhouse*, CBC, 22 March 1956. CBC Winnepeg, 1958.

"Encounters." MS. Williams Lake Coffeehouses, 1960-1970.

The Jack and the Joker. Edmonton: University of Alberta, Department of Extension, 1944.

Lament for Harmonica or *Maya*. Ottawa: Ottawa Little Theatre Play ser. I, catalog no. 10, 1959. Also in *Ten Canadian Short Plays*, edited by John

Stevens (New York: Dell Publishing, 1975), CBC-TV Montreal, 14 February 1960. CBC, Shoestring Theatre, Recorded December, 1978.

"The Lodge." MS.

"Niobe House." MS.

"One Man's House." MS. Chapel Hill, 1938.

Pasque Flower. Carolina Play-Book, 12 no. 1 (1939), 7-20. Also in "Women Pioneers." In *Canada's Lost Plays*, edited by Anton Wagner (Toronto: Canadian Theatre Review, 1979), Vol. 2.

The Rainmaker. Edmonton: University of Alberta Extension Department, 1946; Toronto: Playwrights Coop., 1976. Also in *Canada's Lost Plays*, Vol. 3, ed. Anton Wagner, "The Developing Mosaic." Toronto: Canadian Theatre Review, 1980.

"Remembrance of Miracles." MS.

Stampede. Edmonton: University of Alberta, Department of Extension, 1946.

Still Stands the House. New York: Samuel French, 1939. Also in *American Folk Plays*, edited by Fred. H. Koch (New York: Appleton Century, 1939); *International Folk Plays*, edited by Samuel Selden (Chapel Hill: University of North Carolina Press, 1949); *Eight One-Act Plays* (Toronto: Dent, 1966); *Encounter: Canadian Drama in Four Media*, edited by Eugene Benson (Toronto: Methuen, 1973); *The Carolina Play Book;* edited by Fred. H. Koch (Chapel Hill: University of North Carolina Press, 1939); *Canada Books of Prose & Verse*, no. 5, Toronto: Ryerson, 1950; *Book of Canadian Plays*, edited by Emrys Jones (Saskatoon: University of Saskatchewan Press); *Transitions* (Vancouver: Commcept Press, 1978); *Prairie Playhouse*, CBC Toronto, 5 March 1953, 1955. In *Inquiry Into Literature* 1, Collier Macmillan, 1980; in *The Prairie Experience*, ed. Terry Angus, Toronto: Macmillan, 1975; in *Literature in Canada*, Vol. 2, edited by Douglas Daymond, Leslie Monkman, Toronto: Gage, 1978.

The Stranger. Canadian Drama/L'Art Dramatique Canadien, 5 no. 2 (1979).

Widger's Way or *The Face in the Mirror*. Toronto: Playwrights Co-op, 1976.

Younger Brother (Thirteen Episodes). George Salverson *Prairie Playhouse*, CBC Edmonton, August-September 1960.

2. Musicals

"Look Behind You, Neighbor." Comp. Chet Lambertson, Edson H.S. Auditorium, Edson, Alberta, 2-3 November 1961.

Mirage, Comp. Gary Walsh and Steven Bengston, Greystone Theatre, University of Saskatchewan, Saskatoon, 24 May-8 June 1979. In *The Collected Plays of Gwen Pharis Ringwood*, Enid Delgatty Rutland, ed., (Ottawa: Borealis Press, 1981).

"The Road Runs North." Comp. Art Rosoman, Jr. Secondary School Auditorium, Williams Lake, B.C., 7-17 June 1967.

"The Wall." Comp. Bruce Haak, CBC Winnipeg and Edmonton, 1952.

3. Children's Plays

"Anchor to Westward." MS. Edmonton, 1951.

"The Bells of England." *Radio School Scripts*, CBC Vancouver, 7 May 1953.

"Books Alive." *Right on Our Doorstep*, CBC Edmonton, 7 December 1951.

The Dragons of Kent. MS. Edmonton: Dept. of Education, Alberta, 1936.

"The Fight Against the Invisible." *Science on the March*, no. 7, CBC Edmonton, 13 November 1945.

The Golden Goose. (An adaptation). MS. Cariboo College, 1973. In *Children's Plays* (Toronto: Playwrights Co-op, 1980).

Health Highways for Children. CBC Edmonton. "Frontier to Farmland" (30 January 1952); "Ten Hours a Night" (14 November 1952); "Beware the Germ" (18 November 1952); "Stand Tall" (25 November 1952); "A Fuss About Food" (2 December 1952); "Stop and Think" (9 December 1952).

Heidi. (An adaptation). CBC Vancouver and Toronto, 1959.

"The Lion and the Mouse." (An adaptation). MS. Cariboo College, Williams Lake, B.C., 1964.

The Magic Carpets of Antonio Angelini. Toronto: Playwrights Co-op, 1979. In *Six Canadian Plays for Children*. Toronto: Playwrights Coop, 1980.

New Lamps for Old (MS. lost). "Beethoven, the Man Who Freed Music"; "Oliver Cromwell"; "Galileo, Messenger of the Stars"; "Henry the Navigator"; "Socrates, Citizen of Athens"; "Nansen of the North"; "Prometheus Must Bring Fires"; "Girdle Round the Earth"; "Valley of Ignorance"; "Florence Nightingale", "Out of the Land of Bondage." CKUA Edmonton, 1936.

"The Play's the Thing." *Creative Writing*, CBC Vancouver, 1954.

"A Polished Performance." *Creative Writing*, CBC Vancouver, 1954.

"The Potato Puppet Twins." MS.

Red Flag at Evening. Edmonton: University of Alberta, Department of Extension, Youth Training Schools, 1940.

Saturday Night. Edmonton: University of Alberta, Department of Extension, Youth Training Schools, 1940.

The Sleeping Beauty. (An adaptation). In *My Heart Is Glad*, bk. 2. Edited by Gwen Ringwood. Williams Lake: Saint Joseph Indian School, 1965. Also in *Children's Plays* (Toronto: Playwrights Co-op, 1979).

"So Gracious the Time." CBC Edmonton and Toronto, 1954.

"The Three Wishes." (An adaptation). MS.

4. Novels

"Pascal." MS.

Younger Brother. New York: Longmans Green, 1959.

5. Short Stories

"Clock Time." MS.

"The Day the Loons Came Back." MS.

"Excursion" or "Think of it as a Challenge." MS.

"Get Along Little Dogie." In *Wide Open Windows*, edited by Franklin L. Barrett, pp. 212-25. Toronto: Copp Clarke, 1947.

"Home Base." *Family Herald* 33 (27 September 1962), 62-63. Montreal: Montreal Star Co.

"The Last Fifteen Minutes." In *Stories With John Drainie*, edited by John Drainie. Toronto: Ryerson Press, 1963.

"The Little Ghost." In *Canadian Short Stories*, edited by Robert Weaver and Helen James. Toronto: Oxford University Press, 1952. Also in *Cavalcade of the North*, edited by T. Norah Costain (New York: Doubleday and Company, 1958); *Puerto Ricans Read in English*, edited by Lola Brown, pp. 70-77 (Rio Piedras, Puerto Rico: Puerto Rico Junior College Foundation, 1971); CBC Edmonton.

"Little Joe and the Mounties." *Family Herald* 8 (14 April 1966), 78-79. Montreal: Montreal Star Co.

"Mr. Finnburley and the Nesting Swallows." MS.

"Mr. Gunderson and the President of the Republic." MS.

"Portrait of Miriam." MS.

"Restez, Michelle, Don't Go." CBC Vancouver, 1977.

"Some People's Grandfathers or Sammy Joe and the Moose." In *Stories from Across Canada*, edited by B. L. McEvoy. Toronto: McClelland and Stewart, 1966. Also in *Family Herald*, 3 (31 January 1963), 44-46; *Sammy Joe and the Moose* (Williams Lake: Local publisher, Artist, Joe Poole, 1973); Glenview *Signposts*, 1 January 1975, pp. 162-67; Glenview, Illinois: Scott Foresman and Company; *A Sense of Place*, edited by Theresa M. Ford (Edmonton: Western Canadian Literature for Youth, 1979). In *Inquiry into Literature* 2, edited by Fellion & Henderson, Collier Macmillan, 1980.

"So Gracious the Time." CBC Edmonton, Toronto, 1954.

"The Snow Princess." MS.

"Supermarket." MS.

"The Truth about the Ten Gallon Hat." With Elsie Park Gowan. CBC Edmonton, 1949.

"The Will of the People." MS.

6. Poetry

"Afterwords." *Atlantis*, 4, no. 1 (1978), 164-65.

"For Elizabeth." In *Remember Elizabeth*, edited by members of the Theatre Department, p. 16. Edmonton: University of Alberta Press, 1974.

"Love Poetry: addressed to her husband overseas, Second World War." MS.

"Oh Canada, My Country." MS.
"The Road." *Tribune* (Williams Lake, B.C.), 1958 centennial edition.
"Sandy." *Carolina Play-Book,* 10 no. 4 (1937), 102-4.
Unpublished poetry. MS. 1936-1976.

7. Essays and Articles

"The Adjudicator Says." *Gateway,* 35, no. 17 (15 February 1945), 4-5.
"Drama in the Open: The Carolina Playmakers: 1918-9—1938-9." *Carolina Play-Book,* 12, no. 2 (June 1939), 37-41.
"Elizabeth Haynes and the Prairie Theatre." MS.
"Excursion." MS.
"The Frogs, the Chairs, the Cherry Orchard, and Laura Secord." Speech to Dominion Drama Festival, Vancouver, 1964.
"A Gallery of Faces." MS.
"Geneva." MS.
"Hilt Ryland." MS.
"Joan Baird." MS.
"Notes to Myself." MS.
"Plans for a Lighthearted Novel." MS.
"Portrait of a Woman." MS.
"Real People I Think About." MS.
"Ringwood Talks About Her Life and Work." In *Stage Voices,* edited by Geraldine Anthony, pp. 90-110. New York and Toronto: Doubleday & Company, 1978.
"Rumination While Browsing Through Roget's *Thesaurus.*" MS.
"She Demanded Greatness." In *Remember Elizabeth,* edited by members of the Theatre Department, pp. 5-6. Edmonton: University of Alberta Press, 1974.
"Simon." MS.
"Some Memories of the Theatre in Alberta." MS.
"Some Tall Tales from the Alberta Hills." MS.
"So You Want To Be An Actor." *University of Alberta Radio Lectures.* "Ten Lessons in Theatre," Department of Extension, CKUA, Edmonton, 1939-1940.
"Theatre Rededicated." *Carolina Play-Book,* 11, no. 4 (1938), 95-97.
"Trouping to the North." *Carolina Play-Book,* 11, no. 4 (1938), 111-14.
"The Well Adjusted Parent." MS.
"Women and the Theatrical Tradition." *Atlantis,* 4, no. 1 (1978), 154-58.
"Writers' Workshop." MS.

8. Edited Book of Indian Folklore

My Heart Is Glad. Edited by Gwen Ringwood. Vols. 1-2. Williams Lake: *Tribune,* 1964-1965.

9. Correspondence: A collection of letters written and received over a period of forty years concerning people involved in theater, 1936-1981, in the Ringwood Archives, University of Calgary Library, Calgary, Alberta.

SECONDARY SOURCES

ANTHONY, GERALDINE. "Gwen Pharis Ringwood." In *Stage Voices*. New York: Doubleday & Company, Inc., 1978, pp. 86-89. A brief introduction to Ringwood's style, with a bibliography and chronology.

———. "The Magic Carpets of Gwen Pharis Ringwood." *Canadian Children's Literature* 8:9 (1977), 84-89. An article emphasizing the techniques of good children's drama, using for examples the techniques employed by Ringwood in her play *The Magic Carpets of Antonio Angelini*.

———. "The Plays of Gwen Pharis Ringwood: An Appraisal." *Atlantis* 4:1 (1978): 132-41. An analysis of the regional drama of Ringwood and its folk elements.

———. "The Ringwood Plays of Social Protest." *Canadian Drama* 5:2, (Fall 1979): 112-28. An analysis of Ringwood's later work and its emphasis on social protest.

BENSON, EUGENE, ed. *Encounter: Canadian Drama in Four Media*. Toronto: Methuen, 1973, pp. 30-53. An anthology of radio, film, television, and stage plays. It contains Ringwood's stage play *Still Stands the House* with a short introduction.

BRODERSON, GEORGE L., ed. *Dark Harvest*. Toronto: Thomas Nelson and Sons Limited, 1945. Ringwood's play wih an excellent foreword by Broderson containing a fine description of the play, notes, acting suggestions, and questions.

———. "Gwen Pharis—Dramatist." *Manitoba Arts Review* 4 (Spring 1944): 3-20. A superb appraisal of Ringwood's plays: *Still Stands the House, Pasque Flower, Dark Harvest, The Courting of Marie Jenvrin*.

Conference Across a Continent. Toronto: Macmillan of Canada, 1963. This 521-page book opens with a laudatory account of Ringwood's musical "Look Behind You, Neighbor." It points out that this play epitomizes the whole intent of the conference in the musical's evocation of the history and spirit of the town of Edson, Alberta. The book is an account of H.R.H. The Duke of Edinburgh's Second Commonwealth Study Conference on the Human Consequences of the Changing Industrial Environment in the Commonwealth and Empire. 13 May-6 June 1962.

GARD, ROBERT. *Grassroots Theater*. Madison: University of Wisconsin Press, 1955. An excellent study of regional drama in America with one chapter devoted to Canadian drama. This chapter contains a long letter from Ringwood to Gard, a lyrical description of Canada.

———. *Johnny Chinook.* New York: Longmans Green and Co., 1945. A collection of tall tales and true of the Canadian West. Gard encouraged Ringwood to use like material for her plays.

———. *A Time of Humanities.* Madison: Wisconsin Academy of Sciences, Arts, and Letters, 1976. A history of the Humanities Division of the Rockefeller Foundation, covering the years 1932-1950, with special reference to the director, David Stevens, and his promotion of regional and folk drama. Ringwood's work was supported by this foundation.

GOWAN, ELSIE PARK. "History Into Theatre." *Canadian Author & Bookman* 51:1 (Fall 1975): 7, 8. An original essay on the writing of stimulating historical plays with examples taken from Ringwood's musical, "Look Behind You, Neighbor."

"Gwen Pharis Ringwood: Alberta Graduate." *Gateway* (University of Alberta student newspaper) 35:17 (15 February 1945): 3. An article in general on the Ringwood plays, and on Broderson's review of her work.

HENDERSON, ARCHIBALD, ed. *Pioneering a People's Theater.* Chapel Hill: University of North Carolina Press, 1945. A series of articles by such noted people as Frederick Koch, Paul Green, Samuel Selden, and others connected with the Carolina Playmakers. A memorial to Fred Koch and a survey, summary, and appraisal of the accomplishments of the Carolina Playmakers.

HINCHCLIFFE, JUDITH. "*Still Stands the House:* The Failure of the Pastoral Dream." *Canadian Drama* 3:2 (1977): 183-91. Demonstrates how Ringwood creates a new myth native to the new land.

JONES, EMRYS, ed. *Canadian School Plays.* Toronto: Ryerson Press, 1948. An anthology of Canadian plays suitable for student performances.

———. "Courting of Marie Jenvrin." *Winnepeg Tribune,* 1941. A review of this play in which Jones describes it as one of the most appealing one-act plays ever written on a Canadian theme.

KLINCK, CARL, ed. *Literary History of Canada.* Toronto: University of Toronto Press, 1965, pp. 639-40. This article offers a good review of the play *Still Stands the House.*

KOCH, FREDERICK H. "American Drama in the Making." *Carolina Playbook,* 1936, pp. 79-84. A commencement address delivered at the University of North Dakota, 11 June 1935, giving a broad view of American folk drama and its initiation by Koch at the University of North Carolina in 1918 and the University of North Dakota in 1914.

———, ed. *American Folk Plays.* New York: Appleton Century, 1939. An anthology of eighteen American folk plays, one Mexican, and one Canadian prairie play by Ringwood.

———, ed. *Carolina Playbook.* Chapel Hill: University of North Carolina Press, 1937-41. A journal devoted to the plays of the Carolina Playmakers. Gwen Pharis was totally responsible for the selection and editing from 1937-39.

MAYORGA, MARGARET, ed. *The Best One-Act Plays of 1942.* New York:

Dodd Mead, 1943. An anthology of one-act plays containing Ringwood's play *The Courting of Marie Jenvrin*.

NOONAN, JAMES. "A Review of *Stage Voices*." *Queens Quarterly* 86:2 (1979): 362-64. This review contains references to Ringwood's work.

ORCHARD, IMBERT. "Widger's Way." *Edmonton Journal*, 11 March 1952. A review of Ringwood's play produced at Studio Theatre, University of Alberta.

PACEY, DESMOND. *Creative Writing in Canada*. Toronto: Ryerson Press, 1967, p. 272. The author remarks on the fact that Ringwood has written and had produced a number of fine dramatic portrayals of the Canadian West.

PEERY, WILLIAM. "American Folk Drama Comes of Age." *American Scholar* 11:2 (Spring 1942): 149-57. An intelligent article pointing out the weaknesses that lessen the critical theories of folk playwrights and their overcoming of them.

PERKINS, DON. "*Mirage* Opens at Greystone." *Star-Phoenix* (Saskatoon), 25 May 1979, p. 37. A critical and appreciative review of Ringwood's premiere performance of her new musical *Mirage*.

SANDEMEL, FRANCES FOX. "The Conception and the Creation: A Critical Evaluation of the Work of the Carolina Playmakers." M.A. thesis, University of North Carolina, Chapel Hill, 1941. A stimulating study of the folk play as taught by the faculty at Chapel Hill.

SELDEN, SAMUEL. *Frederick Henry Koch: Pioneer Playmaker*. Chapel Hill: University of North Carolina Press, 1954. A tribute to the pioneering work done by Frederick Koch in the field of folk playwriting by Samuel Selden, a great leader in the same field.

———, ed. *International Folk Plays*. Chapel Hill: University of North Carolina Press, 1949. An anthology of nine folk plays by dramatic art students at the University of North Carolina. It includes Ringwood's play *The Courting of Marie Jenvrin*, with a brief introduction by Selden.

SPEARMAN, WALTER, with the assistance of Samuel Selden. *The Carolina Playmakers: The First Fifty Years*. Chapel Hill: University of North Carolina Press, 1970. An interesting account of the history of the Carolina Playmakers with a few brief references to Ringwood's productions at Chapel Hill.

SPER, FELIX. *From Native Roots*. Caldwell, Idaho: Caxton Printers, 1948. An excellent study of American folk drama.

TAIT, MICHAEL. "Playwrights in a Vacuum." *Canadian Literature* 16 (1963): 5-18. An intelligent and perceptive article on Canadian playwrights such as Ringwood, and their problems in producing professional plays.

THOMPSON, BRUCE. *Williams Lake Tribune* (Williams Lake, B.C.), 23 June 1971. A short but appreciative review of two new plays by Ringwood, *The Stranger* and *The Deep Has Many Voices*, which premiered at the opening of the Gwen Pharis Ringwood Outdoor Theatre, Boitanio Park, Williams Lake.

TOVELL, VINCENT. "Dark Harvest." *University of Toronto Quarterly* 16 (April 1947): 266-67. An excellent review of the Ringwood style in her play *Dark Harvest*.

URSELL, GEOFFREY BARRY. "A Triple Mirror." Microfilm no. 722, 144.1. M.A. thesis, University of Manitoba, October 24, 1966. In the Metro Library, Toronto. A correct though not very original explication of Ringwood's plays along with those of Merrill Denison and Robertson Davies.

WAGNER, ANTON. "Gwen Pharis Ringwood Rediscovered." *Canadian Theatre Review* 5 (Winter 1975): 63-128. An intelligent and sensitive essay on Ringwood's contributions to Canadian drama.

WEAVER, ROBERT, and JAMES, HELEN, eds. *Canadian Short Stories*. Toronto: Oxford University Press, 1952, p. 75. An anthology of short stories containing Ringwood's story "The Little Ghost."

Index

Aberhart, William, 22
Ahlf, Marguerite, 99
Alberta Folklore and Local History Project, 37, 72-73
Alberta Provincial Drama Festival, 46, 58, 74
Alberta, University of, 24, 25, 30, 37, 73, 83-84, 88, 94
Alexander, Wm. Hardy, 24
Allen, Fred, 135
American Folk Plays, 60
Anatol Cycle, 36
Anderson, Maxwell, 40, 62
Andrews, Allen, 61
Antigone, 126
As for Me and My House, 57
Association For Canadian Theatre History, 95
Atwood, Hugh, 154
Atwood, Margaret, 56-58
Autumn Garden, The, 127

Bailey, Howard, 58
Banff Rustic Theatre, 46, 83
Banff School of Fine Arts, 25, 30-33, 72-73, 87-88, 134
Barker, Billy, 95, 102, 105-106
Bear, The, 85
Begbie, Judge Matthew, 103
Benavente y Martinez, Jacinto, 161
Bengston, Steven, 107
Bill, Desmond, 100
Billy Club Puppets, 87, 91
Blackfoot Indian Reservation, 23-24, 111, 114
Blood Indian Reservation, 21, 33, 114, 142
Blood Wedding, 120, 127, 129-30
Brecht and Weil, 80
British Columbia Drama Association, 29
British Columbia Centennial, 95, 102-103
Broadus, Dr. Edmond, 24
Broderson, George, 45, 63
Burgess, Mary Ellen, 46

CBC Radio and TV, 30, 59, 72, 74, 88, 116, 134-36, 147, 153-54
CFRN-TV, 97
CKUA Radio Station, 25, 134, 159, 164
Calderon de la Barca, Pedro, 134, 161
Calgary Stampede, 80-84
Calgary Eye Opener, 73-74
Cameron, Donald, 32, 37, 46, 84
Canadian Short Stories, 153
Cariboo College, 29, 137
Cariboo Indian School, 29, 114
Carman, Bliss, 27
Carmichael, Franklin, 32
Carnegie Foundation, 30
Carolina Play-Book, The, 25, 40, 42, 63
Carolina Playmakers, 34, 61, 70
Carr, Emily, 32-33
Cary, Joyce, 90
Cat on a Hot Tin Roof, 127
"Cathedral Mountain," 34
Chautauqua Festival, 22
Chekhov, Anton, 23, 63, 85, 112, 114, 127, 131, 165
Cherry Orchard, The, 63, 127
Childs, Floyd, 46, 58
Coffeehouses, 161-63
Conference of Inter-American Women Writers, 160
Corbett, E. A., 25
Cornell University, 37
Coulter, John, 115
Cowan, Vivien, 20, 164
Cowboy Songs, 80
Craig, Gordon, 78

Dakota Playmakers, 35
Davis, Harry, 58
"Doc Snider's House," 33
Dominion Drama Festival, 30, 58, 160
Dona Rosita, 53
Donnellys, The, 110
Double Hook, The, 57
Douglas, Lieutenant Governor, 103

Edmonton Journal, 100
Edson Leader, 97
Edwards, Bob, 73-75, 82, 167
"Encounters," 161-63
Eric Hamber Trophy, 29

Family Herald, The, 154
Finch, Robert, 55
Finley, Ethel, 58
FitzGerald, Lemoine, 33
Flath, Louis, 58
Follows, Ted, 83
Fruits of the Earth, 66-68

Gard, Robert, 19, 26-28, 37-38, 72-73, 76, 80, 97, 140, 164
Gault, Lynn, 39, 41, 58
Gauntlett, Doris, 135, 164
Germaine, Sister, 29, 161
Gerussi, Bruno, 83
Gowan, Elsie Park, 30, 32, 58, 83, 88, 95, 134, 167
Grassroots Theatre, 37
Green, Elizabeth Lay, 40-41
Green, Paul, 36, 41, 73, 82
Gregory, Lady, 34
Group of Seven, The, 20, 26-27, 30, 32-34
Grove, Frederick Philip, 20, 56, 58, 66, 68
Gwen Pharis Ringwood Theatre, 32, 116
Gwillym Edwards prize, 46

Haak, Bruce, 95-96
Hardy, W. G., 24
Harris, Lawren, 32-33
Hawthorne, Pamela, 131
Haynes, Elizabeth Sterling, 19, 24-25, 30-31, 38, 47, 97, 134, 159-60
Hellman, Lillian, 127
Hemingway, Ernest, 79
Henderson, Archibald, 36
Hirsch, Sam, 39, 46, 49
His Boon Companions, 41
Horse's Mouth, The, 90
House of Bernarda Alba, The, 127, 131
Howard, Rietta Bailey, 39

In Abraham's Bosom, 36
Irish Literary Revival, 34, 50

Jackson, A. Y., 32-33
James, Florence, 83-84
Jardine, Vivian, 101
Johnny Chinook, 37, 76
Johnston, Frank, 32
Jones, Emrys, 88

Kaasa, Walter, 59
Kansas, University of, 37
Kawartha Festival, 30, 94
Kerr, Tom, 59, 76-77, 103, 111, 123-24
Koch, Frederick H., 19, 25, 34-43, 70-72, 82, 97, 164
Kristjanson, G., 147

Laidlaw, Mary, 58
Lambertson, Chet, 95, 97
Lampman, Archibald, 27
Lardner, Ring, 153
Lismer, Arthur, 32-33
Little Theatre of Medicine Hat, 58
Ljungh, Esse, 136
Lomax, John A., 80
Lonely Voice, The, 155
Look Homeward, Angel, 122
Lorca, Frederico Garcia, 53, 87-91, 115, 120, 127, 129, 131
Love of Don Perlimpton, The, 91

MacDonald, J. E. H., 32-33
McKreath, J. T., 74, 98
Maeterlinck, Maurice, 78
Manitoba Arts Review, 45, 63
Manitoba, University of, 63
Marriage Proposal, 85
Marriot, Sheila, 25, 134
Martin, Robert Dale, 39
Medea, 116, 120
Mellen, Peter, 33
Mengel, Ruth, 58

Metis Indians, 114
Midnight, 37, 80
Miller, Henry, 151
Mitchell, W. O., 20
Montana, University of, 50
Mourning Becomes Electra, 52

N. D. W. T. Company, 110
Nash, Richard, 76
National Multicultural Theatre Association, 29
"Native Prairie Plays," 35
Nelson, Esther, 83-84
New Play Centre Competition, 30, 131
No Smoking, 161
North Carolina, University of, 25, 34-37, 58, 63, 159
North Dakota, University of, 35

O'Connor, Frank, 155-56
O'Neill, Eugene, 50, 52
Ontario Multicultural Theatre Association, 137
Orchard, Robert, 88, 94
Ottawa Little Theatre Playwriting Competition, 63, 116
Ottawa, University of, 160
Our Town, 76-77, 96, 98

"Painter of the Prairies," 33
Parker, Darice, 39
Parker, John, 39-41, 61
Pharis, Blaine, George and Robert, 21, 145, 147
Pharis, Leslie, 20, 23-24, 43, 134
Pharis, Mary Bowersock, 20, 21, 24
Pioneering a People's Theatre, 36
Plautus, 88, 93-94
Playmakers Theatre, 46, 49
Playwrights Co-Op, 124
Pot of Gold, The, 88, 93
"Prairie Playhouse," 88
Pratt, E. J., 27

Rawling, Marjorie Kinnan, 141
Read, Carleton, 46
Reaney, James, 110
Remember Elizabeth, 30
Remember to Remember, 151
Riders to the Sea, 36, 50, 78
Riel, 115
Ringwood, Gwen Pharis: Alberta Folklore, 37-38, 72-84, 89-94, 97-104; biography, 20-30; British Columbia settings, 102-107, 113-32; Canadian directors of Ringwood plays, 59-60, 74-75, 83-84, 88, 94, 98, 101, 103, 123-24, 131; Carolina Playmakers, 34-37, 39-44; children's early stage plays, 133-34; children's educational radio plays, 134-36; children's Christmas play and adaptations, 136-37; children's multicultural play, 137-39; classical drama influences, 88-94, 116-20; Coffeehouses, 161-63; education, 22-24; essays, 159-60; folk comedies, 42-46, 70-94; folk tragedy, 50-69; Indian folklore, 161, 113-20; influence of Frederich Koch and North Carolina professors, 39-42; influence of western Canadian writers: Frederich Philip Grove and others, 56-58, 66-68; influence of Ukrainian people in Alberta, 28, 84-88; novels, 140-153; poetry, 160-61; prairie theatre, 30-34; religion, 22, 24; Saskatchewan setting, 70-72, 107-112; short stories, 153-58; social protest plays, 46-50, 113-32

STAGE PLAYS:
"Chris Axelson, Blacksmith," 40-46, 49, 68, 70, 74, 84, 89-90, 164, 166
Courting of Marie Jenvrin, The, 26, 49, 70-72, 84, 165
Dark Harvest, 27, 32-33, 40-41, 50, 61-69, 164-67
"Days May Be Long, The", 40, 69
Deep Has Many Voices, The, 23, 78, 113-14, 120-24, 129, 145-46, 165-69
Drowning of Wasyl Nemitchuk, The, or *A Fine Colored Easter Egg*, 41, 49, 70, 85-89, 94, 120, 165-67
"Encounters," 161-163
Jack and the Joker, The, 70, 73-75, 82, 84, 90, 94, 165-67
Lament for Harmonica or *Maya*, 24, 33, 49, 113-20, 165, 167
"Lodge, The", 23, 30, 32, 49, 113-14, 120, 127-31, 146, 165-67

"One Man's House," 40, 47-49, 68, 74, 84, 164, 166, 168
Pasque Flower, 32, 40-41, 49-50, 60-68, 164-67
Rainmaker, The, 23, 32, 70, 73-79, 82, 84, 89, 94, 98, 165, 167
"Remembrance of Miracles, A", 49, 78, 113-14, 120, 124-27, 165-68
Stampede, 32, 37, 49, 70, 73, 75, 79-84, 94, 165, 167
Still Stands the House, 25, 32-34, 40-41, 49-62, 67-68, 164-69
Stranger, The or *Jana,* 24, 33, 49, 113-20, 165, 167
Widger's Way or *The Face in The Mirror,* 24, 30, 41, 49, 70, 88-94, 107, 165, 167

MUSICALS:
"Look Behind You, Neighbor," 23, 78, 94-95, 97-102, 165, 167
Mirage, 23, 30, 78, 94-95, 97, 107-11, 165-68
"Road Runs North, The," 23, 34, 78, 94-95, 97, 102-107, 111, 115, 165, 167
"Wall, The", 94-98, 166-68

COFFEEHOUSE MINI-PLAYS:
"Compensation Will Be Paid", 162-63
"Seal Hunt," 163
"Strictly Confidential," 163
"Thing to Do Is Integrate, The," 163
"Wail, Winds, Wail," 162
"zzzzzz," 162

CHILDREN'S PLAYS:
"Adventure With Books," 135
"Bells of England, The," 135
"Beware the Germ," 135
"Books Alive," 135
Creative Writing Series, 135
Dragons of Kent, The, 133-34
"Fight Against the Invisible, The," 134
"Frontier to Farmland," 135
"Fuss About Food, A," 135
Golden Goose, The, 137
Heidi, 136
Health Highways for Children, 135
"Lion and the Mouse, The," 136
Magic Carpets of Antonio Angelini, The, 29, 137-39
"New Lamps for Old," 25, 32, 134
"Potato Puppet Twins, The," 135
"Polished Performance, A," 135
"The Play's the Thing," 135
Red Flags of Evening, 133-34
Sleeping Beauty, The, 136, 161
"So Gracious the Time," 136
Saturday Night, 133-34
Science on the March, 134
"Stand Tall," 135
"Stop and Think", 135
"The Three Wishes", 136
"Ten Hours a Night," 135

NOVELS:
"Pascal," 23, 140, 147-53, 165
Younger Brother, 21, 140-47, 153, 165

SHORT STORIES:
"Clock Time", 154
"Death of Einstein, The", 23
"Excursion," 154
"Get Along Little Doggie", 140, 153-54, 157
"Home Base", 140, 153-54, 156
"Last Fifteen Minutes, The", 140, 154
"Little Ghost, The," 140, 153-54, 157-58
"Little Joe and the Mounties," 140, 154, 157
"Mr. Finnburley and the Nesting Swallow," 154
"Mr. Gunderson and the President of the Republic," 155
"Portrait of a Woman," 154
"Restez Michelle, Don't Go," 154, 156
"Snow Princess, The", 154
"So Gracious the Time," 136, 154
"Some People's Grandfathers," 140, 154-56
"Supermarket", 154
"Will of the People, The", 154

POETRY:
"Afterwards," 161
"Cariboo Trail, The," 161
"Fragments," 161

"Oh Canada My Country, " 161
"Road, The," 161
"Sandy", 42

ESSAYS AND ARTICLES:
"Adjudicator Says, The," 159
"Alberta is My Birthright," 159
"Carolina Playmakers, The, 1919-39," 159
"Drama in the Open," 159
"Elizabeth Haynes and the Prairie Theatre," 160
"Frogs, the Chairs, the Cherry Orchard and Laura Secord, The," 160
"Joan Baird: Homemaker," 160
"Notes to Myself," 160
"Rumination While Browsing through Roget's *Thesauraus,* " 160
"So You Want to be an Actor," 159, 164
"Some Memories of the Theatre in Alberta," 159
"Some Tall Tales from the Alberta Hills," 159
"Well-Adjusted Parent, The," 160
"Women and the Theatrical Tradition," 160

INDIAN FOLKLORE:
My Heart is Glad I, II, 161

Ringwood, Dr. John Brian, 25-26, 29
Risk, Sidney, 83
Roberson, Robert, 61
Roberts, Charles G. D., 27
Rockefeller Foundation grant, 34, 37, 40, 73
Rodgers, Vivian, 58
Ronald, Holt Cup, 25
Rosenberg, David, 46
Rosoman, Art, 95, 102
Ross, Sinclair, 56, 58

Saint Joseph's Oblate Mission, 29, 114, 136
Salverson, George, 147
Saskatchewan Arts Board, 84
Saskatchewan, University of, 30, 95, 107
Schnitzler, Arthur, 36
Scott, D. C., 27
Scott, F. R., 26
Selden, Emily Crow, 39-41, 49, 52, 61, 147
Selden, Samuel, 35-36, 39-41
Settlers of the Marsh, 56-57
Shoemaker's Prodigious Wife, The, 87-90
"Shoestring Theatre," 116
Smith, A. J. M., 26
Smith, Betty, 39, 41, 49, 55
Stage Voices, 87, 160
Stango, Clive, 31, 103
Stevens, Dr. David, 37
Survival, 56-57
Synge, John Millington, 34, 36, 50, 78

Tallman, Dr. Frank, 55
Thomas, Dorothy, 23
Thomson, Tom, 32
Thurber, James, 154
Tovell, Vincent, 83
Tree Grows in Brooklyn, A, 39
Tyo, Jack, 46

United Farmers Organization of Alberta, 21

Varley, Frederick, 32
Veach, Vivien, 49
Victoria, University of, 97

Wagner, Anton, 63
Walsh, Gary, 107
Ware, Nigger John, 81-84, 167
Washed in the Blood, 39
Watson, Sheila, 56-58
Weaver, Robert, 153
Weber, John, 83-84
Welch, Cora, 23, 114
White, Kitty, 58
Who Has Seen the Wind, 20
Wilder, Thornton, 76-77, 96, 98
Williams Lake Players Club, 94, 103, 136, 162
Williams Lake Tribune, 102, 119, 123, 161
Williams, Tennessee, 127
Winnipeg Multicultural Festival, 30
Winterset, 62

Wismer Collection, 114
Wolfe, Thomas, 122
Wynn, Earl, 61

Yearling, The, 141
Yeats, Wm. Butler, 23, 34, 50
Yerma, 115